PRAISE FOR
THE ORGANIZATIONAL RESILIENCE HANDBOOK

'Graham Bell provides an interesting an[...] resilience and lays out the wide-ranging ar[...] happened over the years. It is important to be able to argue from several angles, and this handbook uses case studies to demonstrate the many and varied approaches that have been adopted in the pursuit of resilience.'
Derek Mowbray, Organization Health Psychologist

'This book offers a detailed and thought-provoking look at organizational resilience, with a broad range of case studies and global insights. It places a focus on strategy and delivering commitments to stakeholders, the role of leadership in organizational resilience, the importance of continual learning and everything else in between.'
Janette Kirk-Willis, Positive Psychology and Resilience Coach, Founder of Positively Flourishing

'Provides a practical approach to using the information we gather to move from risk to resilience management. Organizations of any kind will benefit from the focus on transforming risk reviews and assessments into strategic hints. In these days of great change and external pressures, organizations will need a form of intelligent design applied to allow businesses to not only survive but excel. This book provides that.'
Cosimo Pacciani, former COO of Algebris and former CRO of the European Stability Mechanism

'Managing the Covid-19 pandemic has taught us and is continuing to teach us many lessons about resilience. Not least of these is that the responses have been widely varied in terms of the levels of preparedness displayed by different countries and the corporates and entities within them. It is also apparent that a much greater priority needs to be given to organizational resilience in the future, particularly as we face the challenges of climate change and other aspects of global instability that will continue to throw up

shocks, predictable and unpredictable. *The Organizational Resilience Handbook* provides an invaluable and timely framework for assessing the resilience of an organization and to help its leaders enhance their preparedness in a way which is not threat-specific. Above all, it makes the point that any resilience strategy must be holistic and recognize the inter-dependencies that the organization faces.'
Lord Toby Harris

The Organizational Resilience Handbook

A practical guide to achieving greater resilience

Graham Bell

Publisher's note
Every possible effort has been made to ensure that the information contained in this book is accurate at the time of going to press, and the publishers and author cannot accept responsibility for any errors or omissions, however caused. No responsibility for loss or damage occasioned to any person acting, or refraining from action, as a result of the material in this publication can be accepted by the editor, the publisher or the author.

First published in Great Britain and the United States in 2020 by Kogan Page Limited

Apart from any fair dealing for the purposes of research or private study, or criticism or review, as permitted under the Copyright, Designs and Patents Act 1988, this publication may only be reproduced, stored or transmitted, in any form or by any means, with the prior permission in writing of the publishers, or in the case of reprographic reproduction in accordance with the terms and licences issued by the CLA. Enquiries concerning reproduction outside these terms should be sent to the publishers at the undermentioned addresses:

2nd Floor, 45 Gee Street	122 W 27th St, 10th Floor	4737/23 Ansari Road
London	New York, NY 10001	Daryaganj
EC1V 3RS	USA	New Delhi 110002
United Kingdom		India

www.koganpage.com

Kogan Page books are printed on paper from sustainable forests.

© Graham Bell, 2020

The Organizational Resilience Model® is a registered trademark.

The right of Graham Bell to be identified as the author of this work has been asserted by him in accordance with the Copyright, Designs and Patents Act 1988.

ISBNs
Hardback   978 1 78966 186 6
Paperback 978 1 78966 184 2
Ebook   978 1 78966 185 9

British Library Cataloguing-in-Publication Data

A CIP record for this book is available from the British Library.

Library of Congress Cataloging-in-Publication Data

Names: Bell, G. J. (Graham J.) author.
Title: The organizational resilience handbook : a practical guide to
   achieving greater resilience / Graham Bell.
Description: 1 Edition. | New York : Kogan Page Inc, 2020. | Includes
   bibliographical references and index.
Identifiers: LCCN 2020009029 (print) | LCCN 2020009030 (ebook) | ISBN
   9781789661842 (paperback) | ISBN 9781789661866 (hardback) | ISBN
   9781789661859 (ebook)
Subjects: LCSH: Organizational resilience. | Organizational change. |
   Strategic planning.
Classification: LCC HD58.9 .B445 2020 (print) | LCC HD58.9 (ebook) | DDC
   658.4/06--dc23
LC record available at https://lccn.loc.gov/2020009029
LC ebook record available at https://lccn.loc.gov/2020009030

Typeset by Hong Kong FIVE Workshop, Hong Kong
Print production managed by Jellyfish
Printed and bound by CPI Group (UK) Ltd, Croydon CR0 4YY

CONTENTS

About the author ix
Foreword by James Arbuthnot x
Preface xii
List of abbreviations xv
Author's note: Resilience thinking during a pandemic xvii

Introduction 1

Background and approach 1
Contextual setting 4
A meaningful definition 5
The value of building resilience 6
What resilience looks like 7
A flexible model 8
The need for assurance 9
Links to other topics 10
Improving resilience capability 11
Conclusion 12
Endnotes 14

01 Contextual setting 15

Material science 16
Something which can be built and destroyed 18
Standards compliant 20
Data vulnerability 22
Consultancies 24
Societal influences 26
Conclusion 28
Endnotes 30

02 Definitions and references 34

Event-focused definitions 38
Event-plus approaches 41
Soundbite or cryptic references 44
False analogies 47
My own definition 51
Illustrative reference sources 55
Conclusion 60
Endnotes 62

03 Reasoning and benefits 64

The significance of our approach to risk 65
Why it pays organizations to be ambitious 69
Compliance as a strategic issue 72
Responding well in a crisis can directly influence short-term and long-term success 74
An enthusiasm for change is essential 77
The role of leadership 80
Continuous learning is the key 83
The organization is more than the sum of the parts 86
Does size matter? 89
Trust seems to be coming back into fashion 91
Conclusion 95
Endnotes 98

04 Case studies 102

Case study 1: The collapse of UK retailer House of Fraser in 2018 105
Case study 2: The on-track success of the Mercedes Formula One team 109
Case study 3: The re-invention of retail by Alibaba and others 114
Case study 4: BP a decade after the explosion in the Gulf of Mexico 2010 118
Case study 5: The impact of the WannaCry virus in 2017 123

Case study 6: The continued resilience of London's transport network 126
Conclusion 131
Endnotes 134

05 The Organizational Resilience Capability Model® (ORCM) 140

The resilience maturity scale 142
The features contained within the ORCM 148
The concepts contained within the ORCM 156
The elephant in the room 169
Conclusion 170
Endnotes 172

06 Assessment and reporting 175

The provision of assurance 177
Selecting the correct assessment strategy 179
Planning and the assessment process 183
Data gathering and analysis 187
Assessment practices relevant to the 'concepts' contained within the ORCM 191
Applying capacity measures to the 'features' within the ORCM 196
Options for reporting 197
Scoring, charts, infographics and grading 202
Benchmarking performance 205
Conclusion 208
Endnotes 210

07 Other key issues and ideas 212

Compliance in a period of technological revolution 214
The capability to deliver transformational change 218
The relationship between resilience and safety 223
The importance of security 228
Investing in resilience 233
Other models 236

Conclusion 241
Endnotes 244

08 Application and implementation 247

Improvement strategy 249
Resources and capabilities 253
Programme delivery 257
Organizational design (and re-design) 263
Data and information management 266
Conclusion 271
Endnotes 275

Index 277

ABOUT THE AUTHOR

Graham Bell has 30 years' international experience in management, training and consultancy roles, covering manufacturing, telecoms, transport and energy sectors. This includes extended work assignments in the United States and Middle East, and leadership roles within a FTSE Top 25 company. He delivers an existing qualification course on organizational resilience, regulated by Ofqual, and ran his first public training course over 20 years ago.

Through the eyes of a business leader, consultant and trainer, Graham has developed a deep understanding of organizational resilience and followed its growth into the mainstream of management and academic thinking. Having been exposed to numerous models and tools over the years, he has been responsible for establishing and improving resilience capability in a number of organizations.

Graham runs his own consultancy company and actively supports the work of several professional institutes.

He is a Fellow of the Institute for Strategy, Resilience & Security (ISRS), at University College London (UCL), and is also a Fellow of the Institute of Strategic Risk Management (ISRM).

FOREWORD

Books are sometimes described as timely. This one is overdue – a factor of the existential new challenges we face. For the first time in global history mankind has become dependent on networks and technologies essential to the survival and wellbeing of our ever-increasing population. But those networks and technologies are inherently vulnerable to threats. In a world where everything is becoming connected to and dependent on everything else, a failure in one part of our systems could bring about cascading failures elsewhere, and it will become increasingly hard to see where it will end.

So we need to make ourselves more resilient. Resilience is a concept that invites many questions, including, 'Resilience in the face of what?' but true resilience is a strength that allows an organization to survive and, if possible, prosper in the face of anything thrown at it. It is a mistake to rely only on identifying single threats and putting in place mitigating strategies – valuable though that exercise can be. A preferable approach is to identify a range of behaviours that allows your organization to adapt and flex in the face of challenges that are inherently unpredictable.

How can we encourage such an approach? The key to the answer to the question can be found in this book. It involves diversity of thought. And diversity of thought, the avoidance of group-think, stems from the diversity of the thinkers. This means that any organization's management needs to be drawn from a wide range of pools of talent, and that involves diversity of background, experience, gender and whatever else might be relevant to the organization.

And the development of resilience requires courage, the courage to face head-on the fact that bad things will happen. In the film *Kelly's Heroes* the wonderful character Oddball says, 'Why don't you knock it off with them negative waves? Why don't you dig how beautiful it is out here? Why don't you say something righteous and hopeful for a change?' There is, of course, a place for optimism. Without optimism we would never have reached the moon or decrypted the human genome.

But there is also a place for pessimism. Without pessimism we would not have fire insurance, which involves the sensible precaution of recognizing that things might go wrong and it is good to spread the risk. Optimism can be taken too far. We don't like thinking about bad things, and governments and organizations sometimes feel they need to assert that everything is going well. But if we fail to acknowledge the existence of vulnerabilities, we'll fail to deal with them. And governments that fail to talk openly about vulnerabilities will not face the pressure from the voting public to address them.

This book presents the Organizational Resilience Capability Model®, a valuable concept which gives at the very least a starting point in how to approach the many and varied challenges associated with broaching the subject of resilience in any organization. And it encourages the notion of assurance, because a model of resilience that has not been exercised, tested and assessed is one that is unlikely to 'withstand first contact with the enemy'.

And the best bit about putting into practice the suggestions contained here is that instead of having at the back of your mind the vague worry that there is a risk out there that has not been addressed but which is too difficult to think about, you dispel 'them negative waves' with the knowledge that you will be ready to deal with the bad things that will happen. Oddball will be pleased with you.

James Arbuthnot
Lord Arbuthnot of Edrom
Chairman of Electricity Resilience Ltd and former Defence Minister

PREFACE

As my own interest in resilience has increased I have come to accept that most references to the topic, be that in literature or through media outlets, are in fact only references to *aspects* of resilience – to individual characteristics or elements contained within what should be, for organizations at least, a broad, strategic scope. As such, the majority of references to resilience appear very limited or skewed and frequently lacking in ambition; some references even appear to be inappropriate. This book seeks to make sense of the subject and to provide answers to the following questions: What is resilience, from an organizational perspective? What does it look like and how can it be measured? How can an organization improve its resilience capability?

For many people, resilience is restricted in application to the management of climate risks, and for others it enjoys a regular place in describing an individual's ability to withstand negative forces or their persistence at a particular task. Even those practitioners and academics who are concerned primarily with the study of *organizational resilience* routinely demonstrate an inability or unwillingness to coalesce around a single definition or approach to the subject. I firmly believe that resilience, at an organizational level, should always be approached as a strategic concept and one which speaks to the organization's success in managing its risk environment. As we know from real-world examples, organizational resilience is fundamentally about strength, competitiveness, re-shaping and growth.

It is against this background that the idea for the book first came into being, and it did so at roughly the same time as I began developing a formal qualification course, which has since been launched and registered with Ofqual – this is the Office of Qualifications and Examinations Regulation which regulates qualifications, examinations and assessments in England. Both this book and the course build upon a unique model which I created in 2018 for the

LIST OF ABBREVIATIONS

AGOR	Australian Government's Organizational Resilience (AGOR) website
AHAW	Affinity Health at Work
AI	Artificial intelligence
AR	Augmented reality
BC	Business continuity
BCI	Business Continuity Institute
BCMM	Virtual Corporation's Business Continuity Maturity Model®
BNEF	Bloomberg New Energy Finance
BSI	British Standards Institution
CDSE	Center for Development of Security Excellence
CEO	Chief Executive Officer
CNI	Critical national infrastructure
COO	Chief Operations Officer
CPNI	Centre for the Protection of National Infrastructure
CSOs	Civil society organizations
DHS	US Department of Homeland Security
DRJ	*Disaster Recovery Journal*
EECS	European Union's European Economic and Social Committee
EIU	Economist Intelligence Unit
EPA	US Environmental Protection Agency
F1	Formula One
FEMA	Federal Emergency Management Agency
HBR	*Harvard Business Review*
HoF	House of Fraser
HROs	High reliability organizations
HSE	Health and Safety Executive
IIA	Chartered Institute of Internal Auditors
IPO	Initial public offering

JV	Joint venture
M&A	Mergers and acquisitions
M&S	Marks and Spencer
MAAs	Mutual aid agreements
MP	Member of Parliament (UK)
NAO	National Audit Office
NHS	National Health Service
OECD	Organisation for Economic Co-operation and Development
ORCM	Organizational Resilience Capability Model®
PECB	Professional Evaluation and Certification Board
PS-Prep	Voluntary Private Sector Preparedness Accreditation and Certification Program
REAG	Resilience Expert Advisory Group
ROs	Resilient organizations
SMEs	i) Subject matter experts; ii) Small and medium-sized enterprises
TfL	Transport for London
UI	User interface
WEF	World Economic Forum

AUTHOR'S NOTE:
RESILIENCE THINKING DURING A PANDEMIC

A colleague, Dr David Rubens, was presenting at an institute gathering in February 2020, reflecting on how the label 'unprecedented' had come to be used almost routinely in respect of natural disasters and other crisis events. At that point, the full manuscript for my book had already been submitted and the new coronavirus remained little more than a developing story for many people outside of China. It was something which still seemed rather remote and limited to a handful of domestic cases who had travelled abroad – it was actually the day before the outbreak in northern Italy first came to people's attention. Fast forward just a few weeks and the World Health Organization (WHO) had declared the Covid-19 outbreak a pandemic. The magnitude and long-term significance of the crisis quickly began to emerge in that period and 'unprecedented' suddenly had a new point of reference from which to be applied.

As the crisis took on a global form during March 2020, it became clear that many large, complex organizations – some of them famous brands and market leaders – would only remain viable if allowed to operate within fundamentally different regulatory and legal parameters and/or with massive direct financial support from governments. The fate of countless smaller organizations looked no less precarious, and many simply shut down or were forced to do so. During this period, new models rapidly began to take shape, not least in respect of education and learning and in hospitality, and whilst many sectors saw short-term demand fall to zero, others received an unexpected fillip either through new orders or the ability to re-tool.

This is no short-term event or one with only localized impact. The societal context within which every organization operates has been changed forever by the 2020 pandemic, but what is particularly useful for students of organizational resilience is how the scale and velocity of this crisis can help us better appreciate the strategic nature of the subject and also to recognise how we can best contribute to the demands of post-crisis learning. As emphasized repeatedly within this book, resilience is much more than any singular event or indeed an organization's response to it. Nevertheless, history is littered with examples of organizations which have been undone by specific events – something which has taught us that the less resilient the organization, the bigger the focus on shocks and the recovery effort which follows them.

Crises tend to expose organizations in unique ways, be that in relation to long-term capacity for innovation or the ability to successfully execute short-term adjustments and redirect resources. When faced with a crisis, most organizations eventually realise that they have to do *something*, and it is precisely this ability or capacity to do things and to generate the desired effect which tends to be exposed. I always describe resilience as a strategic capability, but as part of this it is typically the organization's short-term abilities which are tested most severely during a crisis and it is of course these which need to be the focus of immediate post-crisis learning activity.

Effective learning and post-crisis action need to be supported by a framework for considering how the organization has been actually been exposed, and it is the study of resilience which can provide exactly that. Organizations will be rushing to re-establish themselves in the post-crisis environment in 2020/21 and a simple, adaptable frame can be useful in helping them better understand weaknesses in respect of awareness, oversight and decision making, for example. Organizations will then be better able to plan for and deliver genuine improvements in resilience capability using the real-world models and approaches described in this book.

One crucial aspect of societal and organizational resilience, and one underlined by the Covid-19 outbreak, is of course *personal* resilience – the characteristics and behaviours of individuals and how these contribute to health and wellbeing, amongst other things. This is worthy of mention here for two reasons. Firstly, it is a reminder of just how transferable the language of resilience is between the personal and organizational context and of how relevant personal success is to that of every organization – something many organizational psychologists have been telling us for years. Secondly, the Covid-19 outbreak represents a crisis in which individuals are forced to deal with an unimaginable shock and one for which they were, for the most part, wholly unprepared. But they have done so within the most unusual of societal and community circumstances, at least in more developed nations, as both critical infrastructure and the machinery of government remained largely intact.

To return to the label with which I began, the levels of societal interruption associated with the 2020 pandemic are truly unprecedented, as will be the eventual scale of economic contraction for many in the years ahead. This global crisis has exposed societies and the organizations we are all familiar with in ways that few, if any, had envisaged, and in ways that no event has done before. The organizations which boast resilience will be those able to demonstrate strength and evidence growth, and those which reshape in order to secure a competitive position. These will be the case study organizations for students of resilience in the mid 2020s and beyond.

Finally, whilst this note has been written in a rather detached way, and deliberately so, I fully appreciate that the Covid-19 is likely to represent a tragedy for many people – it may well turn out to be a personal tragedy for me. However, if you are reading this during a time of crisis, any crisis, I would urge you to embrace resilience thinking – it is only by having clarity about what resilience is that you can hope to select the best course of action now and build true capability going forward.

Graham Bell
July 2020

Introduction

Background and approach

Some practitioners and scholars might have you believe that 'resilience' needs little or no introduction. Surely, they might argue, we know everything we need to know about the subject already – everybody understands what it means to be resilient, don't they? I would strongly suggest otherwise. The inconsistency of application, both at an organizational level and in everyday language, plus the divergence of claims, theories and ideas means that we should absolutely have it properly explained to us – and explained to us simply and clearly, and in a manner which then allows us to do something with it. Organizations need to understand where they stand in respect of resilience and they need to know which capabilities they have and which they lack. This book is intended for managers and specialists who wish to benefit from practical guidance and easy access to resilience tools – guidance which is practical and easily understood, and which does not oversimplify or confuse. It should also serve to provide senior managers and Board members with a robust reference source to help inform strategy and resilience decision-making.

Whilst scholars continue to debate the true meaning of resilience, and not just in the context of both commercial and non-commercial organizations, practitioners can often find themselves struggling to understand the topic in a way that they can articulate and discuss with the Board. Worst still, they can find themselves at the mercy of some anonymous consultancy firm and working against a jealously guarded and opaque framework or model, the detail of which they will only get to glimpse each time they agree to pay for a 'service'. In seeking to address these challenges, this book presents resilience within a realistic and up-to-date context and introduces the reader to a unique and trademark-protected maturity and self-assessment model which can then be applied, unaided. The model, the Organizational Resilience Capability Model® (ORCM), is applicable to any organization, regardless of size or complexity, and to any sector – commercial, governmental, charitable, educational or voluntary.

Resilience has been widely adopted as a term and is used frequently as a descriptor of convenience in the news media. At an organizational level it is most commonly applied in respect of assets or networks and the ability of those asserts or networks to withstand a disruptive event – the term is effectively reduced to a commentary about a particular vulnerability, such as a power outage or flooding, reflecting its early heritage from material science. At a societal level, many references are limited to the management of climate risks or to the robustness of urban infrastructure and what this means for city dwellers. Resilience is also widely used in relation to an individual's ability to withstand negative forces or to their observed persistence and ability to complete a particular task. As will become clear in the following chapters, organizational resilience should be viewed as a strategic concept and one which speaks to the successful management of Board-level risk. When we think about resilience we should be doing so in terms of the organization's strength, competitiveness, re-shaping and growth, and not simply as an event-focused concept or an aggregation of individual high-performers.

Undeniably, organizations can be, and often are, undone by specific events, or at least find themselves severely tested by them. It is surprising just how careless some organizations actually appear to be in exposing themselves to threats, for example by running unpatched operating systems against a background of known intelligence about cyber-attacks – I am referencing here an authoritative post-event report which found that suitable risk-related information was not made available to senior management in the case of the NHS's vulnerability to WannaCry ransomware.[1] However, the point here is that the 'undoing' of the organization and the specific causal event associated with it, whatever that might be, is not really what resilience is about.

Resilience introduces us to a series of critical relationships both inside and outside of the organization and it allows us to better appreciate the complexity and interconnectedness of the organization's capabilities. These capabilities are essentially a reflection of what the organization has available to it or what it can create, and how it does things or the way in which it elects to go about its business. Considerations of resilience capability force us to take a holistic view and one which considers the long-term prospects for the organization.

To return to the event-scenario and the effect this might have on the organization, an appreciation of resilience allows practitioners and senior managers to consider destabilizing or disruptive events within the correct strategic context. That is, the organization's response to an event, and indeed the circumstances which led to it having an impact in the first instance, are of interest to us in so far as they affect the organization's long-term success. Studying resilience encourages us to consider events, and the organization's success or otherwise in responding to them as simply a component of what is a much broader set of capabilities.

Another fact which readily presents itself is the ability of some organizations to post successes, again and again, during periods of uncertainty and rapid change. Many of these organizations are not simply passive in their respective environments, responding only when specific criteria have been satisfied or to specific triggers or warning signs. Rather, like the online giant Alibaba or sportswear company Nike,[2] they are themselves the very agents of change, delivering groundbreaking new products or services, creating entirely new markets and resetting customer expectations and behaviours in the process.

And just as resilience cannot be restricted to one or two key components, there is no simple recipe or standout ingredient for delivering long-term success for organizations, despite what many commentators would have us believe. In reference to specific examples of organizational growth, much has already been written about the importance of leadership or the need to create a climate and culture which supports innovation, but the reality is these are themselves merely components of resilience capability. Of course, we should celebrate success by seeking to understand how learning can be extracted and shared, but care should always be taken not to ignore the unique circumstances within which success has been delivered within a particular organization – the significance of leadership or a culture of innovation can easily be misunderstood and wrongly applied. To allow this to happen risks the creation of an unsustainable and non-transferable vision of resilience capability, focused upon a particular characteristic or limited set of circumstances.

Finally, in approaching the contents of the book, it is worth suggesting that the reader steps through each chapter in sequence, as summarized in the remainder of this introduction. There is a temptation, particularly with management books, to cherry-pick specific elements or to dive straight into some of the specific detail, such as the maturity model or assessment detail in this case. However, I believe there is real value to be had from digesting the subject in the order that it is presented here, and certainly the detail of the maturity and assessment model, outlined in Chapter 5, is likely to make a lot more sense when considered against the context, definitions, benefits and case studies outlined in Chapters 1, 2, 3 and 4.

Contextual setting

Chapter 1 provides a brief explanation of the current and historical context within which the subject of resilience is set. Resilience has a long history and many of today's practitioners may think of its heritage in terms of business continuity or asset management. Whilst our efforts to conclude a working definition need to be cognizant of that heritage, at least in facilitating a compare-and-contrast level of understanding, the main focus here is on establishing the breadth of the subject, its relevance to long-term success and its importance to Board-level decision-making. Trying to align a definition specifically to business continuity or crisis management, for example, would simply miss the point. In addition, the book is not intended to provide a complete research summary – there are several academic papers published on the internet which provide encyclopaedic reference sources – but the citations included within these initial chapters do provide both a comprehensive guide to the topic and introduce the breadth and depth of resilience studies over a significant span of time.

A meaningful definition

Landing on a definition for Organizational Resilience is an important and challenging task, and one which is tackled head-on in Chapter 2. In endeavouring to understand and apply resilience thinking, we are fortunate in not being short of background information – from articles and books to countless research papers and slide presentations, many of which are freely available online. However, contributions to this topic are routinely made from a restricted or skewed perspective and because there is no widely accepted definition or true standard for resilience, contributors feel (and I count myself within this group) able, if not almost obliged, to present their own thoughts and ideas using novel frameworks or models. The absence of a singular, universally accepted definition or perspective frees us to explore and then present on the topic, each in our own way.

Additionally, Chapter 2 provides an introduction to various information sources which may be of help to the reader, and to some of the models and competing definitions for resilience which exist. In suggesting a definition for organizational resilience, I am acknowledging the 'evolution of thinking' which has taken place over recent years and helping to ensure that practitioners can feel confident that they have something which is both practical and enduring. The definition of resilience provided in these pages is also a positive one, and one which reflects the fact that it is built upon the organization's success in managing its strategic risks – it is a definition which has much more to do with whether the organization is capable of delivering on its social responsibilities and promises made to shareholders, than it has to do with the management of operational events.

The value of building resilience

Practitioners should see themselves as being able to lead a discussion at Board level on the subject of resilience, undertake assessments of capability in complex organizations and propose meaningful improvement actions to address identified weaknesses. Building on our robust definition of resilience in Chapter 2, a big part of being able to hold a strategic-level conversation on resilience is having the confidence, born of knowledge of course, to articulate the benefits associated with improvement in capability.

The key to unlocking those potentially difficult conversations – and let's face it, any conversation at this level can be difficult – is to understand just how resilience can be misinterpreted and mis-sold. Unless working in a particularly enlightened environment, it is quite likely that practitioners will be having to steer the conversation by repeatedly correcting and revisiting elements of the discussion and carefully challenging those around them to reduce the scope for confusion and delay. This might all sound a little melodramatic, but organizations ignore the importance of consistent understanding and informed decision-making at their peril, as is frequently evidenced in their results.

Chapter 3 shines a light on to some of those elements needed to build the benefit case for investment in resilience, and in doing so provides the practitioner with valuable references for some of the components of resilience capability which are so often either missing or mistakenly viewed as being more important than they actually are. One of the most important considerations in seeking to create a constructive and honest approach when considering resilience is to ensure that the context and background for the organization – effectively its 'starting position' – is also consistently understood. This requires the organization to reflect on the realities of, for example, change fatigue, available skills and the likely competition for scarce improvement resources.

What resilience looks like

One of the most effective ways to illustrate a concept such as resilience is to provide the reader with access to case studies – that is, named organizations, quotations and well-anchored anecdotes which reference characteristics or behaviours which are relevant to our definition of resilience and which can help in confirming its meaning. This approach, however, is not without its challenges – the most obvious one being the identification and selection of suitable case study material and providing examples which are neither contentious nor vague.

The detail of Chapter 4 introduces a number of case study organizations, six of which are examined in detail. This selection is sufficient to provide a pointer to most of the key components suggested by our definition. For example, the strategic nature of resilience capability is highlighted, and organizations which are clearly enduring, or which can claim a significant degree of success, are presented alongside some of those which have already failed. As mentioned already, learning opportunities are available to us from each of these examples; however, the most value is derived from the way each allows us to re-state and reinforce our resilience definition.

One of the best case study examples of the last decade is provided by BP; going forward this may well be joined by Boeing, depending on the fallout from the 737 MAX grounding and how this affects the company's medium- and long-term prosperity. The fact that BP continues to be a leader in the global energy sector despite having to fund truly colossal damages following the events in the Gulf of Mexico in 2010 represents an extremely strong statement of resilience capability. It is also one which allows us to unpick our definition, namely strength and re-shaping being more relevant in certain examples, and competitiveness and growth more relevant in others. In addition to BP, Chapter 4 details case study examples relating to the UK retailer House of Fraser, the Mercedes Formula One team, Chinese online retail giant Alibaba, and London's integrated transport network.

A flexible model

The capability model outlined in Chapter 5 provides both for a resilience maturity scale and an adaptive assessment framework. The Organizational Resilience Capability Model (ORCM) is multi-dimensional and can be applied to reflect the particular circumstances of any organization, regardless of size, sector or complexity. As mentioned earlier, many practitioners find themselves having to deal at arm's length with resilience assessments via whatever interface they enjoy with external consultancy firms – this interface often being a distant and unproductive one. By presenting and explaining the detail of the ORCM, readers now have access to a tool which can be applied in order to help Board members understand resilience capability within their own organizations and to support how the most appropriate improvement actions can be selected and driven forward.

The ORCM contains a simple, yet effective maturity scale, and one which employs the language of persistence – that is, the organization's staying power – in order to create familiar labels for each of the six defined steps. These labels are in fact deliberately simple, as labels often need to be. As with other elements within the ORCM, interpretation and further descriptors are required in order to bring the resilience maturity scale to life, and the reader may find sporting analogies particularly helpful in this regard, as this can allow us to more fully embrace the notion of a competitive organizational environment.

The ORCM defines the 'what' and the 'how' of resilience capability, presented as two distinct dimensions, each containing a defined list of components. Chapter 5 examines each of these in detail and approaches each from numerous perspectives, allowing the reader not only to obtain a comprehensive understanding of the model but also to select the most appropriate interpretative position – that is, the position around which the conversation between the Board and practitioner takes place. The ORCM is defined in respect of nine primary components. Four of these are intended to reflect the feature-set of the organization and those characteristics which define it, and the remaining five components are more reflective of the organization's behaviours and actions. In full, the list of ORCM components is as follows:

FEATURES

- results;
- skills;
- personality;
- strength.

BEHAVIOURS/ACTIONS

- direction;
- awareness;
- approach;
- learning;
- resources.

The need for assurance

For our purposes, assurance should be an exercise aimed at providing the organization's Board with an independent view on how effectively strategic-level risks are being managed and how this is aligned with the Board's risk appetite, be that implied or stated. Approaching assurance provision from this standpoint ensures that it remains an exercise consistent with our understanding of resilience and one which requires an effective and well-informed assessment process to support it. Having spent much of my career involved with assurance and assurance-related activities, I would always argue that any level of assurance is better than none at all; however I would always encourage practitioners to set for themselves and their organizations the highest level of expectation in respect of quality and consistency of approach.

For assurance to be truly effective, assessment criteria and practices need to be clearly defined, suitably knowledgeable and competent assessors need to be available and an appropriate level of information needs to be accessible to support the exercise. Above all else, the relationship between assessor (and therefore also practitioner) and the Board needs to be one defined by openness and honesty – providing the assessor has sought to ensure that any conclusions are accurate and representative, he/she should be able to present and report informed opinions and recommendations against the ORCM (or other assessment model) without fear of pressure or repercussion.

Chapter 6 provides an overview of assurance provision within organizations and highlights the importance of developing a clear assessment strategy for addressing resilience risks. This strategy should be informed by reference to a range of factors, from the skills available to the organization in carrying out an assessment, through to the quality and accessibility of performance information. The chapter addresses the elements of a typical assessment process and provides detailed guidance on how to assess against the various components identified within the ORCM. Finally, specific examples are provided in respect of Board-level reporting and how the picture of resilience capability can best be captured and presented.

Links to other topics

In digesting the information contained within this book, I would hope that readers, if nothing else, are able to enhance their understanding of the subject and feel better able to consider resilience risks alongside all the other aspects of organizational activity. One of the most effective ways to consider resilience, and therefore also to communicate it, is to do so through other topics. Due to the breadth of resilience risks this is actually quite a straightforward task and one best achieved through reference to subject areas and risks which the Board are already familiar with, such as security and compliance, or the well-documented emergence and impacts of new technologies.

Chapter 7 provides linkages to several topics and potential issues which practitioners can use to their advantage. For example, there are a number of similarities between resilience and safety, and also between resilience and security. Such similarities, however, need to be exploited with care so as to avoid any interpretation of resilience being viewed as a tactical or event-focused subject. Other linkages work specifically to emphasize the strategic value of resilience thinking, such as the implications for compliance due to the application of new technologies. Chapter 7 also considers the business case for resilience investment, both as a response to weaknesses identified within an organization and as part of a wider societal approach.

One of the obvious challenges for practitioners, and indeed for Board members, concerns the variety of often inconsistent material which is presented under the heading of 'organizational resilience'. Whilst detail of my own, unique maturity and assessment model, the ORCM, is presented within Chapter 5, exposure to other specific models can prove to be extremely useful and help to engage with a wider, sometimes sceptical or poorly informed audience. For these reasons, some of the thinking associated with two such alternative approaches is provided within Chapter 7. However, when I use the term 'alternative', both of these approaches, presented by Resilient Organisations and Cranfield School of Management/BSI, share many of the same fundamental principles as the ORCM, and should therefore be approached by the reader as being complementary and informative, rather than truly alternative.

Improving resilience capability

In many ways, improving resilience capability is what the book is here to support and where its true value lies – delivering a well-informed and structured assessment of resilience capability is probably the easy bit. The application of resilience thinking and the push to close those gaps which the Board are comfortable need to be closed is where the hard work really begins. The good news is that many of the challenges associated with resilience are common to other risks and other areas of strategic focus – that is, the need for clear direction, positioning in respect of existing activity, an appreciation of the organization's skills, resources and structural constraints, etc.

One of the more obvious points highlighted in Chapter 8 relates to the way in which improvement activities need to be positioned within a coherent forward plan, and one which provides clarity around future assessment and monitoring of resilience performance. All too often, assessment activities are left 'hanging', regardless of which risk area is under consideration. Admittedly, it may be difficult to provide meaningful signals with regard to resilience until such time as the initial capability assessment activity has been considered, but certainly no Board should ever commit improvement resources without knowing what the next steps are likely to involve.

Change and adaptation are constant companions for those of us who invest time in assessing resilience capability and helping organizations to better manage their portfolio of strategic risks. Chapter 8 allows the reader the opportunity to think about transformational change by reference to some very practical considerations, such as how improvement programmes are delivered and how the organization's data capabilities might influence the way forward. Such considerations, however, only really have meaning when set against the Board's ambition for change, and it is this which provides the glue for the chapter as a whole.

Conclusion

Within these pages, Resilience is positioned firmly as a broad, strategic concept and one which requires an assessment approach which is both flexible and adaptable. Perhaps predictably, I would claim that this book and the resilience capability model outlined within it is a necessary response both to the looseness of thinking on the subject and to the two main organizational failings which can be identified time and again – a failure to learn, and a failure to pay attention. It is these failings, relative of course to the degree of success achieved, which go to define much of what we understand as resilience capability and the level of maturity which can be claimed by an organization.

It may sound a little harsh or dismissive, describing the thinking around resilience as loose, and this does mask the fact that some individual pieces are particularly strong and undoubtedly help to take the subject forward; however, the writing on the subject in many cases is far from convincing. Many contributors remain wedded to the notion that to understand resilience one simply needs to look at the strength of an organization's assets, its contingency plans, the personal attributes of a certain cadre or the quality of its incident response. Others attach themselves, limpet-like, to an individual component, such as leadership, and promote this as the singular most important thing that every organization must attend to if it is to achieve any degree of resilience.

Anecdotes about leadership style, for example, can be both informative and entertaining, but practitioners and Board members don't need fantasies or convenient stereotypes, and they don't need to become obsessed with business celebrity either – what they need are practical tools which can help with establishing and delivering their own improvement efforts. There is also a very real risk that as practitioners we assume that leadership, or indeed any other singular component, is equally important for every organization whatever its level of resilience maturity might be, just because we have identified it as a primary influencer in a specific case. Every organization is different and at a different point in its resilience journey and our assessment and maturity model needs to reflect as much.

As defined within the ORCM, learning is something which can be studied and described in relation both to individuals and to organizations. As it happens, it is also one of those components of resilience capability which attracts the most agreement amongst scholars and practitioners. Like many readers, I have experience of organizational culture which effectively provided the antithesis of learning, and one which was routinely characterized by arrogance and an astonishing disregard for the value of experience. Thankfully, an organization's true learning credentials can be easily tested and so the opportunities for being able to claim something which isn't actually the case should therefore be limited. To begin to understand where an organization has got to in respect of learning, it may therefore be helpful to consider some familiar topic areas such as incident investigation, project delivery and the quality of handovers.

In some form or other, failure to pay attention is a weakness demonstrated by many organizations, from lack of awareness associated with emerging threats or neglecting the importance of commercial acumen, through to the quality of the information upon which the organization's decision-making depends. Whilst the failure to learn effectively represents one dimension within the ORCM, acting as a proxy almost for many of the identified resilient behaviours and activities, failure to pay attention represents the other. And whilst certain skills or financial numbers might represent obvious pointers for organizations, as would asset health, other features of organizational activity which speak to resilience can be neglected. One only has to consider BP's questionable safety record ahead of the Gulf of Mexico disaster or Volkswagen's previous disregard for regulatory compliance to get a sense of how a lack of attention can affect resilience capability.[3]

Endnotes

1 National Audit Office (2017) Investigation: WannaCry cyber-attack and the NHS. 'The Department and its arm's-length bodies did not know whether local NHS organisations were prepared for a cyber-attack.' Available from: www.nao.org.uk/report/investigation-wannacry-cyber-attack-and-the-nhs/ (archived at https://perma.cc/JDU9-QVT8)

2 Amelia Heathman (2019) *Evening Standard*, 22 January. Available from: www.standard.co.uk/tech/nike-app-at-retail-shopping-tech-future-a4044766.html (archived at https://perma.cc/RN4S-CRXG)

3 Enrique Dans (2015) *Forbes*, 27 September, www.forbes.com/sites/enriquedans/2015/09/27/volkswagen-and-the-failure-of-corporate-social-responsibility/#710a55254405 (archived at https://perma.cc/VKY8-N4NH); and Christoph Rauwald (2019), *Bloomberg*, 23 August, www.bloomberg.com/news/articles/2019-08-23/vw-fired-204-staff-for-breaching-rules-in-compliance-crackdown (archived at https://perma.cc/VPL6-4JBT)

1

Contextual setting

It is the history of resilience, and how and by whom the term is used, which contributes massively to being able to establish a working definition and one which is fit for an organizational setting. Resilience is certainly the most versatile of terms, referred to in relation to countless aspects of everyday life and scientific study, from mental wellbeing and the natural environment, to the structural integrity of buildings and even the behaviour of public figures. Due largely to its material science heritage, I would suggest that many people, practitioners and non-practitioners alike, possess a subconscious understanding of the term and apply it in the first instance as one would to the properties of a physical material – that is, applied as a label to something which can resist force and which can retain and/or regain its original function or shape.

It is certainly not my intention to present a detailed or anywhere near complete overview of historical developments in this field, nor to provide the reader with a comprehensive bibliography. Other authors and researchers have done this very successfully already, and as part of applying resilience to different areas, such as child psychology and food security.[1] However, before looking at the way in which organizational resilience should be defined, which is the subject of Chapter 2, I believe that our understanding benefits from taking the time to consider a number of contextual points. An appreciation of these points is essential to how we then seek to position resilience, and these are points which have greatly influenced the body of knowledge which was developed around the subject, and which continues to do so.

Resilience as a descriptor for how materials behave – a descriptor of physical things and of properties which can be observed and predicted – is the first such contextual point worthy of attention. The second relates directly to its application at an organizational level and the notion that, again as a property, resilience is something which can be attended to and potentially improved. This chapter will also touch upon a handful of other influences, such as an organization's ever-increasing vulnerability, or so it would seem, to cyber-attack or system breakdown and what this means for its ability to control data. However, no review of organizational resilience and the context within which it is considered would be complete without a specific mention of business continuity and the often-associated drive towards certification and compliance.

Material science

The term 'resilience' has a long history of use and appears to be an increasingly common accompaniment to many workplace and everyday discussions. It comes originally from the Latin *resilire*, meaning to recoil or rebound, and is therefore widely to be considered 'a notion borrowed from material sciences describing the ability of a material or a system to recover after a deformation' (Dahlman, 2008).[2] Regardless of how else the term has been or is being applied, as mentioned above, I remain convinced that this constitutes most people's reality and therefore governs how it is generally received and understood. Doubtless there are psychologists out there who would be better able to explain the processes through which words and meanings become embedded in this way. Further, it is only by then comparing this with more enlightened definitions for organizational resilience that we come to see just how inappropriate and limiting a 'mechanical' approach actually is.

Resilience has its roots in the study and observation of materials and finds easy application to physical structures, for example, and to what a structure can withstand before it fails – it is not so well rooted in the study of adversity, as it is commonly understood, be that personal, social or economic. Although straightforward, a material science perspective is actually severely bound and can prove itself to be extremely limited. Considering resilience as a mechanical property would pretty much eliminate any opportunity for change when applied in an organizational context – and if we are denied the opportunity to change, we would, presumably, also be denied the opportunity to grow. Just as fundamentally, it is only through a particularly formal application to material or mechanical science that one is exposed to any true measure or unit of resilience – we are rarely so fortunate with casual references. In most cases, the reference to resilience is made whilst offering no suggestion as to how quickly or effectively recovery can be achieved, or how often, or at what cost. It hardly needs me to highlight the importance of each of these considerations from an organizational perspective.

It may have been the advances in civil engineering and increasing reliance on physical structures to everyday life which created the circumstances for resilience to become so popular and widely applied. This certainly suggests how it came to find such favour in relation to communities and urban settings and also to the natural world and ecology. Also, when viewed as a specific objective or goal in the design of something, it quickly becomes much more than simply an abstract property. Much in the same way that project management benefited from the application of models and principles, so too engineering resilience, as characterized by the common reference to the 'four Rs' of resilience: 'resourcefulness' and 'redundancy' defining the means through which enhanced resilience is achieved, and 'robustness' and 'rapidity' the desired end-state.

It is within this context that we can better appreciate the application of the term 'resilience' to areas which include the ability of infrastructure to withstand natural disasters – those studies and reports published following hurricane Katrina or super-storm Sandy in the United States rely heavily upon it.[3,4] It seems to be this kind of event which consistently increases our exposure to 'resilience' in text and everyday language, and somewhat paradoxically, it does so by often reducing the application back to its most basic and essential parameters – how we can improve our capacity to withstand and respond to significant events. As highlighted later in this and the next chapter it is the predisposition to emphasize events and the reaction to them which offers a key differentiator in our considerations of organizational resilience.

Something which can be built and destroyed

There is a complexity and subtlety to organizational resilience which is difficult to ignore, as illustrated time and again in the numerous and varied contributions to the topic. I touch upon the role of leadership in relation to building and maintaining resilience, for example with the Mercedes motorsport case study in Chapter 4, and in doing so highlight that determining its importance, or indeed the importance of a specific individual, is really not at all straightforward – a challenge echoed by many authors, such as Jim Collins.[5] However, it is probably foolhardy to deny that leadership must, in any conceivable context, have at least *some* influence over resilience performance.

This point underpins a simple truth about resilience – and yes, some of it at least is relatively simple – that is, as is true of the organization, resilience can be built and it can be destroyed; or rather it can made or broken; improved upon or diminished. An organization can be undone, and its core capabilities can be individually or collectively undermined. This then, is not a point about the role of leadership per se, but rather recognition that resilience capability is something which can be attended to and influenced, be that through the deliberate actions of a specific individual, leader or otherwise. As such, our expectations about organizational resilience, and therefore our approach, should be that it can be measured and described and that it can be monitored and enhanced. All of this might sound rather elementary to many readers, but it is a crucial contextual point – as practitioners we are, therefore, engaged in something which is both practical and real. This is more about facts and figures than it is about conjecture, assumptions, speculation and guesswork, and resilience capability is something we should expect to have presented to us accordingly.

This should all come as welcome news to many readers, particularly those familiar with systematic and defined approaches used within project management, accounting or assurance, and most importantly, those familiar with the management of risk. As covered in later chapters, and specifically Chapters 6 and 8, establishing that resilience exhibits both form and scale highlights the need for assessment and reporting of capability. It also, therefore, suggests there is potential for the organization to plan for and deliver improved (resilience) performance. This, of course, means seeking to establish improvement priorities and having those challenging discussions about which activities need to be started and which existing programmes of work may need to be changed or abandoned.

It is an obvious point, but, depending on our definition of resilience, it follows that it is management who are doing the building or destroying – it is the organization's management group which has primary responsibility for resilience capability, from team leader and supervisor through to the Board, and the other way around. The tools and resources necessary for the task therefore need to include much more than simply a Board-level paper and an assessment model – as controllers and administrators, managers need to be intimately involved with all aspects of resilience capability, from the initial review of headline performance information through to establishing an assessment strategy and the design and delivery of improvement plans.

The climate and culture of the organization represent its reality in a way that official policies and advertisements never can, and as a subset of this, management culture within an organization is something which we should be keen to highlight and explore. No decision regarding resilience capability or its assessment should be attempted without due consideration of the norms and practices which describe management culture, as it is this which may determine if any hard-won improvements are actually embedded. Culture does not have to become a toxic issue or an obstacle for it to warrant our attention as practitioners – the expectations and values which are reflected in everyday experiences will be critical ingredients in understanding resilience capability.

Standards compliant

To be absolutely clear, compliance is not a dirty word, and I would not encourage anyone to consider it principally in terms of either a restraint or barrier. Ethical and compliant positions are actually essential components of resilience maturity – together they permit freedom of movement, nourish precious network connections and contribute massively to the preservation of value in any organization. To understand this point, one only has to ask the shareholders at Volkswagen,[6] Siemens,[7] Danske Bank[8] or Olympus[9] – organizations which have seen stock value diminish or reported significant bottom-line impacts due to reputational damage and/or the imposition of fines or other penalties.

Whilst important national and local differences exist in this regard, the context within which resilience is approached by many organizations is heavily influenced by business continuity considerations and the drive towards compliance with external standards. More accurately perhaps, the approach is heavily influenced by business continuity practitioners and the belief that: a) resilience and business continuity are simply interchangeable terms: and b) that the discipline associated with external certification efforts brings with it significantly more benefit than it actually does. In some organizations the context is influenced by other standards, for example those relating to security or fire safety, but the argument remains fundamentally the same.

It might make more sense to take each of these points separately, but they are often so intertwined that I tend to approach them as simply representing different sides of the same coin. Business continuity is an event-focused concept, described by Bhamra (2016) as 'essentially returning a business to "business as usual", and nothing more'.[10] It offers nothing in respect of transformation or growth and can only therefore ever be a component of resilience capability, albeit a very important one in some cases. The benefits of compliance with ISO 22301 or other external standards are notoriously difficult to measure, particularly where there is no specific requirement to achieve certification, for example as might be dictated by a contract. Many organizations are also reluctant to measure and monitor the true costs associated with compliance.

The ability to continue delivering products and services in the face of disruptive events is recognized as a strength in many organizational settings. Whilst openly acknowledging the importance of business continuity and the contribution that it makes to building and maintaining resilience capability, I offer the following two perspectives as a way of helping the reader to counter any confusing signals which may be apparent within the organizations they work with. Firstly, compliance isn't everything, not even for business continuity. Secondly, alternative approaches do exist.

In 2010, and in response to the report by the National Commission on Terrorist Attacks Upon the United States, also known as the '9/11 Commission', the Federal Emergency Management Agency (FEMA) of the US Department of Homeland Security (DHS) published details of a preparedness and assessment programme, called the Voluntary Private Sector Preparedness Accreditation and Certification Program (PS-Prep).[11] Quite a mouthful. This programme directly references a number of standards, which now includes ISO 22301, and various models, tools and services have been associated with it – one being the Virtual Corporation's Business Continuity Maturity Model (BCMM)®.

The latest version of the BCMM offers insight into two separate but critical contextual points, namely the true scope of organizational resilience (and the reader will take my earlier comment about terms being used interchangeably) and the significance of standards compliance – it being the latter point which is of particular relevance for now. The BCMM offers six levels of business continuity maturity, the fourth of which is labelled as Standards Compliance. The way the BCMM is constructed allows for a particular interpretation of the language and elements presented across a number of separate standards, but crucially it identifies specific aspects of maturity which are above and beyond that which can be expected upon achieving compliance.

It is also useful for practitioners and Board members to appreciate that alternative approaches are available and that external certification (or even an informal 'alignment') with standards may not be an appropriate route for many organizations. Various blogs, articles, conferences and websites, effectively characterized by Adaptive BC, capture a reaction to the perceived preoccupation with delivering compliance with standards and regulatory requirements.[12] Some of the solutions offered by this group of contributors appear to be quite radical, but these frequently translate into a more value-oriented overall approach, and one which is simply less prescriptive than that found, for example, in ISO 22301.

Exercising of planned contingency arrangements offers a great example of an alternative approach, and one which can be applied in almost any organization. Traditionally, business continuity exercises have been designed to test the adequacy of prescribed arrangements or simply the assumptions or targets upon which they have made and have been deliberately scheduled to satisfy the requirements of a particular standard or certification regime. However, if the organization was focusing its resources into addressing known weaknesses and to the improvement of resilience capabilities, then it is quite likely that a different type of schedule would emerge, one emphasizing the need to bolster decision-making capabilities of certain managers, for example.

Data vulnerability

Many organizations are seeing an increased focus on vulnerabilities associated with cyber-attacks – in fact, it might be difficult to find one that was not. This coincides with an increased number of large, global companies losing control of sensitive data through exposed system weakness, errors or the deliberate act of an insider, and examples are easy to identify:

- Between February and March of 2014, eBay requested that 145 million users change their account passwords due to a breach that compromised encrypted passwords along with other personal information.[13]

- In 2017, controls at Equifax were breached, putting the data of over 143 million Americans and many people in other countries at risk. At the very least, several hundred thousand identities were stolen. Although Equifax did not announce the breach until 7 September, the breach took place several months prior, in May 2017.[14]
- In September 2018, Facebook announced that it had discovered an attack that exposed the personal details of 50 million accounts (later revised down to 29 million), including those of co-founder Mark Zuckerberg and chief operating officer Sheryl Sandberg. The attack also gave hackers access to other services that people logged into using their Facebook account, such as Instagram, Spotify and Airbnb.[15]

According to figures for 2018 published on the Breach Level Index website, nearly 6 million records were lost every day that year in the UK, with malicious activity from outside of the organization accounting for over half of that total.[16] The contextual relevance of this for organizations is difficult to deny and it forces practitioners and Board members to consider data vulnerability in terms which go much deeper than simply IT budgets and firewalls. For example, as practitioners we need to ensure that our assessment framework for resilience capability adequately captures the contribution and importance of data to how the organization operates and therefore the value which should be placed upon it. Similarly, Board members must be provided with full visibility of potential sanctions and accurate assessments of how long-term reputational damage can be affected by fines and penalties, such as the US $700 million settlement reported in the Equifax case.

As highlighted a number of times within this book, having access to meaningful performance information is just as important for our assessment of resilience capability as having a flexible and comprehensive assessment framework – the latter being next to useless without a flow of usable and accurate data. One of the challenges with 'data' for many organizations is that it often remains the preserve of a technical and operational elite. There may be few people in the organization who actually understand what data is generated (and why), how it is used (and by whom), where it is kept and what arrangements are in place to keep it safe and secure.

Organizations often appear to be very wary of data-related issues and for many the immediate reaction to a problem includes some degree of denial, be that internally or even to customers and regulators. The lack of transparency and understanding of data issues, such as the organization's level of dependency on third-party cloud service providers, can also impact what decisions are made in response to an incident. These decisions can also suggest a lack of understanding when it comes to the organization's own customers. The following extract, reported in the *Wall Street Journal,* is particularly relevant in this respect:

> Google exposed the private data of hundreds of thousands of users of the Google+ social network and then opted not to disclose the issue this past spring, in part because of fears that doing so would draw regulatory scrutiny and cause reputational damage, according to people briefed on the incident and documents reviewed by the *Wall Street Journal* in October 2018.[17]

The software 'glitch', as reported above, led to personal data belonging to 500,000 members of the social network not being properly protected. Google announced at the time that it was ending access to the service to the wider public.

Consultancies

Another valuable contextual point relates to the expansion in resilience-related consultancy services, the availability of online content and other material and to promotional events or activities which seek to make a connection to resilience thinking. Some of this comes from familiar sources, such as the Big Four accounting firms, whilst some is provided by more specialist firms, technical institutes, publications or academic institutions. Regardless of how we might view consultancy practices, as practitioners and scholars of the subject we should at least acknowledge the contribution they have made through publishing such a volume and variety of information, highlighting issues of common concern and in creating the circumstances in which we can more easily come together to improve our understanding.

Some firms have a particular service which they are keen to advertise under a 'resilience' banner, and this may well highlight an inherent event-bias as new material or reports (often rather grandly, and misleadingly, referred to as 'white papers') frequently associate with a natural disaster or other crisis. Alternatively, firms might sponsor academic work or carry out their own surveys in order to promote themselves and their ideas and models. As will become clearer during the next few chapters, not only does the description and definition of organizational resilience differ one consultancy to another, but the services being offered tend to be limited to specific components of resilience risk, being tailored towards technology, supply chain, operations, network health or employee engagement and psychological wellbeing, to name just the main ones.

Being able to differentiate by reference to event-bias should allow us to better appreciate the relevance of a particular service offering within the unique context of those organizations that we work with, but it is equally important to be able to understand what knowledge and tools are actually being made available by the consultancy firm as part of their engagement with us. This matters to the organization both in the short and medium term. As referenced within Chapter 6, the manner in which any assessment is undertaken is also of critical importance.

When commissioning assessment work with external consultancies, Boards should be doing so as part of a clear strategy for how resilience capabilities are to be monitored and reported on going forward. It is simply unrealistic to expect any organization, however talented their practitioner community might be, to monitor and report on resilience capability by seeking to mimic an initial assessment which they were not party to and/or by reference to a model of which they lack any detailed understanding. And yet, anecdotally at least, this is precisely what happens on a regular basis. If the organization confirms the use of a particular external provider for its assessment of resilience capability, then its potential long-term reliance on that same provider should also be openly addressed, assuming the Board wish to know how capability and maturity are actually changing over time.

One interesting development concerns the way in which some of those offering consultancy or related services describe their own increased focus in resilience as a natural extension to traditional subjects. The Business Continuity Institute (BCI) and the *Disaster Recovery Journal* (DRJ) have both positioned activities, badged as 'resilience', in this way, and have done so very deliberately and explicitly within their advertising.[18,19] This is not to pass judgement on the quality of the services being offered, but rather to highlight that this journey to resilience, or rather this particular route, is one which will be familiar to many readers, and which therefore may have a particular relevance to it.

Societal influences

Societal considerations should be tremendously important for any organization, but this reference is certainly not about establishing why some individuals are more resilient than others or highlighting aspects of social adversity or deprivation which require some form of outside intervention. Societal influences are important because of what they define and how they influence the environment in which organizations operate. These influences are many and varied and range from how an organization is able to access local resources to the changing national and international regulatory and statutory environment – crisis preparedness, for example, is just one small component of what is important in societal terms. The timing of societal influences is also worthy of note as they often land with different groups of stakeholders almost simultaneously. For example, how employees are affected by the increasing focus and recognition of an emerging environmental concern is not always easy to establish or predict, but the timeframe for such things will be very similar for all groups, be that shareholders, political policy-makers, employees and customers.

Societal considerations cover a vast range of topics and disciplines, from infrastructure planning and the work done by the Rockefeller Foundation and the Organisation for Economic Co-operation and Development (OECD) and others in promoting 'resilient cities', through to collectivism and local political issues and international movements highlighting issues such as globalization or climate crisis.[20, 21] Simply dismissing societal influences as multifarious and complex and therefore just too difficult to think about is not an option if we are to take resilience capabilities seriously. Practitioners should be focused on seeking to establish what these influences actually look like and should be doing through the unique lens provided by the organization they work with, mapping influences to stakeholders and marrying these with the elements of the resilience assessment model they intend to use.

Whilst much has been made of how local infrastructure planning fares when tested by natural disasters, it seems likely that the emergence of new philosophies and social movements will provide an increasing area of focus in the timeframe through to 2030 or beyond. Whilst Board members should not be concerned with trying to predict the future, the way in which strategy is informed by trends and the drivers of change is likely to have a huge impact on the organization's long-term prospects. Studies such as that produced by the European Union's European Economic and Social Committee (EECS) provide valuable insight into some of the likely challenges over the coming years, albeit focused on how they might affect civil society organizations (CSOs).[22] Whilst trends such as those relating to demographic change and digitization might be relatively easy to model, the significance of populism or environmental concerns, and the pace with which such influences change, perhaps illustrates some of the limitations of such analysis.

CSOs are generally viewed as those organizations which occupy the space between government and the public, but not including most private commercial enterprises. As an influencing force it is perhaps easy to neglect CSOs, largely due to their disparate nature, how they are variously defined or because of how they are sometimes staffed. However, this group of organizations has significant economic muscle, a proud history of social innovation and not only do they interface in some way or other with almost every other type of organization, however informally, its members are often well educated and highly motivated by specific beliefs or causes – and they are all potential customers and voters and friends or partners of those who work in more 'traditional' organizational settings.

For any organization, periods of rapid social change can afford significant opportunities as well as challenges. The increasing pressure on fossil fuel producers and users seems likely to produce a genuinely transformative change in many aspects of society at some point in the not too distant future, and organizations should be alive to this. They should also consider the pace and pattern of change, for example in relation to the adoption of clean energy technologies, and what this means for corporate strategy. Reported in the *Guardian* in 2019, Michael Liebreich, the founder of the research group Bloomberg New Energy Finance (BNEF), noted the following (in relation to replacing old technologies with new):

> The first 1 per cent takes forever, 1 per cent to 5 per cent is like waiting for a sneeze – you know it's inevitable, but it takes longer than you think – then 5 per cent to 50 per cent happens incredibly fast.[23]

Conclusion

It is unlikely that many readers will be approaching resilience simply in absolute terms. The performance and capabilities of the organization only really make sense within a particular setting and relative to a certain point in time. Beyond this, resilience takes the organization on a journey of discovery, and our job as practitioners and scholars of the subject is to provide the tools and guidance which will be needed on the way.

This chapter has highlighted a number of contextual references which should be relevant to most organizations, from how data is used through to wider societal influences and political movements.

However, by its very nature, context speaks to the organization's unique history, make-up and position relative to others within its industry or immediate environment. As such, it would never be possible to highlight all of those contextual points which might be relevant, nor to suggest those which might be particularly important or even critical. To make this point in a slightly different way, a number of authors and commentators have made the point that resilience can only make sense when a comparator is applied – as referred to by Carpenter *et al* (2001) as the resilience of 'what to what'?[24]

In accepting resilience as a relative concept, it is also important to appreciate that resilience capability is likely to be influenced differently by certain parts or levels within the wider organization, particularly those organizations which operate at scale: that is, it might demonstrate a degree of capability in certain areas which is not to be found in others, even if these areas interact closely. Similarly, organizations can fail even if many of their parts are considered to be 'resilient'.

A definite commercial perspective and one which highlights business failure and survival is probably a useful way to consider 'context' in concluding this chapter. The statistics for businesses which cease to trade, and in particular small businesses, are quite startling. According to the US Bureau of Labor Statistics, some 20 per cent of small businesses fail in their first year, and 50 per cent will have failed in their fifth year.[25] Now, we've always had small businesses and we've always seen shifting consumer patterns and periods of uncertainty and crises come and go, but it is fair to say that the scale and pace of change in 2020 is something new – it is a different kind of change and at a different pace and is increasingly tied in some way to technology and our increasing dependency on it.

For many organizations it is the sensitivities associated with new technology which provide one of the most recognizable and relevant contextual elements for their consideration of resilience. The sharpness of focus around this element is helped by the fact that it is easily measured and frequently reported upon. As highlighted by the Verizon 2019 Data Breach Investigations Report, some 27 per cent of organizations experienced breaches caused primarily by unpatched systems and software.[26] Commenting on the same report, the following quote from the Tripwire website nicely sums up the significance of such vulnerabilities in a resilience and risk context:

> Finding vulnerabilities is just a part of an effective vulnerability management programme. It is important for organizations to focus on building a programme instead of deploying a tool. Vulnerability management has to include asset discovery, prioritization and remediation workflows in order to be effective at reducing risk.[27]

This chapter should encourage the reader to consider resilience by first seeking to understand the circumstances within which the organization finds itself: its make-up and its surroundings, its networks and its dependencies, as well as its recent history and plans for the future. This then forms the basis for one of the most significant challenges in studying and applying resilience, and the subject for the next chapter – establishing a definition which can be understood and then successfully applied.

Endnotes

1 *Building Resilience for Food and Nutrition Security: Definitions of resilience* (2013). Available from: www.2020resilience.ifpri.info/files/2013/08/resiliencedefinitions.pdf (archived at https://perma.cc/SHH6-QARF)

2 Dahlman, O (2018) *Towards a Resilient European Supply Chain*, 16th OSCE Economic and Environmental Forum, Part 1: Maritime and inland waterways co-operation in the OSCE area: Increasing security and protecting the environment, 23 January. Available from: www.osce.org/eea/30458?download=true (archived at https://perma.cc/G56B-VMYM)

3 Tierney, K and Bruneau, M (2007) *Conceptualizing and Measuring Resilience: A key to disaster loss reduction*, TR News 250, pp 14–17 (May–June). Available from: onlinepubs.trb.org/onlinepubs/trnews/trnews250_p14-17.pdf (archived at https://perma.cc/5476-UF64)

4 Wakeman, T and Miller, J (2016) *Lessons Learned from Super Storm Sandy*, UTC Spotlight, University Transportation Centers Program, No 104 (November). Available from: www.transportation.gov/sites/dot.gov/files/docs/spotlight_1116.pdf (archived at https://perma.cc/S864-2D6R)

5   Strella, K and Reinken, B (2015) Interview with management thought leader Jim Collins, Egon Zehnder, 24 February. Available from: www.egonzehnder.com/insight/interview-with-management-thought-leader-jim-collins (archived at https://perma.cc/W4H3-K6XH)

6   Jolly, J (2019) Volkswagen emissions scandal: mass lawsuit opens in Germany, *Guardian*, 30 September. Available from: www.theguardian.com/business/2019/sep/30/volkswagen-emissions-scandal-mass-lawsuit-opens-in-germany (archived at https://perma.cc/FK9K-6JFP)

7   Venard, B (2018) Lessons from the massive Siemens corruption scandal one decade later, *The Conversation*, 13 December. Available from: theconversation.com/lessons-from-the-massive-siemens-corruption-scandal-one-decade-later-108694 (archived at https://perma.cc/BZ2T-KCLD)

8   Gronholt-Pedersen, J (2018) Danske Bank's compliance head quits after 'intense' work over Estonia scandal, *Reuters*, 11 July. Available from: uk.reuters.com/article/uk-danske-bank-moves/danske-banks-compliance-head-quits-after-intense-work-over-estonia-scandal-idUKKBN1K117W (archived at https://perma.cc/7JWK-MXMZ)

9   *Financial Times* (2011) Background: Olympus scandal, 10 November. Available from: www.ft.com/content/00907f78-ecaa-11e8-89c8-d36339d835c0 (archived at https://perma.cc/Q324-7YS4)

10 Bhamra, R (ed) (2016) *Organizational Resilience: Concepts, integration and practice*, Florida USA, CRC Press, p xvii, referenced by BCI. Available at: www.thebci.org/news/what-is-organizational-resilience.html#_edn3 (archived at https://perma.cc/DD4M-GU4F)

11 Kean, T and Hamilton, L (2004) *The 9/11 Commission Report*, 22 July. Available from: www.9-11commission.gov/report/ (archived at https://perma.cc/EAR7-UTTW)

12 Lindstedt, D and Armour, M (2016) Adaptive BC Manifesto and other information. Available from: www.adaptivebcp.org/ (archived at https://perma.cc/V7Y4-ET9R)

13 Peterson, A (2014), eBay asks 145 million users to change passwords after data breach, *Washington Post*, 21 May. Available from: www.washingtonpost.com/news/the-switch/wp/2014/05/21/ebay-asks-145-million-users-to-change-passwords-after-data-breach/ (archived at https://perma.cc/BSL9-FTQ4)

14 Leonhardt, M (2019) Equifax to pay $700 million for massive data breach. Here's what you need to know about getting a cut, *CNBC*, 22 July. Available from: www.cnbc.com/2019/07/22/what-you-need-to-know-equifax-data-breach-700-million-settlement.html (archived at https://perma.cc/FSJ2-PXBC)

15 Isaac, M and Frenkel, S (2018) Facebook security breach exposes accounts of 50 million users, *New York Times*, 28 September. Available from: www.nytimes.com/2018/09/28/technology/facebook-hack-data-breach.html (archived at https://perma.cc/K44G-W6W9)

16 Data Privacy and New Regulations Take Center Stage (2018) and other information. Available from: breachlevelindex.com/ (archived at https://perma.cc/P96E-ARZF)

17 MacMillan, D and McMillan, R (2018) Google exposed user data, feared repercussions of disclosing to public, *Wall Street Journal*, 8 October. Available from: www.wsj.com/articles/google-exposed-user-data-feared-repercussions-of-disclosing-to-public-1539017194 (archived at https://perma.cc/5TVY-MLK6)

18 The title of the BCI education month events for 2019 was 'Building Resilience'. Available from: www.thebci.org/event-detail/event-calendar/education-month-2019.html (archived at https://perma.cc/CX5L-3N9S); The title of the BCI education month events for 2018 was 'Discovering Organizational Resilience'. Available from: www.thebci.org/event-detail/event-calendar/education-month-2018.html (archived at https://perma.cc/FMN5-VJ6Q)

19 The title of the DRJ Fall 2018 conference was 'Reimagining Business Resiliency'. Available from: www.drj.com/images/conferences/fall2018/DRJ_F18-24pg.pdf (archived at https://perma.cc/8DSK-G6N2)

20 Reference to the 100 Resilient Cities organization (which concluded on 31 July 2019) and the City Resilience Index. Available from: www.rockefellerfoundation.org/our-work/initiatives/100-resilient-cities/ (archived at https://perma.cc/NMW9-CY7V)

21 Reference to the OECD Resilient Cities project. Available from: www.oecd.org/cfe/regional-policy/resilient-cities.htm (archived at https://perma.cc/CZW6-L46A)

22 *The Future Evolution of Civil Society in the European Union by 2030* (2018). Available from: www.eesc.europa.eu/en/our-work/publications-other-work/publications/future-evolution-civil-society-european-union-2030 (archived at https://perma.cc/B9PB-HNPG)

23 Ambrose, J (2019) Rise of renewables may see off oil firms decades earlier than they think, *Guardian*, 14 October. Available from: www.theguardian.com/environment/2019/oct/14/rise-renewables-oil-firms-decades-earlier-think (archived at https://perma.cc/N9PF-VK48)

24 Carpenter, S, Walker, B, Anderies, J and Abel, N (2001) From metaphor to measurement: Resilience of what to what?, *Ecosystems*, 4, p 765. Available from: doi.org/10.1007/s10021-001-0045-9 (archived at https://perma.cc/HLG3-7ZJF)

25 McIntyre, G (2019) What percentage of small businesses fail? (And other need-to-know stats), Fundera, 20 November. Available from: www.fundera.com/blog/what-percentage-of-small-businesses-fail (archived at https://perma.cc/U9YN-J6Y2)

26 Verizon 2019 Data Breach Investigations Report. Available from: enterprise.verizon.com/resources/reports/dbir/ (archived at https://perma.cc/L3VG-XNNN)

27 Lapena, R (2019) Unpatched Vulnerabilities Caused Breaches in 27% of Orgs Finds Study, *Tripwire*, 3 June. Available from: www.tripwire.com/state-of-security/vulnerability-management/unpatched-vulnerabilities-breaches/ (archived at https://perma.cc/4NPP-23QJ)

2

Definitions and references

In addition to introducing a variety of definitions for organizational resilience, and of course presenting one which provides the common thread for the remainder of the book, this chapter provides an introduction to various information sources which may be of help to the reader. In doing so, it also serves as an introduction to some of the various models, frameworks and approaches which exist elsewhere. Some definitions effectively pre-date the current focus on organizational and societal resilience, but nonetheless, most provide us with an important reference point and their analysis and dissection undoubtedly promotes a better appreciation of the wider subject. With regard to models and frameworks, it is reasonable to expect that one approach or research perspective will resonate with readers more than others and therefore provide particularly useful insight or learning. This is not to devalue my own maturity model and self-assessment framework presented in Chapter 5 – far from it – but simply to recognize that just as different learning styles might allow us each to understand a particular point but in different ways, so too alternative approaches to considering resilience might allow us to reach a better appreciation of its meaning, and to do so more quickly.

I must begin this chapter by admitting to something of an inner conflict in respect of definitions. As I frequently explain to clients or training course delegates, there is a danger in getting 'hung up' on the detail of definitions, particularly when presented with a number of them, and when each appears to conflict in some way, one to another. It can at times feel rather ridiculous to expect grown adults to attach themselves to a particular meaningful phrase, and to remember it 'off by heart' much in the way we were made to do at school. However, there is a bigger part of me which recognizes the value in being able to differentiate between alternative definitions and to have the ability to recall a clear, impactful phrase or sentence which can then be used in conversation or elsewhere. After all, this book, if nothing else, is an exercise in application – being able to apply a working definition in a real-world environment and in a way that leads to measurable improvements in resilience capability.

The other key point to make in respect of definitions is that they allow us to emphasize what resilience is not, as well as what it is, and in doing so these alternative definitions and references actually allow us to rehearse many of the discussions which take place on the topic within organizations, frequently of course at Board level. The ability to explain resilience in a meaningful and consistent way is essential. To be able to differentiate between resilience and other aspects of risk- or event-focused concepts, such as business continuity, gives the practitioner a distinct advantage and one which can be vital in moving things forward within an organization. The scope for misunderstanding when considering resilience is actually quite significant and reference back to a single differentiating definition can greatly reduce the likelihood of conflict and delay.

A basic search on the internet provides us with a variety of working definitions for resilience, and with a little care this can be narrowed more effectively to 'organizational resilience'. However, it takes some effort to appreciate the full breadth of definitions which have been put forward over recent years. Some definitions are easily accessible via Wikipedia or online dictionaries, and others are presented quite openly by consultancies or government agencies. Other, equally or indeed more valuable, contributions remain buried in academic papers, articles or books, such as this. Each of those definitions selected for inclusion in this chapter provides an opportunity to examine a specific area of focus, and therefore to discuss a particular strength and weakness. It is certainly not intended to provide an encyclopaedic list – in presenting my own, clear definition of resilience, other definitions are therefore included largely for illustrative purposes.

One likely observation when faced with my own definition of organizational resilience is just how different it is to many 'everyday' meanings of the term, but also how easy that makes the differentiation to other topics. There are several reasons for this, although all connected, and these points can be used to test the validity and relevance of pretty much any definition of resilience we are likely to come across. Many definitions, for example, are undeniably operational or tactical in nature, and most of these ultimately revolve around the seriousness of a particular event and the affects that this potentially has on an organization. Not surprisingly therefore, many definitions also focus on avoidance or failure or at least the limitation of damage of unexpected and unwelcome events. It is only by elevating resilience to a strategic concept that notions of growth and success become apparent, and many existing definitions are simply not at this level.

Some definitions also exhibit common shortfalls which can be seen in any topic or field of study – that is, their creators simply re-order some of the words in the hope that they then make more sense, or swap out one or more of the words and replace them with others which then also require some degree of interpretation. An example of a simple swap-out: 'organizational resilience' becomes 'how we build an enduring enterprise'. At first glance this definition appears to be quite attractive, after all it is short and easy to remember. But of course, we deserve much more than this by way of a definition – it actually gives us nothing new – and the use of 'enduring' simply provides us with a focus in time, and a single focus at that.

Additionally, some definitions of resilience may not be specific, or indeed intended to be applied in the first instance within an organizational context. Again, the listing on Wikipedia provides a useful reference point in this regard, and not only because various potential applications for resilience are conveniently presented in one place. Whilst the application is often clear, based on the subject of the work or the other references in the surrounding text, we should always seek to be fair in our assessment of definitions proposed by others and not to hide or misrepresent their intended meaning. Having said that, we can still usefully employ resilience definitions originally made for personal or societal applications providing that we are clear about our intention and any issues which this new application might present. For example, a statement or definition of resilience which is clearly and specifically intended to be applied at an individual (ie personal) level may still add value to our understanding of organizational resilience. An alternative intent should certainly not disqualify it from consideration here.

As part of formal academic endeavours or otherwise, anyone seeking to undertake a literature review in this field will probably come to a couple of early conclusions: firstly, others have been here before you; and secondly, simply deciding what to include is going to be quite a challenge. External reference sources provide us with insight into alternative perspectives or interpretations, so allowing a more effective comparison across a series of alternative definitions. They also provide an aid to understanding by highlighting developments or historical context for the subject and between them they point to the sheer diversity of thinking.

Whilst this chapter introduces three specific sources, including one from national government, practitioners may also wish to give some thought to those sources which have a particular relevance for the organizations with which they work. In doing so, external sources should be expected to contribute in some way to the following, which has many similarities with how case study material should be approached (see Chapter 4):

- historical, national or commercial context within which resilience is considered;
- definitions which might be suitable for a particular organization;
- particular characteristics or components which may be of interest;
- reference to other applications, such as resilience from a personal or societal perspective;
- examples of how improved capability can be delivered and measured.

Event-focused definitions

How an organization responds to a crisis or some other disruptive event, and of course its success in preventing them in the first place, is likely to have some effect on its activities, and therefore on its results, and ultimately even on its long-term success. And as we build our definition of resilience, we should be very clear in acknowledging these points – we should certainly not allow ourselves to get into the business of denying their relevance. However, we should be seeing an event, even a crisis event, as merely a component of organizational resilience and therefore we need to be very careful in how this is reflected in the language and terminology we choose to employ.

If our definition speaks to events in some way, and assuming we are not attempting to list *all* possible components, it suggests that we are highlighting events deliberately, so as to emphasize their importance. Perhaps we intend for them to be viewed as 'first amongst equals', or as alpha components when it comes to resilience? Perhaps not. One particular event-focused definition of organizational resilience is provided on Wikipedia:[1]

> The ability of a system to withstand changes in its environment and still function.

This definition employs 'change' in the shape of an event and does so without necessarily implying a crisis event. It is, however, unashamedly event-focused. We are perhaps to assume that change in this context should incorporate all events, even significant ones, but the reader is really left to address that for themselves. Having planted an event-focus in the centre of the definition, we are also treated to the very specific notion of the organization being able to withstand some sort of pressure or external force. This, of course, is taken from the classic event life cycle used frequently in business continuity and disaster recovery approaches, but it remains a very specific and exclusive element within the overall life cycle. This part of the definition, therefore, speaks directly and clearly to resilience's material science heritage and conjures up images of a substance being subject to an unspecified deformative force – the idea being that some materials are better able to retain their shape or functionality in such environments than others.

Even without considering the definition as a whole, I would argue that the rather narrow reference to events and to the characteristics of substances marks this out as totally unsuitable for our purposes. The definition effectively limits the ability of an organization to influence the environment within which it operates – the organization is presented as entirely reactionary, effectively waiting for change to happen around it and then seeking to limit any negative effects such changes might have. Interestingly, this has echoes of Darwinian evolution theory, where genetic mutation takes place without any conscious input, direction or awareness by the organisms involved. This is hardly a realistic position from which to study a typical organization, I would suggest, and not one which reflects the experience of most readers.

Having just dismissed the usefulness of event-focused terms, perhaps it seems rather odd to pose the following questions: What about other elements of the classic event life cycle? Are these not equally important and worthy of inclusion in our definition? Well, at least this might provide a more useful, if still incomplete and skewed narrative. One of the challenges with any definition, at least one which we hope to be of use, is the sheer space (aka number of words) necessary to list or describe every possible element or permutation. For the event life cycle, this is not completely impossible, but it still results in a definition which can feel overly long and baggy. Our definition would likely need to include a number of elements in the form of a list, presumably with some additional wording either side of this in order to provide context and positioning – otherwise it would indeed simply be a list. Such a list might include the following: anticipate, prevent, withstand, respond, recover, learn. Again, not an impossible list to include as part of a definition, but challenging, nonetheless.

With the first part of the Wikipedia definition focused on events and anchored very much within engineering and material sciences, the second part of the definition, in just two words, falls foul of an equally common mistake – it effectively captures the organization in time, prohibiting growth and extinguishing any notion of organizational development or expansion. For the organization simply to 'function', we must abandon any ambition we may have had, and our approach must concentrate instead simply on protecting vital functions and establishing suitable contingency arrangements should those functions ever be interrupted.

Business continuity is an event-focused concept, which is essentially concerned with returning a process or function to its original position following an interruption – it is essentially restorative in nature, and no amount of polish can disguise this fact. Whilst some business continuity practitioners may argue otherwise, there is no tangible ambition present beyond reclaiming a business-as-usual, or more accurately a business-before-interruption position. It therefore follows that if we are considering transformational change or even more tactical business improvement, we are unlikely to achieve this from a business continuity standpoint. So, the idea that a business is simply 'functioning', as referred to in the Wikipedia definition, is likely to be something which is at, or even below, business-as-usual levels.

'Functioning' implies that some of the organization's processes are simply dormant or on hold. New product development perhaps, marketing, financing, contract reviews, recruitment, training, even business planning and the setting of next year's budget – all of these activities may have ceased. To my way of thinking, functioning suggests that only those activities required for statutory or regulatory purposes are being undertaken, or perhaps those stipulated within minimum contractual terms.

Therefore, if we compare the Wikipedia definition with my own – resilience being defined by the organization's strength, competitiveness, re-shaping and growth – we see that the contrast is indeed stark. The definition offered on Wikipedia remains silent on all but one of the elements within my definition, and then it only suggests a very limited aspect of organizational capability which might be considered as 'strength'.

Event-plus approaches

The AGOR definition

Drawn from a source perhaps unfamiliar to many readers, the following definition is reflective of arguably the most common approach to organizational resilience, and one which still broadcasts its business continuity and crisis management heritage. Whilst there are several elements of the following definition which are to be applauded, and it is certainly more enlightened and comprehensive than most, the references to aspects of change and risk do feel rather like add-ons – an attempt perhaps at differentiating organizational resilience from these other concepts but without any true conviction:

> Organizational resilience refers to a business's ability to adapt and evolve as the global market is evolving, to respond to short-term shocks – be they natural disasters or significant changes in market dynamics – and to shape itself to respond to long-term challenges.[2]

The definition is provided courtesy of the Australian Government's Organizational Resilience (AGOR) website. In dissecting this definition, it is probably sensible to begin with the central reference to 'shocks'. This is a very deliberate word and is usually intended to be a grown-up or contemporary reference to crisis events, and an attempt to elevate them to a more strategic level. Shock is an increasingly popular reference as a simple substitute for crisis, but it is often intended to convey something in addition – not only a modern approach but also one which suggests an intimate or expert knowledge on the part of the user of technical areas, such as financial systems.

Predictably, many of the same criticisms which are levelled at event-focused definitions, can also be applied to those I have termed as event-plus. But there are unique elements to describe here. For example, what about things which are not shocks – things which should have been anticipated and prevented? I would also argue that many more organizations have either failed or thrived as a result of changes in their core market, poor service delivery or lack of liquidity than have done so as a consequence of 'natural disasters'. And yet these two very different considerations are presented as a) equal or equivalent and b) only as shocks.

So, back to the beginning of the AGOR definition and the words 'adapt' and 'evolve'. The notion of adaptation clearly signals an open acceptance of change and that the organization will be different as a result. Evolution, although clearly being applied without any reference to a scientific position, also signals change, but is more often taken to be a more targeted reference to gradual and/or managed change, possibly over the medium or longer term, and we should perhaps assume that is how it was intended in this case. It may appear to the reader that I am being unnecessarily precise with how these words are used, after all words such as adapt and evolve are used routinely and it could be argued that their meaning requires no additional discussion.

However, I would suggest that our definition of resilience is an important and challenging one to establish, and that the slightest confusion or misdirection can lead to long-lasting difficulties for us as practitioners. Both adaptation and evolution are essentially gradualistic in nature, which is a potential problem in itself, but both are also generally passive and reactionary, which is perhaps an even bigger problem. For an organization to react to events is quite normal, and indeed for many organizations this would be a regular, if not indeed a daily event. However, we would expect an organization to also have a deliberate impact on its environment – to create and influence, at least in part, the context within which it operates. We want our organizations to be innovators and pioneers, and these are not traits one normally associates with those which wait or remain dormant – we want our organizations to make it rain and not simply to grow to a genetic script once the ground has been soaked.

As indicated above, the nature of change itself and the experience which many organizations have of it is not always best described as gradual, or indeed successful. Change can obviously be sudden and unexpected, but even well-planned change events routinely involve periods of intense activity which peak around commercial handovers, product releases, decommissioning dates or the launch of new operating systems. References to change, as readers can attest to themselves, are indeed frequently gradualistic and it remains unclear as to why that might be. It is also unclear why the constant nature of change is often omitted from commentary and definitions. Either way, we are regularly left with the suggestion of only smooth, even developments, implying that the organization also has the time and warning necessary to always make controlled responses.

The reference to 'shape' within the definition is a welcome one, and one which immediately creates a sharp contrast to the 'rebound mentality' maintained by many commentators. In many ways the use of 'shape' is stronger and more certain than that simply implied by 'change', the reason being that it is outcome-focused. As an activity or event, change is immediately recognizable, but the result, success or value associated with it are often less convincing, particularly in practice – a change event may have been confirmed via internal communications, but actually being able to witness or recognize what has changed is often missing from our own corporate experiences. The notion of shape feels altogether more conclusive.

The remaining elements within the definition could easily be overlooked, but each is probably worthy of mention. Firstly, 'itself' is an important addition to the overall definition and is so because it places emphasis on ownership. When taken literally, which I assume is how it was intended, it underlines that the organization's shape is largely, if not entirely, within the Board's gift. This might seem like a very obvious point to be making, but it stands in sharp contrast to those definitions which would have us believe that the organization is nothing more than a passenger, responding and reacting to its environment, unable to influence or direct it.

Secondly, the definition speaks to the long term. Surprisingly few definitions offer us anything in respect of timescales, and there is at least recognition here that short-term responses to crisis events or shocks is not really what resilience capability is about. There is also something implicit in longer term horizons which confirm our thinking is at a strategic rather than operational level. Thirdly, by introducing 'challenges', the AGOR definition positions the organization's resilience thinking alongside that of wider risk concepts, which is of course exactly where it should be.

Other event-focused definitions

The following definitions are also, in one way at least, event-oriented and are embellished, albeit in a different way to the AGOR version. As already acknowledged, approaches to organizational resilience which centre around events, shocks and the response to them are certainly popular, and these are just two further examples:

> Anticipate, prepare for, respond and adapt to incremental change and sudden disruptions in order to survive and prosper.[3]

> The ability to survive a crisis and thrive in a world of uncertainty.[4]

We have touched upon the crisis or shock-oriented language used in both of these additional definitions, but there is also a separate and very important belief which connects them: that surviving the crisis somehow affords space for the organization to 'thrive' and 'prosper', not just to continue on its original path. However, as presented here, neither of these definitions offer us even a hint as to how this would actually be achieved or what additional attributes or capabilities might be required in order to achieve it. After all, being able to avoid a tackle doesn't necessarily put you in a winning position. In fact, as headline definitions, both appear to be rather naïve and somewhat detached from commercial reality.

Soundbite or cryptic references

By their very nature, soundbites are succinct and memorable, but they can also prove to be rather valueless, other than to offer an alternative 'spin' or perspective. Arguably, therefore, the two definitions immediately above contain an element of soundbite to them, specifically in respect of the reference to 'thrive' and 'prosper' (which when put together does sound like something from a famous US TV sci-fi series from the 1960s). It is only through dissection and analysis that we can determine if such definitions are as insubstantial as they might first appear.

The following references are typical of this group of entries, as they hardly qualify as proper definitions at all, and each also falls foul of a classic definition-related mistake – words are re-ordered and/or simply replaced with others requiring further discussion or interpretation. 'Building an enduring enterprise' is referenced by the Economist Intelligence Unit (EIU),[5] and 'success through persistence' by the Business Continuity Institute (BCI) and others. Whilst there is merit in recognizing that resilience capability is something which can, and therefore also needs to be constructed, the first of these references provides no indication of what this might look like or what components or ingredients might be required to achieve it. However, of the four words on offer to us, the use of 'enduring' is surely the most powerful. Endurance, as a noun, is undoubtedly a characteristic closely associated with resilience, and is commonly interpreted as a measure of strength or energy. Used as a verb, it also strongly implies a long-term application or permanency.

The downsides of using 'endurance' or 'enduring' are two-fold. Firstly, it does, at least for most of us, require some interpretation and it can generate a number of different meanings. For example, not everybody will have taken the time to clearly differentiate between 'endurance' and 'persistence', both of which can be used as measures. Secondly, 'endurance' and 'enduring' both lack a reliable anchor in relation to efficiency or effectiveness. For instance, longevity can be achieved in a variety of ways, some more appropriate and ultimately successful than others, and some more resource-intensive than others. The long-term functioning of an organization provides no clue as to how or indeed whether wider organizational goals have been achieved. Therefore, to offer 'an enduring enterprise' as a way of helping us to appreciate resilience is largely meaningless.

When presented in formal text, the following maxim appears rather clichéd, and even though it is grounded very clearly at a personal (rather than organizational) level, I share it for several very good reasons:

> Persistence and resilience only come from having been given the chance to work through difficult problems.[6]

Firstly, as mentioned a number of times in the book, there is generally value to be had in seeking to apply pointers and references from personal resilience to the study and improvement of organizational resilience, or at least being open to their application in that way. Secondly, it allows us to examine the alternate meanings of 'persistence' and 'resilience', and also their connection. Thirdly, the above reference speaks directly to the importance of learning, something which is central to our appreciation of organizational resilience.

Whilst connections between personal and other areas of resilience, including organizational and societal, are usually quite easy to identify, these are not always so obvious when dealing with definitions. Simply by virtue of why they are required and how they are used, definitions are typically quite specific, and therefore a definition for personal resilience will use language and terms which are tailored to that particular application. The reference above is a little more generous in that it is only loosely tailored to the capabilities of individuals – the tailoring is implicit rather than explicit. It is therefore relatively straightforward to think about an organization having to deal with problems both internally and externally, and how such experiences manifest themselves in respect of the organization's structures, behaviours and actions.

Persistence is not to be confused with resilience, although it represents an extremely important characteristic – so much so that it forms the basis for the ORCM maturity labels outlined in Chapter 5. Persistence is largely task- or activity-oriented, whereas resilience is more achievement- or outcome-oriented, and also multi-dimensional. Persistence, for our purposes, can be defined as the willingness and ability to continue with something or in a particular direction, and (likely) to do so in the face of some undefined opposition or difficulty. At an individual level persistence is often associated with traits or personal qualities, but it is certainly not used exclusively in the positive – the desire to keep going at a task, whilst perhaps admirable in many ways, may be accompanied with high direct and indirect costs and may turn out ultimately to be (self-) destructive.

To note, the labels used for the ORCM maturity scale in Chapter 5 are deliberately task-oriented and have the advantage of being clear and memorable. Employing the language of persistence allows the maturity scale to focus attention on success and the long term and provides a simple platform from which to consider the complexities of resilience capability.

As for the learning aspects of the above definition, whilst this is welcome, it still sounds a little old fashioned – the flavour is very much 'what doesn't kill you makes you stronger' and the approach sounds almost parental in tone. That said, any emphasis on the importance of learning helps us to better explain the concept of resilience; however, we should perhaps be a little more realistic when considering how knowledge is managed within a typical organization. Corporate knowledge, even that which is retained by individuals, is not always experiential in origin – how the organization identifies, orders, secures and disseminates knowledge will provide the basis for much of what individuals call upon in the course of their everyday duties.

False analogies

Ironically, perhaps even this heading, 'false analogies', requires a definition of its own. Simply stated, I am referring here to occasions when the reader is presented with a comparison or claim, which upon further investigation actually turns out to be misleading or simply implausible. There is nothing necessarily malicious or deliberate about such things – they may simply be misplaced or applied incorrectly due to a misunderstanding. I am also very aware that such things can also be the subject of carelessness – a reference applied due to its apparent convenience or because it has become fashionable elsewhere.

The following quote is the basis for one such analogy. I believe that Darwin's work itself is much misquoted, so I have been careful to attribute these particular words to Megginson, albeit in direct reference to Charles Darwin's *Origin of Species* from 1859:

> It is not the most intellectual of the species that survives; it is not the strongest that survives; but the species that survives is the one that is

able best to adapt and adjust to the changing environment in which it finds itself.[7]

The use of 'evolve' and 'evolution' is relatively common in relation to studies of organizational resilience, and to a lesser degree, so too are references to Darwin or Darwinian ideas. Given that in almost every case the authors who use these words feel no need to explain what is actually meant, we should presume that references are usually to a gradual period of change, and therefore to an organization's capability in this respect. References to 'evolve' tend not to be accompanied by suggestions of anything sudden or even disruptive – perhaps most readers would also recognize the use of 'incremental' in any further expansion of a definition.

Given the above, which I believe provides a reasonable and defendable summary of the position both in respect to how 'evolve' and 'evolution' are used and interpreted, I try hard to avoid direct or indirect references to either for the following reasons. Firstly, the Darwinian heritage, which I would suggest informs most people's understanding, even if this may only be at a subconscious level, provides a wholly inappropriate starting point for considerations of not just resilience, but also of how organizations actually operate – it is as misplaced a starting point as 'bouncing back'.

Darwinian evolution, widely (but not universally) acknowledged to provide a cornerstone for our understanding of life on Earth, is based around two distinct ideas: the first being genetic mutation; and the second being natural selection, and modes thereof. Mutations occur in a random and uncontrolled way, outside of any direct influence or awareness on the part of the organism concerned, and mutations present themselves not in the here and now, but only through the changed physical or behavioural characteristics of future generations. Does this sound in any way like a typical organization, regardless of its size or commercial orientation? I would suggest there simply isn't a Board which would describe its stewardship of the organization as being intentionally random, chaotic or uncontrolled. Darwinian evolution does not describe conscious and deliberate adaptation or re-shaping.

Natural selection suggests that changes or 'variations' which demonstrate value to the organism within a particular environment will endure – beneficial changes are 'preserved', to employ a Darwinian word, as they help the organism to survive and/or to reproduce. When applied in an organizational context, this theory suggests that changes are released blindly and in great volume, with no prior expectation as to how many may prove to be advantageous – the organization, from the Board down, accepting that each and every change will need to be tried in order to determine its potential value. Those which worked would then be retained and those which did not would be discarded. Now, whilst some change initiatives certainly feel rather chaotic, and I am sure we all have experience of them, the notion that change activities are a complete 'free for all', with no prior consideration to establishing any sort of business case, is surely fanciful.

The second reason for my reluctance to use 'evolve' as a descriptor for resilience is that it tends to misrepresent the nature of change, and the experience which most readers will have of it. Change is rarely so gradual as to be imperceptible or to go unnoticed by those within the organization, and indeed this would be counter to much of what we learn in respect of managing change activities. Change in a Darwinian sense is usually thought of as small, incremental or 'slight', and certainly not fundamental or what we now commonly refer to as 'transformational'. There is also an implied gentleness to evolutionary change, suggesting even that none of those experiencing the change will themselves be disadvantaged by it. When reaching for descriptors we need to select change-related words which reflect both its constancy and importance, but also its unevenness and the potential it has to cause damage and undermine organizational performance. For these reasons alone, and certainly for those of us who have experience of catastrophic systems implementations, 'evolve' really does not feel at all appropriate.

The comments above are not intended to be whimsical or flippant, and nor do I wish the reader to think that I am dissecting words and meanings unnecessarily. The use of 'evolve' has become commonplace, and it appears to be well supported – surely there is no harm in references to evolution, even if such references are sometimes rather casual? But great care is required in respect of our choice of terms, particularly in building definitions and explaining concepts and meanings to others.

One final comment on Darwinian notions of evolution concerns the relationship which the organism, and by inference therefore the organization, has with the environment around it. For the most part, of course, organisms are entirely unable to influence their environment – they are reactionary and responsive in the extreme. Changes and variations which take place from one generation to the next may influence how they are able to respond to or exploit that environment, but there is little or no thought to how the environment itself might be influenced or changed. Again, this is not the reality for organizations, which for the most part seek to consciously influence their environment to the greatest extent possible.

As mentioned later in the book, and by way of further illustration, there is a popular misconception in respect of how resilience at an individual or personal level can and should be translated and then applied at an organizational level. In many cases, this is probably driven by a desire to reduce the challenge of resilience capability down to something familiar and/or extremely simple and manageable, and presumably therefore more marketable. We are left believing that organizational capability will be improved only through focusing on the performance of individuals, and then, probably only a proportion of those individuals whom we have available to us. However tempting the analogy – and the notion of aggregating the capabilities of a few key decision-makers or leaders can obviously sound very attractive – we should remember that the organization is always considerably more than the sum of the parts, and therefore its resilience capability is considerably more than simply the resilience of its people.

Any analogy we decide to promote should be tested and subjected to some rigour. A good proportion of resilience definitions recognize the direct contribution of an organization's people, in respect of culture or skills, for example. Through this we can conclude that many approaches to resilience utilize aspects of behaviours and skills in seeking to understand how resilience performance can be enhanced. However convenient it might be having reached this point to then proclaim that personal resilience is the 'missing ingredient' in unlocking the resilience potential of organizations, we should resist.

The analogy, as rather crudely presented above, passes neither the test of universality nor that of common sense. Some organizations rely on people assets in ways which others do not, and some would be able to affect changes in skills or behaviours more quickly and more effectively than others. Some organizations possess a depth and subtlety of understanding when it comes to personal resilience which others will never attain, and some have already made considerable efforts in respect of leadership decision-making or boosting the psychological wellbeing of staff. The analogy is also peculiarly circular in one important dimension: it still relies entirely on our definition of resilience. If our perspective is a reactive and event-focused one, then we are likely to interpret references to decision-making, for example, as only relating to crises or operational activities.

My own definition

I believe the desire of resilience practitioners has long been the same: to help create the circumstances in which the organization can keep going and ultimately be successful. For many, this has meant an emphasis on those properties which allow organizations to resist pressure and bounce back. However, many practitioners are increasingly aware that it is properties focused on building stamina, creating a dynamic change environment, and promoting growth and the organization's competitiveness which will determine its long-term success. How an organization deals with a crisis event therefore becomes a singular component of overall resilience capability, and in many ways not the most important, at least not most of the time.

The following is my own definition, and the one which supports the detail of the ORCM in Chapter 5, and it introduces the reader to just four key attributes associated with organizational resilience. It also offers something quite different from many other approaches.

I would describe organizational resilience as simply being defined by the following:

> Strength, competitiveness, re-shaping and growth.

If required, there is also a longer version of the same definition, which reads as follows:

> This is not an event-focused concept, but is about strength, competitiveness, re-shaping and growth. It is about how successfully the organization manages its strategic risks.

Even the short version clearly positions resilience considerations at a strategic level and does so without making reference to crisis events or to 'shocks'. As a result, the reader should be left in no doubt that 'bouncing back' is simply not what defines resilience capability for an organization and should certainly not be our starting point as we embark on a journey of understanding resilience. I believe the definition is a powerful one, not because it claims to include each and every conceivable reference or sub-component of resilience, but rather because it points only to those characteristics which have proven absolutely essential for organizations to succeed, whilst avoiding the trap of relying on insincere or empty words, such as 'thrive' or 'survive'. It is also eminently understandable and for the most part requires no additional context or explanation for it to make sense – each word is both immediately recognizable and widely applicable.

Unless seeking to signpost the steps in a cycle, for example, a defining statement is probably not the best place to introduce a lengthy list of things for consideration. After all, the purpose of the definition is to communicate meaning, not necessarily to register content. We are fortunate in this respect, as the resilience model outlined in Chapter 5 does this for us and is a much more appropriate vehicle for considering aspects such as organizational leadership or innovation. By introducing only four outcome-oriented terms in the definition, we effectively avoid any charge that we have omitted something or that we have focused on components which are important to some organizations and not to others.

This definition of resilience remains memorable and requires little, if any, additional interpretative effort on the part of the reader. It is also one which, as noted above, can be used in either a long or short version, depending on circumstances. Of the four principal terms, only 're-shaping' is perhaps slightly unusual, but I would argue it remains recognizable and easy to apply. The notion of re-shaping sits well in an organizational context, both at a structural (ie organizational design) level and in relation to product/service lines, geographical locations and to the organization's wider business model. It is also fair to point to 'competitiveness' as a term which might only make sense within a full-on commercial setting, where its meaning is quite obvious. However, the notion remains highly relevant to almost every organization, providing it is also taken to include cost-effectiveness or even attractiveness. It seems quite likely that all organizations at some point or other will be required to demonstrate they are providing value for money and every organization regardless of the commercial or ownership model which underpins it will be defined by the take-up of its products or services.

In the form of a postscript, it is also worth highlighting that what also makes the concise definition uniquely relevant is that it was born out of on-the-record comments made about BP, including those by its own CEO in 2017 – comments which provided a pointer both to levels of corporate health and to the journey which the company had been on since the disaster in the Gulf of Mexico in 2010.[8] As alluded to further within the case study material provided in Chapter 4, this was one of a number of comments provided in recent years by both the CEO and chairman of BP which were almost triumphant in nature – statements not intended to dismiss or downplay the significance of events in 2010, but rather to celebrate BP's commercial achievements and how it believes it is now positioned to grow and exploit opportunities in global energy markets.

Whilst the words contained within the short version of the definition are clearly intended to speak to a strategic audience, the long version makes this even clearer, and does so through introducing the concept of risk and through positioning 'resilience' firmly as a risk management concept. This point is perhaps equally important as the absence of specific references to crisis events, and is something which will directly challenge those practitioners who subscribe to the 'bouncing back' approach and to those who use the term only to describe a narrow set of organizational qualities or operational capabilities. As mentioned elsewhere in this book, the organization's strategic risk landscape – that which is either created or impacted by the organization's fundamental plans and decisions – is exactly where considerations of resilience should be most apparent. Resilience capability is a function of how risk and uncertainty is considered within the organization, and the definition seeks to reinforce this point and to make it a strategic one.

Returning briefly to cryptic references, where the essence of meaning is likely to remain just beneath the surface and therefore still requires some interpretation, one could argue that such a label should be attached to the ending of my long-form definition. In defence, I would suggest that whilst pithy, the reference to 'strategic risk' is a meaningful one and one which provides specific positioning – it is certainly of more value to the reader than vague notions of 'thriving in a hostile environment', or something similar. The way in which the ending of my definition works, whether or not we think of it as cryptic, is largely as a discrete part or 'support act' and, as such, it does allow a slightly more informal or creative use of language.

Finally, it is worth examining the definition through the lens of personal resilience. Whilst in many ways it is only the context or application which differs, organizational versus personal, the short version of the definition certainly lends itself to considerations of an individual's resilience capability, whether or not that is specifically as an employee or as a leadership figure within an organization. Regardless of how we think about personal skills and behaviours within our organizational or even societal construct, the parallels and the opportunities to employ common language and descriptors are significant. By reference to 'strength and competitiveness', the shorthand version of the definition contains a reference which has real potential for application at an individual level, not in a harmful or negative way, and our reference to 'growth' is clearly aligned to and recognizes the importance of personal development.

Illustrative reference sources

In permitting ourselves to study organizational resilience, we are certainly not short of material to draw upon. Although references are made to other approaches and models throughout these chapters, it is worth highlighting a handful of specific sources at this point as a way of pointing the reader at information which might allow further consideration of our resilience definitions and insight into what practical application involves. It might also be useful at this relatively early stage in the book to employ an external perspective or two before we get too far into the detail of benefit cases, and the self-assessment model itself. One of these sources, the Australian Government's Organisational Resilience website (AGOR), is already used above in our analysis of event-plus definitions. Another, the Affinity Health at Work (AHAW) material, is somewhat different in that it points to a particular emphasis around personal resilience and psychological wellbeing – topics which are referred to frequently both in this book and as part of resilience discussions more generally.

The AGOR website is a valuable source,[9] dedicated to organizational resilience, not least because it contains a high-level health-check tool and provides links to industrial strategies and 'knowledge hubs' associated with partner organizations, such as the Resilience Expert Advisory Group (REAG) and Resilient Organisations (RO). Although the site is unashamedly governmental in its approach, and the emphasis on 'infrastructure resilience' might not seem particularly relevant to some, its perspective on resilience is clearly articulated and its priorities are defined and explained.

The site content should be applauded for making very clear its point-of-departure and definition for resilience and also for touching upon different approaches which organizations might adopt. The AGOR definition and the perspective adopted remain predominantly event-oriented. As mentioned above, the detail is in many ways very 'governmental' in how it seeks to encourage and promote the benefits of organizational resilience, making reference to different branches of commerce and seeking to create linkages between profitability and resilience. In style and approach, it mirrors many other 'campaigning' or single-issue websites, for example those dedicated to improving public health.

Any resource which includes a free self-assessment tool, and certainly one as broad as that offered by AGOR, deserves further investigation. Although the tool, developed by REAG, includes a reasonable level of detail, the user is left to interpret each element in a way which makes sense in their own organization; but as a quick-fire assessment tool, the results are probably most useful in highlighting immediate strengths and weaknesses and therefore as the basis for an initial discussion. The tool introduces resilience by reference to three key attributes, thereafter divided into 13 behavioural indicators (aligning to that promoted by RO). The immediate value of the tool lies not just with access to potential treatment actions, for example, but also in its ability to emphasize the breadth of the topic – it touches upon aspects such as organizational climate, culture, engagement, collaboration, knowledge management, horizon scanning and change management.

AGOR also provides access to a series of guidance documents, including a number of 'position papers' relating specifically to the role of the CEO and to critical infrastructure resilience. The site provides some local context for this information, which should still be of interest to those from other countries, by reflecting on the Australian government's publicly-stated strategy for organizational resilience. In addition, the site seeks to promote a number of 'research priorities', with the aim of supporting academic interest in the subject and thereby the wider body of knowledge which organizations can call upon. Although obviously produced with a domestic audience in mind, as of course is the website as a whole, these priorities provide a particularly useful way of 'testing' our thinking around resilience definitions and include some quite novel references and areas of focus.

The research priorities listed by AGOR include 'dimensions of leadership', 'CEO tenure', 'organizational structures' and the 'role of human resources'. To some degree or other, each of these priorities emphasizes the importance being attached to leadership structure and cultural values in building and maintaining resilience capability within the organization. But it is the particular and quite unusual focus on tenure of the organization's CEO which justifies our attention here. To quote directly from the AGOR site:

> The CEO has a pivotal impact on a range of factors associated with resilience, in particular culture. There has, in recent years, been a trend towards shortening CEO tenure as boards and shareholders pursue short-term profit in favour of long-term sustainability, potentially impacting on an organization's resilience.[10]

Regardless of how the assertion about CEO tenure sits with our own experiences or those of organizations with which we work, the way in which it is associated here with resilience capability should encourage us to challenge the definitions we are exposed to by using similar reasoning. For example, whichever definition or perspective we may be considering, can it be interpreted in a way which reflects a role for the CEO and is it likely to be something which is impacted by Board-level considerations? Does it encourage us to consider decisions in relation to both long- and short-term value creation? As commented on in later chapters, it is easy to over-emphasize the importance of leadership, or in this specific example the tenure of the CEO; however, it is when we elect to promote an event-focused or operationally-oriented definition of resilience that any real disconnect comes into focus.

Consultancies can prove to be an extraordinarily fruitful source of information for both scholars and practitioners. Affinity Health at Work (AHAW) is one such source, and one which places a particular emphasis around employee health and wellbeing. Either directly or indirectly, many of the articles or references available on the AHAW website touch upon the importance of developing resilience capability at an individual level, and the relevance of doing so in respect of organizational-level applications. Listed amongst these is a research report from 2011, authored by AHAW, which offers a summary comparison between personal and organizational resilience, and does so through providing a review of available literature.[11]

The report points to a number of conclusions, each of which has relevance to our considerations of organizational resilience definitions. Firstly, the report highlights that, 'much of the research… examines resilience in the context of reactions to disaster events or periods of dramatic change' and therefore risks failing to adequately reflect the wider commercial and strategic context within which organizations operate. Although this is hardly a surprising conclusion, the evidence (ie more recent research) may have led to a slightly different emphasis if it were conducted today.

Secondly, the report concludes that, 'there is no distinction in studies between small, medium and large organizations nor clarity about whether they were in the private, public or third sector.' This is an important point, and one which certainly draws attention to the applicability of the resilience definitions we choose. Although individual case studies usually provide very obvious references to the type and size of organization in question, it is likely that many practitioners and academics alike remain unclear as to the relevance of such things in relation to resilience capability. Of course, it is not simply a matter of size. To highlight one very specific point, and one where size might well be irrelevant, the organization's recent ownership structure and its regulatory environment are likely to be major influencers on how new products and services are brought to market. As the AHAW report conclusion suggests, to promote 'leadership', or any individual characteristic of resilience capability whilst remaining silent on the organization's surroundings may not lead to the most insightful of approaches.

Perhaps of most use in relation to establishing a robust and flexible definition, the AHAW report introduces a tabular referencing tool, covering characteristics, sources and interventions relevant to both personal and organizational resilience – the 'resilience grid' – and a proposed suite of resilience measures. The tool provides a structure and approach which can be tailored to reflect a range of resilience definitions, even though the characteristics listed in AHAW's grid are heavily skewed towards elements of leadership, culture and traditional organizational (ie structural or departmental) design. As a standalone reference source, the grid and the supporting bibliography includes numerous definitions and outlines suggested by historical research and also points us to topics for which more up-to-date references may be worth exploring, for example in relation to crisis management consultancies and arrangements relevant to critical infrastructure protection.

Although online versions of AWAH's measures table contain an obvious identification error in publication – the orange-shaded section of the table should clearly be titled 'organizational' to mirror that used in the resilience grid – it is an extremely useful reference source in its own right, and somewhat unusual in that this is an area frequently neglected in resilience literature. By including a narrative-rich table such as this, the AHAW report highlights the need to fully understand the detail and structure which sits behind a resilience definition and to be positioned to apply it through reference to potential measures and other information sources.

Finally, as introduced earlier in the chapter, I have included reference to a 2015 study by EIU as an example of how Board-level opinions can be analysed and presented, again primarily for the purposes of testing our resilience definitions.[12] Sponsored by the British Standards Institution (BSI), and in many ways a precursor to the 2017 study by Denyer,[13] this was an independent assessment of senior executives' attitudes, which found that almost 9 out of 10 saw resilience as a priority for their business, whilst 8 in 10 believed it to be indispensable for long-term growth. It also revealed that just a third of CEOs were confident their organization possessed the resilience to survive in the long term.

Opinions, however captured or reported, are notoriously difficult to unpick. For example, it would be naïve to assume that a group of CEOs, or indeed any group for that matter, who offered an opinion on their organization's long-term capabilities was doing so on the basis of deep consensus regarding the definition of resilience. What is important here is not just the headline figures and the soundbite narrative, but also the fact of what the CEOs in the survey were actually being asked to consider. For example, wherever a narrative conclusion is drawn from a 'set menu' or against predefined parameters, the author obviously has some latitude which is not available to the individual respondents. Lists and the detail of quantitative data sources are also frequently used, either explicitly or implicitly, to establish the definition favoured by the author, and this is the case regardless of whether a clear definition statement is also offered to the audience at the time.

This survey report provides a reasonable balance of quotes (including from named individuals) and anonymized data analysis and it successfully reinforces the breadth and strategic nature of the topic, both by virtue of the questions asked and through aligning individual quotations to a series of Board-level considerations and topic areas. As alluded to in later chapters, having made an assessment of resilience capability one of the challenges is then having the opportunity and insight necessary to position that assessment against others in order to enable comparisons to be drawn. This is not simply a challenge due to there being no universally agreed model or framework for assessing organizational resilience but, as highlighted by the AHAW review, there is also an over-reliance on self-assessment activities generally, the results of which are notoriously difficult to calibrate. For Board members, quotes and references linked to specific organizations can serve as a convenient proxy for more formalized benchmarking activities and they have the advantage that they come from that cadre of leaders who, it is presumed, are all speaking a similar language.

Conclusion

One thing is for certain: organizational resilience requires us to adopt a consistent definition, or at least to appreciate the benefit of a common perspective if we are to have any hope of extracting full value from our efforts in this area. As practitioners we are prevented from realizing the benefit of shared learning opportunities by the absence of a common point of reference around which to consider examples of resilience success and failure – a lack of agreement on what constitutes 'resilience', where to look for it and how it can be measured and influenced. We can be assured of the lack of agreement through attempting to seek answers to the following questions: What is resilience? What does it look like? How do I know how resilient my organization is?

To a greater or lesser extent, the lack of an agreed perspective casts a shadow across almost every new survey or publication in this area and acts to reduce the effectiveness of local assessments and improvement activities. It hampers debate with the Board, and it acts to delay and confuse. This, of course, at a time when attachments and references to resilience are becoming ever more popular, be that the 2019 guide to city resilience (BS 67000) or the ever-increasing media attention being given to climate risks. To illustrate, I recently presented myself at the local wellbeing centre for a routine health assessment – something akin to what we (more willingly perhaps) subject our cars to on an annual basis. Prior to one of the tests I was asked, 'so, how resilient are you?' – the test, apparently, was designed to measure certain physiological responses to a simple breathing exercise.

In offering my own definition and perspective on resilience, I am obviously seeking to promote the idea that it is a topic which should be approached by the Board. In doing so, I would also encourage practitioners to have a conversation with members of the Board in order to confirm that this should indeed be the case – after all, early engagement is probably the most effective way of ensuring a positive outcome. Managing strategic risk is increasingly a priority for an organization's Board and we can expect to see risk management practices increasingly integrated or at least aligned with business planning and strategy activities. Introducing resilience capability as a function of how well the organization manages its strategic risks provides an excellent basis upon which to establish a coherent approach.

It is important that practitioners are able to at least categorize existing definitions and to recognize the direction of travel suggested by the latest research. Specific reference sources can help us with the challenge presented by a varied and often loose application of the term 'resilience', and our understanding can be enhanced if we are able to get a better appreciation of the context within which a particular definition was presented or used, be that commercial or historical. Whilst I have offered several reference sources in this chapter, each quite different one to another, there is additional value to be had by simply remaining up to date and abreast of what is happening around us. For example, the guide to city resilience, mentioned above, was published in 2019. It was promoted on the BSI website as follows:

> The standard aims to move cities away from a reactive, response-focused strategy, and ultimately towards a foresight model where resilience is seen as a means of exploiting opportunities and anticipating future changes which allow sustained economic competitiveness.[14]

The fact that this reference is specific to cities is largely irrelevant – in fact, it might even prove to be of assistance. The document represents some of the latest thinking, applied to an area of life which has been attracting a good deal of political and corporate attention in countries across the world, including major growth regions in Africa and Asia. Read as a definition for resilience it is certainly more enlightened than many, and from a practitioner's perspective it is simply not something which can or should be ignored. Our engagement with the Board should at least be well informed, and if we can point to reliable, authoritative sources (including those which even touch upon the subject within an urban and societal context) in support of our approach and proposals then we should approach the challenge with some confidence.

This chapter has sought to introduce the reader to a range of resilience definitions and to some typical information sources which can help in determining their potential use and application. I have also presented my own definition of organizational resilience, the detail and substance of which is clearly present throughout the remainder of the book. In recognition of the fact that the Board, colleagues and other stakeholders may need to be persuaded to invest in resilience, Chapter 3 focuses upon the value-proposition associated with adopting or maintaining such a position.

Endnotes

1 References on the Wikipedia website provided on the subject of resilience, under the headings of ecology, social sciences and technology and engineering. Available from: en.wikipedia.org/wiki/Resilience (archived at https://perma.cc/23BQ-NJGF)

2 Definition of organizational resilience on the official Australian government's website. Available from: www.organisationalresilience.gov.au/Pages/default.aspx (archived at https://perma.cc/ZXS4-SFV6)

3 British Standards Institution (2014) BS 65000:2014: Guidance on Organizational Resilience

4 Definition provided on the Resilient Organisations website. Available from: www.resorgs.org.nz/about-resorgs/what-is-organisational-resilience/ (archived at https://perma.cc/KZR2-EXNM)

5 Economist Intelligence Unit (2015) *Organisational Resilience: Building an enduring enterprise*. Available from: www.bsigroup.com/Global/revisions/Org-res-EIU-report.pdf (archived at https://perma.cc/X2Y8-8TWG)

6 Attributed to Gever Tulley, author of *50 Dangerous Things (You Should Let Your Children Do)*. Available from: www.brainyquote.com/quotes/gever_tulley_559476?src=t_resilience (archived at https://perma.cc/QLL5-5KCA)

7 Megginson, LC (1963) Lessons from Europe for American business, *Southwestern Social Science Quarterly*, **44** pp 3–13, p 4

8 Alrawi, M (2017) BP's quiet American Bob Dudley remains a study in resilience, *The National*, 13 July. Available from: www.thenational.ae/business/energy/bp-s-quiet-american-bob-dudley-remains-a-study-in-resilience-1.578145 (archived at https://perma.cc/SAX7-8WHL)

9 The official Australian government's website on organizational resilience. Available from: www.organisationalresilience.gov.au/Pages/default.aspx (archived at https://perma.cc/ZXS4-SFV6)

10 Listed as one of the research priorities on the official Australian government's website. Available from: www.organisationalresilience.gov.au/resources/Pages/default.aspx#_rrp (archived at https://perma.cc/6UC9-EJ6B)

11 Affinity Health at Work (2011) *Developing Resilience*. Available from: www.cipd.co.uk/Images/developing-resilience_2011_tcm18-10576.pdf (archived at https://perma.cc/F92R-RWEA)

12 Economist Intelligence Unit (2015) *Organisational Resilience: Building an enduring enterprise*. Available from: www.bsigroup.com/Global/revisions/Org-res-EIU-report.pdf (archived at https://perma.cc/X2Y8-8TWG)

13 Denyer, D (2017) *Organizational Resilience: A summary of academic evidence, business insights and new thinking*. Available from: www.cranfield.ac.uk/som/case-studies/organizational-resilience-a-summary-of-academic-evidence-business-insights-and-new-thinking (archived at https://perma.cc/736G-88R9)

14 British Standards Institution (2019) BS 67000:2019 City resilience guide. Available from: www.bsigroup.com/en-GB/standards/Information-about-standards/bs-670002019-city-resilience.-guide/ (archived at https://perma.cc/ND25-W7B9)

3

Reasoning and benefits

There is an inevitability about change, and as Jeff Bezos suggested in 2018, an inevitability about failure too – that is failure at an organizational level.[1] So, you might ask, what's the point discussing resilience? If we are doomed to failure, there's no point, right? If the founder of Amazon is to be believed, we might be left thinking there is little that can be done about the longevity of an organization as our energies would be focused simply on delaying the fateful day. It is a kind of organizational or societal fatalism. Alternatively, we could find a successful, enduring organization and seek to appreciate the potential downsides, perhaps. 'What are the drawbacks of success?', we could ask.

This chapter seeks to introduce the rationale, propositions and benefits associated with organizational resilience and also some of the practical considerations which may be important to the practitioner. However, the chapter and the questions implied within it, only make sense if we recognize organizational resilience as a dynamic concept and if we approach it as an open-ended journey or complex series of interactions or changes. At best, achieving a degree of success today guarantees only the point at which we begin again tomorrow and perhaps the degree of confidence we might have in our ability to do it – at worst it guarantees pretty much nothing at all. We are interested here in what could have delivered success for the organization and also what those potential prized outcomes might be. We do not have the time to indulge the notion that failure is somehow unavoidable.

For any given circumstance, senior management's role is to create a vision of what success looks like. As we define it here, resilience is not just restricted to competitive advantage, it speaks directly to the organization's chances of realizing that vision. A resilient organization is one which is constantly re-inventing itself and is defined by being 'always ahead of the curve'.[2] It relishes uncertainty and is supremely creative, it possesses an uncanny ability to turn a negative event into a positive outcome and a commercial success.

This chapter represents a natural follow-on to examining some of the various definitions which exist for organizational resilience. As with the definitions themselves, the way in which different organizations perceive resilience and the potential benefits therein will also vary. The chapter reflects the need the practitioner has to be able to 'sell' investment in organizational resilience, and to pitch that sale at a potentially reluctant or ambivalent buyer, in the form of the Board.

This chapter also serves to introduce some, but certainly not all, of the elements contained within the Organizational Resilience Capability Model® (ORCM) and which are covered in more detail within Chapter 5 and provides a convenient lead-in to the various case studies examined in Chapter 4.

The significance of our approach to risk

Much in the same way that successful, enduring organizations work differently and are significantly more effective when it comes to learning – a 'superior brand of learning', according to Vogus and Sutcliffe – so too does their approach to risk differ.[3] This is true on several levels and creates not just a clear differentiator, one organization to another, but also underlines the benefits to be enjoyed. The way in which resilient organizations approach risk, and the threats and opportunities therein, speaks directly to the prize of success and longevity. And this differentiator is a good deal more subtle than a simple reminder to always treat a risk as a potential opportunity. The following quote places resilience exactly where the Board should be encouraged to consider it:

> Resilience is not just about 'bouncing back from adversity' but is more broadly concerned with adaptive capacity and how we better

understand and address uncertainty in our internal and external environments. The basis of organizational resilience is a fundamental understanding and treatment of risk.[4]

Let us consider the organization's threat landscape. It is widely accepted that for most organizations the threat landscape is increasingly complex – defined by high velocity and unpredictability, and the rapid emergence of novel, physical and non-physical threats. Practitioners need look back only to the period 2012–2016 to realize just how stable that landscape actually was by comparison – a commercial and political landscape which had shown only unremarkable change since the financial crisis of 2008. Institutes, industry bodies, consultancies and others are out there, vying to help us understand this new landscape through surveys and analysis, and governments and other agencies push out regular assessments, warnings and advice for every major commercial sector.

This type of landscape inevitably exposes new vulnerabilities for the organization and is doing so with increased regularity. So, if we are to make sense of it, and successful enduring organizations do just that, we need to remember which risks we should be focused on. Organizational resilience provides an exercise in the successful management of strategic risks. That is, those risks which introduce us to the threats and opportunities presented by the organization's core strategy and business model, and which in turn directly influence strategic decision-making – risks that speak to the organization's fundamental direction of travel and the very beliefs, assumptions and plans upon which it is built. If the landscape is examined only by using the language of 'jeopardy', the organization will inevitably be focused around the care and additional protection required such that individual plans and objectives are not undone.

However, from exactly the same landscape and from exactly the same set of emerging features, the leadership of the resilient organization will draw pointers and ideas which remain invisible to many – strategic opportunities which bring forth new plans and which suggest new products or services or which lead to the creation of new markets. It is these very pointers and ideas upon which the organization will act and around which it will focus its innovative efforts, and as practitioners, this is where we should be steering the discussion with senior managers.

As referenced in Chapter 2 as part of our push to establish a definition, language and terminology are important in any discipline, and this is certainly true for organizational resilience. With a term prone to misinterpretation and overuse it is particularly important that we are clear in our meaning and that we regularly seek to differentiate, clarify and explain. The need to take extra care with the language we choose is also relevant to considerations of risk. If our narrative is limited to how we might counter a particular threat, this is probably indicative of lower resilience maturity and suggests a rather singular focus to our assessments and organizational sensitivities – it is a vocabulary of challenge and not of opportunity. Similarly, if the narrative is primarily one of how we prevent and mitigate threats or how we should quickly recover from disruptions, then we are probably not having a conversation about what it means to be a truly resilient organization.

For those of us who have invested time in heavily regulated environments the following quote should resonate, although it is from a rather unexpected source:

> [Regulation] changes are both opportunity and threat. They are an opportunity because all the old assumptions about what you need to have are swept away and, if you are fleet of foot and smart in dealing with that, you can do better than all the others that are tackling the same change. They are a threat because if you are not as smart and you didn't see how to make the most of these new regulations, then you'll certainly suffer.

The words are from the launch of the 2019 Formula One (F1) Mercedes racing car, and were provided during a widely reported interview by the team's technical director, James Allison.[5] For those of you who do not follow such things, these are high-profile, high-tech businesses employing hundreds of people and with annual budgets approaching the £1 billion mark. The Mercedes team is the fourth most successful of all time and prior to the launch event had managed to stay at the very top of their sport for the previous five years, winning everything that was on offer, year after year – a trend which continued into the 2019 season.

Organizations which lack resilience are more likely to be undone by a specific event, which is why so many definitions still make reference to 'short-term shocks'. It is not so much that the definition or the thinking behind it remains wedded to event-focused concepts, it is more a recognition that dealing successfully with shocks and interruptions is just part of what it takes. The less resilient the organization, the bigger the focus on shocks and the recovery effort following them.

If we are serious about risk and we understand its importance to resilience, then we also need to get serious about reading the road ahead. Horizon scanning, as outlined in the following quote, is about anticipation and optioneering, not prediction, but it still requires consideration of scenarios which are sufficiently diverse and time-frames which are sufficiently progressive that the organization feels equipped to plan for a wide range of possible outcomes. Even if the organization's near-term behaviour might be seen as conservative or of little commercial consequence, its outlook should always be radical and take account of the unconventional and even the extreme:

> Horizon scanning is a systematic process for capturing and monitoring change. The process identifies emerging issues that are on the periphery of current thinking and planning, and provides early warning of how trends and developments may lead to changes in behaviour and create new challenges and opportunities in the marketplace.[6]

For many organizations, what passes for horizon scanning is neither strategic nor is it set beyond the 1- to 3-year limit of most business plans. Nor is it often based on any meaningful intelligence beyond that used for administrative updates to the corporate risk register or gleaned from annual surveys published freely to the internet. So, if horizon scanning is truly about detecting 'early signs' or 'weak signals', then our reporting in 2020 shouldn't simply be reflecting well-documented developments in Blockchain, artificial intelligence (AI) or commercial drones – we should be seeking to detect and consider more novel developments, and in areas not necessarily dominated by technology.

To illustrate, let us consider a potential 'future' which sees the organization needing to recruit candidate numbers and skills in a way not previously experienced. What does population and educational trend data suggest this market might look like in 5, 10 or 15 years' time? What are the latest developments in the recruitment industry, having seen the basic process remain largely unchanged for many years, despite the advent of social media? To date, has the organization itself truly reflected the marked change in career expectations of those joining within the last 5 years, versus those from 15 years ago, and what additional challenges does this present for the future we are now considering? And, given that it is unwise to ignore technology altogether, how might the 'new employment' future (with a significant impact from AI) fit with a high-growth scenario?

Why it pays organizations to be ambitious

Displaying a lack of ambition is a charge which can be levelled at much of what passes for a business plan or project proposal. It seems to permeate almost every floor and every meeting in your typical corporate HQ and even finds its way into businesses born of a fierce entrepreneurial spirit. It behaves rather like a fungus and can be seen growing on the surface of even the most imaginative of ventures. Our engagement around organizational resilience should be based upon ambitions for growth and success and our vocabulary should be one of 'transformation' and 'dexterity'. Anything less than this and we too can be accused of accepting that invisible ceiling which sits between 'struggling to cope' and 'just about doing enough'.

To reiterate a point made in Chapter 2, organizational resilience is not just about bouncing back – it is not a one-dimensional, event-focused concept. If it were, our ambitions absolutely *could* be kept in check. For example, the entire foundation of business continuity is about maintaining those processes deemed worthy of being maintained and supporting a meaningful recovery if things do indeed go badly wrong. Either way, business continuity is a concept and a set of arrangements centred about the status quo – preserving it and returning to it, or a version of it, if at all possible.

Traditional approaches to business continuity, and particularly those which are intended to be nothing more than 'standards compliant', are frequently weak on prevention. It is also completely unrealistic to think that business continuity involves 'coming back better' – if we are thinking step-change improvement or transformation then we are not thinking about business continuity. In such circumstances, by accident or by design, we are actually engaging with the agenda which is organizational resilience:

> Resilient organizations thrive despite experiencing conditions that are surprising, uncertain, often adverse, and usually unstable.[7]

The type of ambition which should frame our interaction with senior management is eloquently summed up by the above quote. We immediately get the sense that here is an organization which will do well, regardless of what is thrown at it. This is an organization which is constantly re-inventing itself, which relishes uncertainty, possesses boundless energy and is supremely creative. By being able to thrive, it also possesses an uncanny ability to turn a negative event into a positive outcome and a commercial success.

So, to put it another way, here is an organization which is always in the right spot. It makes adjustments with great speed and agility and can absorb anything that is thrown at it. Positioning ourselves as needing to 'thrive' firmly dispels any notion that we would be accepting of things carrying on in the way they always have done, and therefore also announces our intention to move beyond the containment of individual events and the status quo – this is an organization with ambition.

We can also view ambition as an extension to the previous point on risk. Take, for example, 'operational resilience', being careful to note the word operational, and not organizational. If we start with a best-average approach to its definition we can see that it too lacks ambition, and this is driven by the way in which risks are considered. The scope of operational resilience commonly extends no further than the mitigation of operational risks – the maintenance of service delivery for customers through emphasizing the need for preventative measures and through determining just how much pressure (or resultant stress) the organization's critical processes can actually tolerate.

Buried somewhere within the intellectual consideration of resilience, and linked to the notion of maintaining service delivery, is the concept of 'stability' and being able to maintain or return to a stable position following a disruptive event. Stability is often referred to within studies of societal resilience. This is clearly not necessarily the same as the 'status quo', although it could be, the implication here being that stability is a prerequisite for delivery of services, or at least a preferred state. But is that realistic, and is it even desirable? Our consideration of resilience touches repeatedly upon the scale and frequency of change and the velocity of emerging risks. Maturity is characterized by being able to pull off constant re-invention.

The focus on ambition is not intended to decry other disciplines or approaches – far from it. Financial services and other sectors may well point to a transformation in their understanding of resilience over recent years precisely because of their focus on preserving delivery to customers. However, the above pattern of limitation can be seen repeatedly across resilience literature and whenever we come across reference to specifics, such as technology resilience, brand resilience or supply chain resilience. Our examination here of organizational resilience should be broad and inclusive and we should be ambitious in our scope and application. We should be suspicious of anything which might be interpreted as being just a temporary response, or a response to something which is itself only temporary.

One last one word on 'ambition'. Organizations should take care not to treat it as some sort of compensatory tool, masking shortfalls in results or skills. As a measure of capability, organizational resilience requires a degree of achievement. As practitioners we have a responsibility to ensure that the models and frameworks we employ to measure that capability and to provide assurance to senior management do not overstate drive and determination, however necessary those behaviours might be.

Compliance as a strategic issue

One of the benefits which should be routinely enjoyed in embracing resilience is a sharper appreciation of how different approaches and mitigation strategies operate within the boundaries of the organization. After all, the organization is, in many respects, a largely closed system – it is unrealistic to think that something new can be introduced, or something taken away, without it having an effect on what is already there. All too often, disciplines and requirements are analysed and discussed in isolation from one another, and/or through a singular lens. The problem here is that the view from within the organization can then become rather blinkered or distorted.

Take 'governance', for example, and its close associate on that side of the office, 'compliance'. Whilst neither of these concepts may always represent the height of fashion in management circles, let us be absolutely clear about what our stance, as practitioners, should be. For the organization to adopt and promote robust and effective governance arrangements is a positive thing, and as such, it should feature prominently in our assessment of organizational resilience and in our measure of maturity.

We will touch upon the trade-offs, the need for balance and the natural 'tensions' which exist shortly, but first we should explore what the compliant mindset is all about and why it has a particular relevance for us here. In many ways, compliance constitutes a deliberate act, but one which can be driven by numerous factors and considerations and one which can have a range of outcomes. There is nothing inevitable about good governance, or a compliant position, and rarely can it be accidental. Similarly, there is nothing inherently weak or limiting with a compliant mindset.

Importantly for a resilient organization, compliance, or to be more accurate 'being compliant', is usually less about fear of sanction and more about seeking a stance which allows the organization to remain free and from which it can then take best advantage of emerging opportunities. Being compliant also permits the organization to shout proudly to regulators, customers and prospective employees about its values and ethical position.

If compliance is viewed primarily as an obstacle or barrier, the decision to ignore it can still prove to be a difficult one. The consequences of non-compliance can be unpredictable and long-lived. In a world with more than enough uncertainty already, the organization's Board would presumably only create more of it, and deliberately embrace a non-compliant stance, if it had weighed all the options very carefully indeed.

To illustrate the point about consequences being unpredictable and long-lived, the UK-based banking and financial services company Standard Chartered announced in early 2019 that it had set aside approximately £720 million (US $900 million) in order to cover potential fines from UK and US authorities.[8] Part of this included a specific fine from the UK's Financial Conduct Authority of £102 million relating to historical control failings. Investigations were said to include activity dating back more than 12 years.

Like it or not, robust and effective governance will be a prerequisite for resilience in most environments. Whilst compliance can help to define and position the organization, it can also provide an important reference point during periods of heightened uncertainty or transformational change. As referenced above, a compliant position is one most likely to equate to a freedom-to-act and therefore the best position from which to exploit new or emerging opportunities. Nevertheless, compliance will often be received in the negative and viewed, rather ironically, as a brake or limiter to freedom, flexibility and responsiveness. It is often considered to be unfashionable and unsophisticated and as representing something which is rather elementary and/or basic:

> There are two core drivers of Organizational Resilience – defensive and progressive – and there are two core perspectives on how resilience can be achieved – consistency and flexibility. Where these have not yet been integrated into a holistic framework, integration, balance and fit (for purpose) are essential.
>
> Senior leaders need to manage the tensions between these four approaches if organizations are to be truly resilient.[9]

Whilst this quote doesn't necessarily seek to address the different interpretations or expectations of compliance, the 'tension quadrant' outlined by Denyer does provide some useful insight into its importance and recognition that it needs to be considered. The manner in which the organization seeks to generate value from its strategic objectives also needs to be considered. For example, what is the organization's stance on driving consistency within its processes and is standardization something it is seeking to promote?

Governance and resilience can make for the best of bedfellows; however, it means more than simply repeating the two words together in the hope that they somehow gel. There is nothing inevitable about good governance, or a compliant position for that matter. These approaches, if nurtured, can influence the organization massively, for example through culture building, and senior management clearly need to be alive to potential threats posed by a standards mindset and to the manner in which it considers consistency.

Responding well in a crisis can directly influence short-term and long-term success

Granted, a famously successful response might do wonders in terms of damage limitation, be that reputation with supply partners, future scrutiny from regulators or the cost of raising short-term finance. Preventing a crisis in the first instance will probably do significantly more for an organization's long-term success and prosperity. The less mature the organization is in terms of resilience the more important the crisis response capability is likely to be, the theory being that resilient organizations are less likely to be underdone by specific events, even really bad ones. To illustrate the point, and to create a useful contrast in respect of the above, let us consider the crisis which BP found itself at the centre of in 2010.

THE BP CRISIS

A catastrophic failure during the underwater drilling process led to the tragic loss of 11 lives and a maritime disaster of unprecedented scale.

The compensation process, according to BP's own figures published in 2019, has amounted to some £47 billion (US $65 billion). This is a colossal amount of money, and one which BP obviously needed to cover. Not only that, the company's reputation for safety and environmental stewardship was in tatters as the case was dragged through the very public glare of the US courts. BP also faced the prospect of losing access to key markets as regulatory and statutory provision was levelled across the sector and as it divested itself of assets and withdrew from some high-profile international investments.

Key elements of BP's crisis response were roundly criticized at the time, and Tony Hayward's (the then chief executive) comments about how he would like to 'have his life back' have passed into communications folklore. The fact that BP remains one of the biggest global players in the oil and gas industry in 2020 pays testament to its resilience as an organization:

> I think we are now stronger and more focused – competitive, as we have to be, but also fit for a future which is changing ever-faster. After this period of re-shaping, we are now getting back to growth.[10]

Organizations should probably avoid taking comfort from BP's survival and apparent ability to thrive. This was certainly an exceptional case. Better, surely, to focus on prevention, on world-leading crisis response capabilities and in seeking to ensure that the type of risks which BP failed to address are properly identified and considered.

Senior management need to be equipped to respond effectively in a crisis situation and have the confidence to make the right strategic decisions whilst under extreme pressure. Structures should be in place to facilitate that response through the body of the organization and the mechanisms required to communicate complex information across multiple stakeholders should be solid and well understood. For all of these reasons, large organizations tend to adopt a very systematic approach, at least at the most senior levels, which perhaps in some ways compensates for their (often) lack of experience in actually dealing with a real crisis.

The inevitability and avoidability of crises are equally well documented, but it is surely the former which can easily be overdone. Prevention works on a number of levels, from containing emergencies and preventing an incident from escalating into a crisis situation, to establishing the conditions within which change can take place without exposing dangerous new weaknesses for the organization. In this regard, and as neatly articulated in the following quote, the Board and non-executive directors have a crucial role in fostering good governance processes and challenging senior management to demonstrate effective early warning systems and the provision of world class intelligence:

> Lapses in recognition occur when leaders remain oblivious to an emerging threat or problem – a lack of attention that can plague even the most skilled executives.[11]

Having returned to the topic of 'horizon scanning', it is also important to recognize these issues as not just affecting large organizations. In a 2018 report, the British Standards Institution (BSI) made specific reference to the apparent weakness in respect of small businesses and the lack of attention to a number of key elements considered important for resilience:

> Their relative neglect of horizon scanning raises key issues, such as whether it is born of ignorance or complacency, and whether it invites unexpected setbacks in the future.[12]

With crisis prevention in mind, specific considerations for the organization might include the following:

- application of data analysis techniques and forecasting models to identify exposures and potentially damaging events;
- challenging the perceptions of senior managers about their own levels of preparedness, using simulations and feedback from independent observers;
- arrangements for corporate social media teams which reflect user behaviours and which maximize the possibilities for early information sharing without requiring senior management input or oversight;
- constantly refreshing the learning potential associated with crisis events and ensuring that senior managers have opportunities to witness them first-hand.

An enthusiasm for change is essential

Change, both inside and outside organizations, lies at the very heart of resilience thinking. It is both incremental and transformational and is frequently baked into the definitions used for the subject. Survey results abound which suggest a significant proportion of senior management believe their organizations are simply ill-prepared to respond effectively to the increasing change-pressure they find themselves under or their organizations are unable to positively influence the rapidly changing environment within which they operate.

In a resilient organization, change is not part of some predictable or forced routine staff are dragged through every few years, and nor are they forced to endure 'mandatory fun' initiatives in order to confirm their enthusiasm or readiness for change. Similarly, the beneficiaries of change are not limited to the favoured few who occupy newly created senior positions or to those lacklustre performers who have been desperately hanging on for their long-service award.

Change inevitably involves the introduction of an unknown condition or new variable, and as such brings with it an element of uncertainty and loss of control. Therefore, if we accept this as a working definition, and I see no reason why we would not, then an enthusiasm for change requires us to embrace the prospect both of being uncertain and of losing a degree of control.

Over recent years we have heard a great deal about 'change readiness' and it has been widely touted as a defining characteristic of resilient organizations. I believe change readiness is only part of what organizations require and being ready for something certainly need not equate to any enthusiasm for it or indeed proficiency in dealing with it. It is the quality of the organization's response and subsequent results which provides the marker for any enthusiasm for the task at hand. Readiness in this context implies only an awareness of change and change-related factors together with the make-up of that change and also perhaps an element of preparedness.

Enthusiasm, on the other hand, speaks more clearly to the organization's proactive stance and suggests an element of actually seeking it out or indeed bringing about a change and making it happen.

Enthusiasm also points to a cohesion and common value set which is not necessarily the case when considering readiness alone. In applying this thinking to the organization, we should also consider the following:

- Avoiding the use of the word 'stress', unless that is specifically what we intend. Change and stress are not the same thing, and the latter is probably best employed as an outcome or measure of resilience.
- The kind and frequency of change we are experiencing will likely have a bearing on how it is received, and it would be naïve to think otherwise.
- 'Resistance to change' is a rather blunt term frequently used to describe staff behaviours, but it may be more helpful to consider those behaviours in terms of a desire for certainty or control and how that will likely manifest itself in any obvious or out-and-out resistance.
- 'Change fatigue' is widely used but is also rather too simple to be of much use as it suggests only a negative reaction and associates this most commonly with the amount (ie the constancy and/or pace) of change, rather than its quality or necessity.
- Rather than recognizing its dynamic and multi-directional nature, much of the historical treatment of change has considered it in a singular and/or temporary dimension, for example by reference to a wave, curve or cycle.
- In addition to the aspects of change which can be experienced internal and external to the organization, it is also useful to consider both the intended and unintended consequences of change activity.
- Change can obviously be superficial and tactical as well as structural and strategic, and as a reaction to external forces, much of the change experienced by staff remains largely within the gift of leadership, both in detail and timing.

In order to further our appreciation of change, and whilst being careful not to overdo the linkages, we are probably best served by seeking to highlight some of the connections between personal and organizational resilience. We will revisit the point throughout this text that there is more to a resilient organization than simply a group of resilient people, but there are some potentially helpful parallels in respect of change which are worthy of exploration.

There is a significant amount of research and literature associated with personal resilience and understanding the habits and traits associated with those who are identified as being resilient or demonstrating resilient qualities. Within this body of knowledge there is widespread acceptance that resilience capability is something which can be developed and that some of these capabilities are directly associated with how change is viewed and/or delivered. There is also common emphasis on the importance of these capabilities within the leadership cadre and of deploying 'change champions' to role-model the desired behaviours within the wider organization at specific points in time.

The benefits associated with developing change-friendly capabilities amongst staff are often presented at both an individual and organizational level. For the individual, these benefits might include higher performance, greater levels of empathy, improved wellbeing and emotional stability. For the organization the benefits are frequently linked to the reduced cost of change activities or the increased speed with which they can be delivered:

> Resilient people are not, however, immune to change; they experience the effects just as anyone would, but they will move through the transition faster and respond more positively. They may come to terms with the change quickly and experience much less turbulence.[13]

In seeking to better understand organizational resilience by reference to personal traits, characteristics and behaviours, I believe the above quote is useful for two reasons. Firstly, it uses language which is clear and transferable, and that is to be applauded. Secondly, it alerts us to one of the main challenges of relying too heavily on these linkages, that being the rather negative association with change and the rather reactive stance suggested for the individual. Whilst this latter point might not be deliberate, it does leave us with the clear impression of an individual who is for ever 'coping' with change, reacting to circumstances and adopting a defensive posture. This is hardly someone who is enthused by the prospect of change, regardless of how little it might be seen to impact them.

Change is uncertainty and it will usually usher in some loss of control. Enthusiasm for change must be the polar opposite of change fatigue and it is absolutely something which organizations should develop strategies to address. Deliberately limiting the amount of superficial change is only one part of the solution, but organizations must be alive to anything which could undermine their wider change efforts. After all, when senior management consider their next routine organization re-shuffle, being seen to reward mediocrity in the workplace will undermine the enthusiasm for almost anything else.

The role of leadership

As introduced in Chapter 1, organizational resilience is rarely an accidental state and is one which can be built and destroyed, the latter perhaps being easier to accomplish if time is short. Resilience is neither the preserve of a particular group nor is it controlled by a particular function or discipline within the organization – it is a truly pervasive concept and capability. However, just because there is no ownership in a traditional, hierarchical fashion, this does not diminish the importance of effective leadership in its development and maintenance. Organizational resilience is, if nothing else, a proactive capability and as such, leaders must be deliberate and creative in their cultural stewardship and energetic in the development of their own competencies and capabilities in this regard.

Regardless of how influential the personal resilience of employees actually is, and this is something revisited later in the chapter, the following quote touches upon some important elements of leadership:

> When an organization is put under pressure, it is their people and how they come together that can make or break the organization.

The prevailing culture and the behaviour and capabilities of leaders can enhance or erode the resilience of all employees.[14]

As we will see in Chapter 5 when we examine the ORCM, leadership influences operate at a number of levels, and this is more than simply ensuring that leaders demonstrate flexibility during times of change and are seen to be enthusiastically embracing ambiguity and uncertainty. This is not even the 'heavy-duty' resilience of senior management referred to by Jack Welch.[15] This is about recognizing that leaders are responsible not only for their own resilience, as indeed are all staff, but also for creating and maintaining the connections and pathways upon which resilience capability is built across the organization.

Leadership as a true influencer of resilience can be identified and assessed and is difficult to fake. Pretending often translates into the withholding of information, as a form of control, from which the leader believes they can emerge 'triumphant and masterful' at a time of their own choosing. The narcissist will therefore view resilience as primarily a leadership condition. Nevertheless, our models and our assessments must be capable of calling-out these behaviours and exposing leadership where it is genuinely weak.

A leader's individual resolutions and values must genuinely chime with the needs of the wider organization and be seen to synchronize at every level and within every function and location. In turn, these resolutions and values must align to the stated vision which is shared across the organization and beyond. Resilient organizations require resilient leaders, but not just as a component. The organization requires resilient people, period. By definition, resilient leaders need to understand what is required of them in order to deliver long-term success. For example, leaders are responsible for the following:

- developing a compelling future vision for the organization;
- creating the structures and mechanisms necessary to ensure that decision-making can be delivered quickly and at the right level to have maximum effect;
- fashioning recruitment and retention activities to ensure best-fit and to ensure development of emotional intelligence and behavioural skills amongst staff.

As a further prelude to Chapter 5, the following elements associated with leadership can also be identified from within the ORCM:

- The PERSONALITY of the organization is greatly influenced by traits exhibited at leadership levels. For example, bias, intolerance or aggression, and the climate which can be fostered as a result and carried forward by staff in discussions with regulators or customers.
- Although somewhat difficult to define, establishing and maintaining a fertile culture is critical for organizations. Made up of values, beliefs and behaviours, what passes as cultural norms within the organization can be the result of intentional effort by leaders just as much as it can be by unintentional neglect, and forms part of what we identify as the organization's APPROACH.
- The list of SKILLS which may provide contributory support for an organization's resilience can be rather long, potentially unwieldy and therefore difficult to unpick. The requirement for some skills will of course be greater than for others within each organizational setting, but a number of these will doubtless be reserved for those at the most senior levels.
- The reference to RESULTS is about how past achievements position or equip the organization to deal with, influence and respond to approaching change – it's about situational positioning and what this means in respect of the organization's stance. The stance the organization chooses to take on compliance is an example of how leaders can directly influence organizational resilience in this way.
- Most obviously perhaps, the DIRECTION for the organization is generally viewed as the preserve of the leadership cadre, as is the provision and allocation of RESOURCES in the pursuit of specific goals and objectives.

Finally, one perhaps less obvious consideration in respect of leadership and organizational resilience is the ability to retain top talent, as influenced by or attributed to those at the most senior levels. Or to put it another way, staff don't always leave organizations, they often leave their leaders. This need not mean that we are necessarily looking at a toxic situation when good people elect to leave, or that the chief is necessarily branded as some sort of ogre, but rather it is recognition that their immediate and personal connections and pathways are important too.

Much has been written about resilience as an entrepreneurial and leadership quality; however, it is the compassion and empathy required to cultivate loyalty amongst the wider leadership cadre which is also important here. Loyalty must be recognized as a factor in an individual's decision-making, for example in whether to leave an organization or to remain and engage with it. Loyalty is probably one of the key attributes that leaders need to cultivate amongst their immediate team and one which could be as valuable to them and the organization as being able to articulate a clear and exciting vision.

As an extension to our analysis of leadership, and as reported below by the GRC Institute, tenure and stability of leadership provides a potentially important and novel ingredient to organizational resilience. The idea that prediction and consistency are important elements for the whole organization, and not just in relation to leadership roles, may suggest that individuals are actively making their own judgements about what it takes to survive or out-live specific characters at the top table:

> When you get a new CEO, they come in and say, I need a new strategy and a new culture. All the pre-existing patterns of prediction get ripped up and thrown away and a different set are brought in.
>
> We don't have to worry what this CEO is saying, we can wait 18 months and there will be another one.[16]

Continuous learning is the key

Learning is the result of a number of related processes, allowing the organization to adapt more quickly and more effectively to changes in its environment, and to influence things in the way that it wishes. One such process involves the management of knowledge, as defined in the following quote, and there are few more important applications of this process than in the delivery of projects and when staff exit the organization:

Managing the corporation's knowledge through a systematically and organizationally specified process for acquiring, organizing, sustaining, applying, sharing and renewing both the tacit and explicit knowledge of employees to enhance organizational performance and create value.[17]

Whilst knowledge transfer should normally be a collaborative and mutually beneficial activity, it can take on a distinct and perhaps one-sided purpose when an individual exits the organization. At this point, knowledge transfer can be viewed as a function of the value assigned to the individual during their employment – and from the individual's perspective, how else could it be viewed? – the purpose of which is to allow further learning to take place, now or at some future point. However, the key to unlocking the potential here is that at the point when the individual announces their intention to leave, the transfer of knowledge should already have taken place.

For example, for resilient organizations, running a simulation in the absence of key staff is no longer about damage limitation or preparing a list of excuses for the subsequent report but rather the application of newly acquired knowledge and gaining confidence in performing new roles. It is about seeking to lose control of knowledge, deliberately, and to see that through and understand how it plays out in real-life situations. The fact of who is accessing the knowledge and when and how that is happening should be secondary to ensuring that the knowledge is current and readily available.

The other example of knowledge transfer comes during the course of project delivery, be that for products, contracts or internal solutions, and particularly when expert resources are brought in. Projects tend to exhibit common failings rather than novel ones, and it doesn't take a genius to work out that learning in a project environment isn't always an effective process – you only have to look at the number of times projects go bad and the fact that so many post-project reviews look alike.

Project management is a recognized skill and requirement for any resilient organization and learning opportunities can easily be identified at critical points within a typical project life cycle. The transfer of knowledge should be keenly felt across the project and be recognized for its contribution to unlocking opportunities and minimizing the risk of delays, unplanned costs or user dissatisfaction. In fact, the learning requirements and knowledge transfer potential of the project should have a direct bearing on how it is managed. For example, a project which is highly complex, or which is for a new customer or in a new territory, should have learning requirements which are more clearly defined than for something which is low value or routine.

Related to the above, another very relevant learning process relates to the pointers or lessons which provide triggers for action and change more generally for the organization, captured in the following quote in respect of lessons from disaster events:

> Lessons are an important source of learning, particularly following specific events. Common structural and behavioural elements which contribute to organizations missing out on the learning potential of events include poor lessons capture and dissemination, lack of resources and a lack of motivation to fix the issues.[18]

THE VW SCANDAL

As widely reported in 2017, following investigations by the Environmental Protection Agency (EPA)[19] and others, the German carmaker Volkswagen (VW) pleaded guilty to criminal charges brought by the US Department of Justice in relation to presenting false emissions figures for some of its diesel engine cars from 2009 to 2015.[20] This fraud was achieved through the installation of software in the engine's electronic management system which was intended to provide certain results only during test conditions, deliberately disguising the results which would otherwise have been returned.

Direct action was taken against VW not only in the United States but in markets from South Korea to India and Switzerland. The company's share price collapsed in the days following the crisis, senior executives resigned or were suspended, the regulatory regime across the sector was thrown wide open and the scandal has since cost VW billions of pounds in criminal fines, compensation and lost revenues.

Whilst cultural obstacles may have been relevant, the learnings from which VW could and should have drawn upon were well documented and appear to have been in plain sight.[21] The failings of large multinational corporations had already been exposed by this point – there would be little new in that respect that would come out of the many investigations into the car maker's activities. Examples of where senior management had presided over a 'good news' culture and failed to appreciate the significance of information which flashed across their desks were well known. The significance of a compliance mindset had also been one which had been misinterpreted before.

Compliance has a special place within the ORCM, as detailed in Chapter 5, and I have already touched upon it in respect of it being a strategic issue. Within the ORCM, compliance also forms what can be referred to as a 'bridging concept', connecting the two complementary dimensions present within the model – it reflects important organizational features and those associated with behaviours and outcomes. From a practitioner's perspective, we should not be ignoring the massive scale of the fraud or its technical detail, but as identified through the *Newsweek* article referenced above, what was it in the culture of the car giant which allowed this to happen? Is this mindset of non-compliance endemic within the organization, and even within the industry? Have regulators turned a blind eye to the practice? How do you recover from that? What are the lessons to be learned?

Attitudes towards compliance provide a critical insight into the prevailing culture within any organization, not least as they can be extrapolated with some degree of confidence across a range of disciplines and risk areas, from financial conduct and governance through to safety and the treatment of staff, leading me to conclude that the presence, or otherwise, of a compliance mindset is a pretty good indicator of resilience capability overall.

The organization is more than the sum of the parts

Is resilience meaningful at an organizational level only because it is being fostered and developed (at an individual level) through the organization's leadership and employees? Or is it the other way around? Chicken and egg, perhaps, and it largely depends on your perspective on what actually constitutes 'the organization'. However, one thing is for certain: in this case, the whole is significantly more than the sum of its parts. This is as true for the organization as it is for resilience. Organizational resilience is not simply a sum game of bringing on gritty employees and it is much more than just the combined resilience of its people or 'culture' or the behaviours and capabilities of its leadership cadre. As an indicator of capability, resilience should not be used to refer to something which is exclusively human:

> The organization's capacity for resilience is developed through strategically managing human resources to create competencies among core employees, that when aggregated at the organizational level, make it possible for organizations to achieve the ability to respond in a resilient manner when they experience severe shocks.[22]

To alert the reader immediately, I have a big problem with the position as outlined above. In isolation, and that appears to be where it is aiming, this statement is no more true than if I were to claim that I could create a complex structure capable of withstanding the worst environmental conditions simply by ensuring that some of my key materials were proven to have inherent strength.

Similarly, there are some novel concepts buried within the detail of what we understand as 'personal resilience' which are particularly relevant for us here and with the alignment to organizational resilience. One such concept is 'speed' – that is, speed and quality of decision-making and response. Speed is critical to the concept of resilience and it works at both an individual and collective level. However, we cannot simply rely on the quickest individual responses to determine the success or otherwise of an outcome. In many cases, we will be expected to take account of the majority, if not all responses, and this will inevitably include some of those which are the slowest. Providing a view based on the quickest responses, or even an average, will likely result in a view of resilience which is skewed.

Much better then to recognize the interconnectedness of it all and to remember that no organization operates in a vacuum. As outlined below by the Professional Evaluation and Certification Board (PECB), resilience only makes sense in the commercial, social, physical, economic and political context within which the organization finds itself, and therefore we cannot simply ignore the external environment:

> The resilience of an organization is a sequence interconnection that depends on the resilience of other organizations, individual resilience, industry, societies and at the ultimate level, countries.[23]

Just because we cannot and must not rely simply on the personal resilience of our people, and we must therefore seek to avoid using it as a proxy for organizational resilience, that is no reason not to invest in it. Absolutely we *should* be seeking to invest and we should also be seeking to ensure that the organization's culture is one in which our people understand their contribution and how that is valued. Paradoxically, one of the ways in which Board members can justify and explain an investment in personal resilience is to exploit the fact that, conceptually, resilience at an individual and organizational level are indeed very similar.

Focus, and therefore investment, aimed at enhancing personal resilience can be pitched at different aspects of behaviour or personality and at different elements within the employment life cycle. However, rather than attempting to unpick personality traits as part of recruitment or development activities, it may be more productive for organizations to focus on mental health or wellbeing as a way of delivering value from any investment, and on ways in which environmental factors can be managed in order to reduce employee stress. Specific considerations for the organization might therefore include the following:

- job roles and structures designed to maximize exposure to fluid, challenging situations, for example by assigning standby roles for staff to perform;
- programmes designed to assess as well as nurture resilient traits, for example through predicting reactions to change in addition to helping employees prepare for it;

- awareness of how individuals consider their own resilience to be constructed, what sources they might rely upon and how their personal reservoir of goodwill can be drawn upon;
- development activities specifically aligned to the model used for organizational resilience and application of the same overall maturity terminology;
- encouraging staff to explore potential limitations associated with their beliefs and behaviours in a safe environment, for example through the provision of proactive and confidential mentoring support.

We will revisit the linkages between resilience at an individual and organizational level a number of times during this book, and certainly as we explore the ORCM in Chapter 5 and other models in Chapter 7. Those linkages are natural and easy and the ability to employ personal resilience to create analogies is a powerful tool when discussing organizational resilience with senior management.

Does size matter?

When we consider what it means for an organization to be resilient, should we be concerned with the number of employees or the spread of the organization's geographical footprint? What about cultural norms associated with operating in different countries and under different legal, political or religious systems? Do the examples in this chapter of BP and VW, both of which incidentally reported healthy profits in 2019/20, suggest that big is beautiful in resilience circles, or even that some organizations are simply too big to fail?

As outlined in Chapter 2, the context within which we approach the study of resilience is of material importance, as is what the organization has been through to reach its current position or state, whatever that might be. We are all the result of our own histories, and the same is true of organizations. However, the size, scale or wealth of an organization is only of academic interest when it comes to making a determination of resilience or an assessment of an organization's resilience maturity. The same rules and considerations apply, big or small, rich or poor, as we will discover in Chapter 5.

Having said that, each organization is likely to display sensitivity to size in some way or other, so in that sense it might matter to them, although size alone is unlikely to provide any sort of defence against a failed business plan, fraud or a string of bad decisions. Take small or medium-sized organizations, for example. We might expect such organizations to feel disproportionately impacted by regulation, whilst also enjoying the benefits of a small and agile workforce. However, some research suggests that hard facts in this regard might be in short supply, with the following commentary published in 2018:

> Resilience research with an overtly SME [small and medium-sized enterprise] focus is emergent. To date, such research has primarily focused upon the individual resilience of the leaders of SMEs, which has often been characterized as little more than a resource to underpin organizational resilience, and on SME characteristics and capabilities, which have often been presented as detrimental to their ability to be resilient. A very limited body of work has considered practical interventions which may improve resilience in SMEs.[24]

Large organizations probably enjoy no automatic advantage in respect of resilience, compared that is to small ones, although much depends on the conditions within which they operate and it is likely that timelines for large organizations may be extended. It is unrealistic and unfair to compare directly, for example by quoting business survival rates or other statistics as few organizations start life as large, well-established outfits. We cannot simply ignore that nearly all organizations need to progress through a start-up or rapid growth and development phase – that is just the reality of it.

If we take the need for growth and development as a given, it is actually not difficult to find examples of where smaller organizations are presented with what appear to be distinct advantages – conditions intended to promote their chances of success and therefore their resilience. Take, for example, the regulatory conditions which are intended to promote new market entrants bidding for work, the additional governmental support afforded to local community initiatives aimed at tackling climate change, or, to be very specific, the support provided for the development of health systems through the World Health Organization's European Small Countries Initiative.

Smaller organizations tend to exhibit a number of characteristics which differentiate them from their larger counterparts. One such being the relevance of what we might refer to as *community* resilience. There are linkages here to aspects of wider societal resilience and to the emerging philosophies of 'collectivism' and 'municipalism' – social movements and trends towards greater local democracy and local control. For example, we might expect to see a greater proportion of small organizations taking advantage of independent (micro) power grids and their exposure to mutual aid agreements being less formalized and tied to a regional geography rather than to an industrial or commercial sector.

The assumption that small-scale operations are better able to respond with speed and agility may be true, but such assumptions should not form the basis upon which we make an assessment of resilience. We may be just as tempted to make assumptions about the primacy of leader resilience within an SME or the inherent challenges associated with raising finance. What matters more from an assessment and maturity perspective is that we take proper account of the organization's tenure – that is, has it been around long enough to demonstrate that it can endure? No amount of flexibility or entrepreneurial spirit can replace brand loyalty or legacy, at least not directly, and certainly not from an assurance perspective.

Trust seems to be coming back into fashion

As introduced above by reference to the GRC Institute article on leadership (see page 83),[25] trust can be recognized as a quality and characteristic very relevant to organizational resilience and even as a necessary ingredient in establishing a resilient culture. Researchers have invested time and resources in attempting to model the elements of trust and to understand the interplay between trust and other cultural influences within the organization.

It appears that the concept of trust finds easy passage into our thinking in this area, and aside from its relevance to data which we will turn to shortly, there are several possible reasons for this. Firstly, I believe there is an ethical dimension which supports the notion of trust and which transcends our study of organizational resilience. Secondly, it may simply be a case of word association – that is, the word is applied largely (and repeatedly) as an accompaniment to another word without any real depth of meaning or understanding. Thirdly, it has relevance due to the increasing maturity in respect of how external supply relationships are managed by the organization and the emergence of notions such as 'trusted supplier' status.

Ethical behaviours and practices have been high on management's agenda for some years, a reaction in many ways to new obligations and the increased threat of sanction by national and international enforcement agencies. Regardless of how effective some of the countless e-learning programmes in this space have actually been, the profile of ethics has undoubtedly been raised, and as a consequence so too has the notion of trust in the workplace. Another key driver, albeit at a more macro-level, has been the response to the 2008 financial crisis, and the level of trust in financial organizations, defined as:

> An employee's feeling of confidence that the organization will perform actions that are beneficial, or at least not detrimental, to him or her.[26]

Quoted by the Organisation for Economic Co-operation and Development (OECD) in a 2018 study on organizational culture, the above definition of trust introduces the notion of a 'social contract' and how this in turn is 'likely to strengthen the organization's ethical focus'.

References to trust, and the need for it to be rebuilt, are inevitably associated with the collapse of Lehman Brothers bank in 2008 and the crisis which befell the global markets immediately afterwards. The bank, the fourth largest investment bank in the United States at the time, had a history dating back to 1850, but was one of those which contributed to excessive risk-taking in the period prior to the Federal Reserve refusing to guarantee its loans resulting in its filing for bankruptcy.

How many times have we seen the following four words used in combination: empowerment, integrity, trust and accountability? When writing on the subject of organizational resilience it is difficult to avoid it, but we should be acutely aware of the trap which so many fall into – simply by repeating words or a combination of words doesn't make them any more relevant or applicable. The coupling of 'trust' and 'accountability' in particular is very noticeable in articles and other literature.

This is not to suggest that references to trust are unnecessary or clichéd, but rather to highlight the importance of proper usage. When thinking about the pairing of 'trust and accountability' I am reminded of a BSI publication which I came across in researching for this book – the *Standards Outlook 2017 – Governance and Resilience*.[27] This exact combination, governance and resilience, is used nearly 30 times in what is a relatively short promotional publication. If you are anything like me, you will be left with the impression that the author is more interested in attempting to create something and to convince you that it is true rather than explaining what it actually means or how you can make it happen.

Trust is the important issue that it is within supply chain management largely because, historically at least, these connections are not fully autonomous or efficient and they have proven incapable of running themselves for the benefit of all concerned. As a result of increasing globalization, societal instability and the complexity of supply chains there is growing interest in what is necessary to minimize disruption and build aspects of resilience into those relationships – something which is reflected within the regular profile given to supply chain risks by senior management, and defined for us by Dubey:

> Resources, capabilities, behavioural uncertainty, trust, commitment and cooperation are the predictors of supply chain resilience.[28]

Trusted status is something which appears very often to be self-awarded within supply chain relationships and/or without reference to the basis upon which such a position is claimed. Similarly, it is probably unclear within many supply chain relationships what significance trust has in the securing or maintaining of contracts, for example, and we would not expect necessarily to see it quantified or recorded. Nevertheless, it would be naïve to assume that organizations are not investing heavily in the quality and longevity of supply chain relationships through the sharing of information, expertise and resources, for example, and also in developing trust at a more individual and transactional level.

Trust in financial services is reported to have increased in recent years, at least by some commentators, and there is certainly widespread agreement that trust matters and recognition that technology has a vital role in building that trust. This leads us nicely on to the topic of digital trust – a concept which is highly relevant to resilience – and also to recognizing that new technology and data is driving change in financial services and the world's monetary systems in a most profound way.

As a measure of confidence, trust is being applied to the digital world with some enthusiasm. This is recognition of the growing imperative to provide protection and security for data and ensuring privacy for employees and customers alike. Whilst it may be tempting to think that some organizations, such as the tech giants, operate above and beyond normal values and are somehow immune from exposure and negative publicity, this is certainly not the reality for most organizations. When the market conditions allow, most of us will recall a time when our choices have been influenced significantly or even primarily by trust.

Brand loyalty and the fostering of long-term relationships is a critical component of resilience, and from a data perspective this includes all the standard elements of trust: security and privacy, reliability, usability, transparency and integrity. The new reality in the digital age is that almost every transaction or activity involves the exchange of personal information – and this is information which we know has a value assigned to it, both by us and by others. The safeguarding of personal information is now an essential requirement and the organization's capabilities in this area must form part of the overall resilience picture which we create and/or seek to assess.

As consumers of products and services we are increasingly aware that our data is being used beyond the immediate or singular transaction or onscreen experience which we participate in, and this is often a painful realization if we then become the victim of a fraud. As this information becomes harvested and used in ever greater quantities so too will our sensitivity to how organizations are able and willing to explain not only the security of data but also how they are acting in our best interests.

Conclusion

'Resilience' captures and sums up our observations of the organization as it is put under pressure from change forces, both internal and external, and as it seeks to influence the environment within which it operates in pursuit of its goals. The organization's ability to deliver success over the long term is a function of many things, not least the speed and agility of its decision-making in facing up to change forces as and when they are encountered. As we have touched upon several times already, resilience is much more than simply the ability to bounce back in the face of adversity, and this holds true at both an organizational and personal level. In fact, I would suggest the notion of 'bouncing back' significantly limits our ambitions when considering resilience and should not be allowed to define our approach – we have shown resilience to be about strength, competitiveness, re-shaping and growth.

When we discuss resilience with the organization's leadership, we should also be seeking to uncover the organization's strategic risk reality – helping senior management to understand the potential disconnect between the risks that it is actually exposed to and those which it feels comfortable with. In turn, this can help to expose the organization's resilience maturity by defining the true nature of fundamental threats which exist, and the value of any opportunity which is potentially being delayed or even sacrificed.

It is unlikely that organizational resilience in relation to a limited type or number of challenges has significant meaning. Today's environment is increasingly characterized by unprecedented economic and political uncertainty, and rapid, unpredictable and often seismic change. It is reasonably safe to assume that no organization will endure if it focuses only on known threats or simply protecting existing markets. As captured below in the following quote, the manner of our engagement with organizational resilience should be expansive and energetic and we should seek to ensure that we describe its value and explain its reasoning using whole-organization language:

> The benefits of becoming a more resilient organization cannot be overstated. Resilience will increase an organization's awareness of its entire operating environment… and provide the capacity to recognize and act upon the threats (and opportunities) of any situation.[29]

In addressing the various elements of organizational resilience, as outlined throughout this chapter, practitioners may wish to consider the following:

- velocity and significance of emerging threats/opportunities, such as regulatory or commercial changes;
- particular vulnerabilities (or sensitivities), such as ageing assets, high-profile locations or a damaged brand;
- criticality of products or services, such as those provided by critical national infrastructure (CNI) organizations;
- organizational stability, including ownership, leadership and financing aspects;
- corporate memory, such as recent data breaches, or learning drawn from other organizations;
- pressure exerted by shareholders, corporate sponsors or other external bodies.

Similarly, the organization should not be considering the needs-case or potential benefits of resilience in a vacuum, and as such it may be necessary to take account of the following:

- organizational structures, the prevalence of organizational change or the potential for change fatigue;
- potential for a resilience focus to be viewed as an attempt at rebadging other failed initiatives;

- ability of a resilience programme to attract and retain scarce resource already committed to other projects;
- possibility that the focus of organizational resilience may be lost or tainted by current Gucci topics, such as 'agile';
- the organization's previous experiences with initiatives or new techniques.

The organization should also pay attention to understanding and recognizing the barriers to success, and just as important, being able to describe what success might actually look like, paying attention to the following:

- knowledge gaps or availability of trained practitioners;
- access to or agreement on an appropriate resilience model or methodology;
- suitable assurance mechanisms and ability to implement appropriate performance measures;
- ability to benchmark resilience performance at an industry, national or international level.

Finally, the organization may wish to explore the following aspects of threat management:

- The organization should be wary of 'threat displacement', whereby one threat simply replaces another, and also 'threat fatigue'. Senior management have a famously limited capacity to discuss risk in any formal sense, often seeing it as an administrative exercise designed to record some evidentiary trail to satisfy an invisible compliance body or faceless auditor.
- The organization should also be wary of 'event fixation', whereby unrealistic or disproportionate emphasis is given to certain scenarios.

This chapter has sought to capture some of the key considerations relevant to the exploration of resilience capability within an organization, and in a way which flows naturally from our examination of resilience definitions. This chapter also forms something of a bridge between two of the three critical questions which, as practitioners, we are constantly in search of the answers to: What is resilience? and What does it look like? The following chapter focuses exclusively on the second of these questions and does so by employing a number of international case studies.

Endnotes

1. Kim, E (2018) Jeff Bezos to employees: 'One day, Amazon will fail' but our job is to delay it as long as possible, *CNBC*, 27 November. Available from: www.cnbc.com/2018/11/15/bezos-tells-employees-one-day-amazon-will-fail-and-to-stay-hungry.html (archived at https://perma.cc/8PEH-F5BU)

2. Lee, A, Vargo, J and Seville, E (2013) Developing a tool to measure and compare organizations' resilience, *Natural Hazards Review*, **14** (1) pp 29–41, February. Available from: www.researchgate.net/publication/273370397_Developing_a_Tool_to_Measure_and_Compare_Organizations'_Resilience (archived at https://perma.cc/FCZ9-QSNY)

3. Vogus, T and Sutcliffe, K (2007) *Organizational Resilience: Towards a theory and research agenda*, IEEE, Man and Cybernetics International Conference (Montreal, QC: Canada), 3418–3422. Available from: ieeexplore.ieee.org/document/4414160 (archived at https://perma.cc/PP4L-4DML)

4. Gibson, C and Tarrant, M (2010) A 'conceptual models' approach to organizational resilience, *Australian Journal of Emergency Management*, **25** (2), April. Available from: www.austlii.edu.au/au/journals/AUJlEmMgmt/2010/27.pdf (archived at https://perma.cc/9R6J-Z54S)

5. BBC News (2019) Mercedes: Toto Wolff says team 'taking nothing for granted', 13 February. Available from: www.bbc.co.uk/sport/formula1/47224163 (archived at https://perma.cc/VXB8-6NKW)

6. Cranfield University and Waverley Consultants (2018) Smarter Regulation of Waste in Europe (LIFE13 ENV-UK-000549) LIFE SMART Waste Project, Horizon Scanning Toolkit. Available from: www.sepa.org.uk/media/367059/lsw-b4-horizon-scanning-toolkit-v10.pdf (archived at https://perma.cc/AMF9-F4Z9)

7. Lengnick-Hall, C, Beck, T and Lengnick-Hall, M (2011) Developing a capacity for organizational resilience through strategic human resource management, *Human Resource Management Review*, **21**, 243–255. Available from: iranarze.ir/wp-content/uploads/2016/10/5503-English.pdf (archived at https://perma.cc/V8N8-7FJ3)

8   Burton, L (2019) Standard Chartered sets aside £688m to cover potential US and UK fines, *Telegraph*, 21 February. Available from: www.telegraph.co.uk/business/2019/02/21/standard-chartered-sets-aside-688m-cover-potential-us-uk-fines/ (archived at https://perma.cc/K2MX-CTB9)

9   Denyer, D (2017) *Organizational Resilience: A summary of academic evidence, business insights and new thinking*. Available from: www.cranfield.ac.uk/som/case-studies/organizational-resilience-a-summary-of-academic-evidence-business-insights-and-new-thinking (archived at https://perma.cc/PP46-Y2ER)

10 Alrawi, M (2017) BP's quiet American Bob Dudley remains a study in resilience, *The National*, 13 July. Available from: www.thenational.ae/business/energy/bp-s-quiet-american-bob-dudley-remains-a-study-in-resilience-1.578145 (archived at https://perma.cc/86SF-TL5K)

11 Watkins, M and Bazerman, M (2003) *Three Steps for Crisis Prevention, Research and Ideas*, Harvard Business School, 7 April. Available from: hbswk.hbs.edu/item/three-steps-for-crisis-prevention

12 British Standards Institution (2018) *Organisational Resilience Index Report 2018*. Available from: www.bsigroup.com/globalassets/localfiles/fr-fr/organisational-resilience/static-banner-images/or-index-2018-final-web2.pdf (archived at https://perma.cc/9L32-E3GS)

13 Hodges, J (2017) Building capabilities for change: the crucial role of resilience, *Development and Learning in Organizations*, 31 (1), pp 5–8. Available from: www.emeraldinsight.com/doi/full/10.1108/DLO-07-2016-0064 (archived at https://perma.cc/2KCZ-P7MB)

14 Seville, E (2018) Building resilience: how to have a positive impact at the organizational and individual employee level, *Development and Learning in Organizations: An International Journal*, 32 (3), pp 15–18. Available from: www.emerald.com/insight/content/doi/10.1108/DLO-09-2017-0076/full/html (archived at https://perma.cc/VZY2-WLUK)

15 Welch, J (2005) *Winning*, HarperCollins. (Referred to as a key characteristic of senior leadership)

16 The GRC Institute (nd), *Trust and Stability in Organisational Resilience*. Available from: thegrcinstitute.org/news/view/2033 (archived at https://perma.cc/Z6DV-VERB)

17 Davenport, TH and Prusak, L (2000) *Working Knowledge: How organizations manage what they know*, Harvard Business School Press, Boston, MA

18 Donahue, A and Tuohy, R (2006) Lessons we don't learn: A study of the lessons of disasters, why we repeat them, and how we can learn them, *Homeland Security Affairs*, No. 2, Article 4 July. Available from: www.hsaj.org/articles/167 (archived at https://perma.cc/5FWM-6KW6)

19 Environmental Protection Agency (nd) Learn About Volkswagen Violations. Available from: www.epa.gov/vw/learn-about-volkswagen-violations (archived at https://perma.cc/K3A3-Z6DG)

20 *Financial Times* (2017) How VW's cheating on emissions was exposed. Available from: www.ft.com/content/103dbe6a-d7a6-11e6-944b-e7eb37a6aa8e (archived at https://perma.cc/3WVN-XUN3)

21 Goodman, L (2015) Why Volkswagen cheated, *Newsweek*, 15 December. Available from: www.newsweek.com/2015/12/25/why-volkswagen-cheated-404891.html (archived at https://perma.cc/B5Z8-S7VA)

22 Lengnick-Hall, C, Beck, T and Lengnick-Hall, M (2011) Developing a capacity for organizational resilience through strategic human resource management, *Human Resource Management Review*, **21**, pp 243–55. Available from: iranarze.ir/wp-content/uploads/2016/10/5503-English.pdf (archived at https://perma.cc/V8N8-7FJ3)

23 Professional Evaluation and Certification Board (2016) *The Importance of Organizational Resilience*, 18 August. Available from pecb.com/article/the-importance-of-organizational-resilience (archived at https://perma.cc/WZ3Q-2VXM)

24 Wishart, M (2018) *Business Resilience in an SME Context: A literature review*, Enterprise Research Centre and Warwick Business School. July 2018. Available from: www.enterpriseresearch.ac.uk/wp-content/uploads/2018/07/Resilience-review-Final.pdf (archived at https://perma.cc/DUH7-RGVG)

25 The GRC Institute (nd) *Trust and Stability in Organisational Resilience*. Available from: thegrcinstitute.org/news/view/2033 (archived at https://perma.cc/Z6DV-VERB)

26 Tan, H and Tan, C (2000) Toward the differentiation of trust in supervisor and trust in organization. *Genetic, Social, and General Psychology Monographs*, **126** (2), pp 241–60. Quoted by Filabi, A and Bulgarella, C (2018) *Organizational Culture Drives Ethical Behaviour: Evidence from pilot studies*. Available from www.oecd.org/corruption/integrity-forum/academic-papers/Filabi.pdf (archived at https://perma.cc/U6WF-B93S)

27 British Standards Institution (2017) *Standards Outlook 2017: Governance and Resilience*. Available from: www.bsigroup.com/en-GB/standards/Standards-Outlook-2017-Governance-Resilience/ (archived at https://perma.cc/G5Q6-XXHL)

28 Dubey, R (2018) *Antecedents of Resilient Supply Chains: An Empirical Study*, IEEE Transactions on Engineering Management. Available from: pearl.plymouth.ac.uk/bitstream/handle/10026.1/9613/Final%20Accepted%20Version_IEEE%20TEM%20Paper%20-%2029%20June%202017.pdf?sequence=1&isAllowed=y (archived at https://perma.cc/7U6Y-RG7Y)

29 McManus, S (2008) *Organisational Resilience in New Zealand*. Available from: core.ac.uk/download/pdf/35459228.pdf (archived at https://perma.cc/J99S-3XFZ)

4

Case studies

Within the context of organizational resilience, and indeed any subject for which there is such a volume of emerging knowledge and range of interpretations, the use of case study material can be particularly relevant and informative. Case studies are useful in illustrating different aspects of resilience theory and help us to explore and reinforce different aspects of our accepted definition. Importantly, they also help us to gain an understanding of what a resilient organization looks like without having to gain access to organization-specific information through some form of assessment, or through having worked with the organization in some capacity.

This chapter introduces a number of international case studies, which include the influential role of Chinese e-commerce giant Alibaba, the continued success of Mercedes Motorsport in Formula One, and the collapse of the UK retailer House of Fraser in 2018. Several of our case study examples make reference to specific crisis events and whilst I am always very careful to emphasize that resilience is not an event-focused concept, I am also the first to acknowledge that how an organization responds to a crisis can have a significant impact on its long-term success and growth potential. The reason for using crisis events can also be explained as it is not the management of the crisis which is our primary focus, but rather what this tells us about resilience capability and the gaps or weaknesses which might be exposed in respect of how the organization manages its strategic risks.

Case studies should create an engaging and informative story for the reader and their value in providing a reference to real-world situations is widely recognized in academia and in management studies. However, the challenges of promoting a particular organization or situation for illustrative purposes are perhaps similar to those associated with volunteering a definition for resilience: that is, they present easy targets for anyone who may be adopting a different perspective or who may be seeking to promote an alternative view. The other main challenge is perhaps that of currency: that is, whether the example is able to stand the test of time. With some care this particular risk can be mitigated away, and even if a once successful organization were to subsequently fail, this should not matter. In fact, we should actually find their fall from grace after the passage of time that much more informative, if we bother to understand the reasons why it happened.

There will always be people who, by virtue of their access, position or other experience, are extremely well informed about a particular event or an individual organization. This is inevitable and not something to be feared when writing or considering material for a case study. In recognition of this, what I can do here is to endeavour to draw references from different sources and reflect alternative perspectives where they are apparent. I will also aim to be clear and consistent with my focus, ensuring that I highlight as many aspects of the organization's resilience landscape as possible and not paying too much attention, as mentioned above, to individual crisis events or how successfully they are managed.

Organizations which are presented as case studies do not have to be the most resilient, and in fact they can appear to be in terminal decline and still exhibit some fascinating and highly relevant traits and characteristics worthy of further examination and discussion. One only has to think about some established religious or faith-based organizations to understand this particular point. The thing which defines case study organizations both collectively and individually is that they speak to resilience in some way and can be positioned by reference to our definition and resilience maturity scale. For example, Mercedes Motorsport speaks to growth and competitiveness more perhaps than the example of BP, which in this context at least speaks specifically to re-shaping and strength.

Before beginning to examine the case studies themselves and touching immediately on the holistic definitions we now have available to us, the BP example is a particularly good one to use as an illustration. It is worth remembering that resilience for many commentators remains little more than the ability to recover from shock or the capacity to cope, and for others reference to resilience is reserved exclusively for considerations of climate risks at a community or societal level. Interestingly, the marine ecosystem in the Gulf of Mexico has proven itself to be remarkably resilient, if only using the rather outdated 'bounce back' definition of the term. That is not to dismiss the concerns raised about longer-term damage; after all, 2010 is not that long ago, but the level of recovery exhibited by the marine environment must be at the higher end of many expectations back then. Incidentally, the internet contains plenty of well-informed commentary which charts the recovery in these natural marine habitats, and also continues to highlight ongoing concerns and long-term impact on wildlife and coastal communities.

The BP story is also capable of supporting multiple areas of focus simultaneously, each of which speaks in some way to the broad perspective of organizational resilience introduced in these pages. Delving into the detail of safety, environmental, commercial and societal aspects of the Gulf of Mexico explosion therefore allows the reader to consider not only how the example supports our definition of resilience, but also how it points to specifics such as crisis management communications, organizational re-design, political engagement and the impact of regulatory change.

Referring back to the definitions provides an extremely valuable way of considering the value and relevance of individual case studies, and can also highlight specific aspects from within the ORCM and the following chapter as a way of introducing their significance. My definition of organizational resilience is deliberately strategic in nature and intentionally broad, characterizing capability in respect of strength, competitiveness, re-shaping and growth. Any organization which could be considered as offering examples or learning relating to resilience will inevitably be unique in terms of its maturity and the context within which it operates. Some will have a long and high-profile history, perhaps synonymous with a particular sector or product, whilst others will be less well known but will have experience which can be still shared.

Finally, it is worth emphasizing that other examples or approaches to case study material should be actively considered by practitioners and scholars of the subject – those case studies offered here are certainly not intended as an exhaustive or definitive list. Some of the most fertile areas for case study material are those experiencing the most change, such as retail and technology, and there are numerous articles and indeed books devoted to the science of business success (and failure). For example, a quick internet search will highlight a number of articles charting the rise, dominance and ultimate decline of Nokia – a firm which helped to define the mobile telecommunications market, and which once boasted a market share of well over 40 per cent.[1] Oxfam, an international aid charity, found itself at the centre of a historical sexual abuse scandal in 2018, the full impact of which has yet to become clear not just for the organization in question but for the voluntary and aid sectors more generally.[2]

Case study material need not necessarily be that which is headline news. The Eastman Kodak Company (Kodak) sought bankruptcy protection in the United States in 2012, having struggled for a number of years with a decline in the use of photographic film and an uptake in digital imaging which it was slow to embrace. Still describing itself as a 'technology company focused on imaging' and despite some residual brand loyalty, rather like Nokia it has fallen from view and continues to restructure and re-shape its business.[3] Practitioners in search of case study examples should also consider how some long-established direct-selling companies have sought to manage the transition from traditional pre-digital selling techniques, such as door-to-door, that would doubtless uncover numerous examples of good practice or informative approaches.

Case study 1: The collapse of UK retailer House of Fraser in 2018

Our first case study is provided by a retailer which had featured prominently on the UK high street for many years. However, it was a business increasingly ill-equipped to compete in a fast-changing environment which was being shaped by growth in new technology and the constant interruption provided by new market entrants. It was also operating in an environment in which traditional customer behaviours could no longer be relied upon. Using business failure as a route to identifying case studies is particularly important with regard to resilience, as this is precisely what defines the organization's persistence and which synchronizes with the labels we use in the ORCM maturity scale, outlined in Chapter 5. Importantly, and whilst success or failure provides our basic parameters, this is not a case study which describes a business being undone by a singular crisis event. In fact, far from it.

The collapse of House of Fraser (HoF) was one of the more memorable events within what were generally harsh trading conditions for UK retailers in 2018. HoF began life as Arthur and Fraser in Glasgow in 1849 and had grown into a large, well-known business with a brand immediately recognized across the country. As widely reported in the news media at the time, when it collapsed into administration it had already posted significant losses for the previous year and had debts of over £1 billion.[4] HoF was viewed as a brand-driven retailer, something which was evidenced by the numerous brands owed money when it went into administration – the detail of what was owed being published in the annual accounts of companies such as Oasis and Mulberry in 2019.[5,6] However, it was not recognized by analysts as a digitally-led company and had only launched its online store in 2007. Its product mix, by virtue of the famous brands which it presented, was often identical to that which could be found elsewhere online, but often more expensive. Another charge commonly levelled at HoF related to a lack of innovation in its store estate and an approach to attracting customers into the stores which wasn't aligned within its core retail offering.

In 2004, the chain was being described by the Interactive Media in Retail Group, a trade body, as one of the UK's 'online laggards' that had 'failed to embrace internet trading opportunities'.[7] In addition, HoF's stores lacked the attraction of many others on the high street and its own brand offering was increasingly viewed as secondary to the large number of concession owners which presented their products in-store. It was also widely acknowledged that HoF simply had too many stores, and instead of slimming or streamlining its estate, more stores had been acquired, often with expensive lease arrangements. HoF also suffered with some well-documented management and ownership issues, including one high-profile failed merger (with Galeries Lafayette).[8]

History and common sense suggest there was nothing at all inevitable about HoF's demise, and the notion that resilience is all about an organization's ability to successfully manage its strategic risks can rarely have found a more appropriate illustration. The fortunes of HoF, and its inability to adapt to changing conditions and to the explosion in internet shopping, can of course be contrasted to other retailers, such as Boohoo – an online fashion retailer born of the very technology and customer relationship which HoF failed to grasp. We should dismiss immediately any charge that somehow Boohoo had an *unfair* advantage in this contest. In fact, we could argue strongly to the contrary that HoF had *every* advantage in establishing and growing an online presence to complement its existing store base and to profit from many years of retail experience.

Boohoo reported a 22 per cent rise in customers in the 12 months (September 2018) prior to HoF's collapse.[9] It had 6.3 million followers on Instagram, a 200 per cent rise in the previous 12 months, and 1.4 million followers on Facebook, up 40 per cent.[10] Boohoo started in 2006 and floated on the stock market in 2014. Expansion has included both the introduction of new ranges and the acquisition of other labels over the three years to 2019. By way of contrast, in 2018 HoF had just 178,000 followers on Instagram. Now, as already mentioned, this is not intended to amount to an unfair contrast between traditional, store-dominated retail and start-ups born of the internet age. Rather, it is presented as being symptomatic of how a well-established and seemingly mature organization can simply lack the knowledge and understanding or simply the agility to take advantage of new opportunities.

It is also not the case that HoF was somehow limited in how it 'defended' itself to the new and emerging online world with which its customers were increasingly engaged. HoF clearly neglected to take advantage of its high-street presence in the way that some of its competitors were able to. For example, customers did not experience the sort of in-store innovations which others were seemingly left to profit from, such as a focus on selling experiences, radical interior designs, alternative workplace ideas for underused floor space or providing valuable retail space to business start-ups.

To help make further sense of the situation in which HoF found itself, it is worth remembering that retail was not the only sector to be hurting. Car manufacturers, for example, were already having to make significant adjustments both to capacity and to product lines in 2018, as the move away from diesel (and towards electric vehicles) gathered pace. It is also important not to view a failure of this type as being restricted to the one, named organization – HoF's collapse inevitably had direct consequences for suppliers. In June 2019, Mulberry, the British luxury bag maker, announced it had taken a £2.1 million hit as a result of the HoF collapse.[11] In announcing its annual results, Mulberry also made reference to the ongoing challenges being experienced in their own particular market segment, noting changes that were being made to its retail model and growth prospects of digital sales and emerging markets in Asia.

The UK retail market alone can provide a number of other potential case study examples, such as electrical retailer Comet, which found itself unable to maintain a cost-leadership position and was widely viewed as providing a poor in-store experience and poor customer service. Although e-commerce has changed the traditional high-street model for ever, the failure of individual retailers such as HoF or Comet is more complex than a simple e-commerce versus 'bricks-and-mortar' equation might suggest. In the case of HoF, other department stores may have simply got the leap on them, suggesting the model itself is not necessarily in terminal decline. Whatever the specifics for HoF, it is clear that in the digital era, retailers must continue to provide compelling reasons for customers to buy in-store and provide an environment and experience which enhances customer loyalty – one only has to walk past a typical Apple store to appreciate what can be achieved in this regard.

A truthful internal assessment of performance or capability can often be a valuable, and sometimes unexpected source of case study information. In November 2018 the CEO of retailer Marks and Spencer (M&S) attracted praise for openly admitting some of the weaknesses in his business, referring to the organization as 'silo-ed, slow and hierarchical', but also claiming that M&S is now becoming a 'faster, more commercial and more digital business'.[12] One analyst commented:

> M&S is admitting its shortcomings and promising to deliver what investors have been screaming at it to do for years. Modernizing the clothing range, focusing on good quality but affordable 'must-haves', and selling more of what people want is reassuring to hear.[13]

Such commentary probably resonates right across the retail sector, although even under new ownership – it was somewhat controversially rescued from administration in a £90 million deal – it may already be too late for HoF.[14]

Case study 2: The on-track success of the Mercedes Formula One team

Motor racing's Formula One (F1) is big business – a high-profile, multi-billion pound enterprise at the forefront of innovation in engineering and technology and one which enjoys a truly global reach. As to be expected within any complex enterprise, measures of success will be many and varied. For some participants, the business of F1 is how they generate their revenue and without it they simply wouldn't exist. For others it provides a convenient shop window – a seductive brand opportunity and a means of promoting their other products or activities. It is fair to say that the simplicity, breathlessness and perhaps vulgarity of motorsport, and indeed many sports, may appear to make it a wholly inappropriate place to seek case study material for the vast majority of practitioners and organizations out there. However, a resilient organization, if nothing else, is one which is defined by its ongoing success.

As a team, and also as the manufacturer of its own engines, Mercedes (or in full, the Mercedes-AMG Petronas team) has dominated F1's racing calendar of recent years, winning each of the championships from 2014 to 2019. In fact, that domination has been so complete as to place enormous pressure on the sport's governing body to introduce new measures to counter what has frequently become a rather unexciting procession at race weekend – after all, a race with no actual racing is clearly not an attractive or sustainable proposition. Some aspects of F1, such as an overall sense of power, speed and acceleration, together with the exercising and discipline which allows a team to change all four wheels on a racing car in under three seconds, have long held an attraction for (perhaps predominantly male) managers and trainers seeking to create learning opportunities for their client organizations. Some have studied the culture and characteristics of F1 teams in great detail, but the recent on-track success for Mercedes has, understandably, attracted a whole new level of interest around the team and, in true celebrity-style, for Team Principal, Toto Wolff.

Periods of single-team domination in F1 are nothing new – in fact they are very much the norm. It is therefore easy to find ourselves asking the wrong questions about resilience in this context. Yes, resilience is all about success, but in such a closely-regulated environment where design and innovation take place continuously and within the narrowest of parameters and where the trophy can only go to one of a number of competing teams, we must be able to apply the notion of 'success' in a way which remains relevant. The competitiveness between sports teams has a sharpness to it, with a particular emphasis on individual victories and a very obvious all-or-nothing perspective when describing an outcome – one team wins, and therefore all the others must automatically 'lose'. It is very 'black and white' in many respects, and of course a victory is what attracts all the positive attention.

Before we examine two specific aspects of resilience by way of reference to this particular case study, it is worth considering the resilience of the Mercedes team beyond their recent on-track successes. Through the team, parent company Daimler has recently celebrated 125 years in motorsport and has been a familiar name in recent

F1 history, both as an engine supplier from 1994 and again since 2010 as the name of a racing team. The team has grown in size and complexity massively from what it was only a few years ago. There are many ways of measuring success in F1, and Mercedes is certainly not the most successful team when measured by number of historical race wins or championship titles. However, it is clear that its current team boss has an outstanding win ratio when compared to his peers, and the team surely satisfies our overall definition of resilience as it has remained competitive for a number of years and has won acclaim for the way in which it has adapted to changes in regulations and for attracting and retaining some of the best drivers and technical expertise available.

To help us position and make full use of the case study, it is probably worth considering the team's recent success through focusing on two discrete aspects of resilience, namely leadership and data. Generic across all F1 teams, the races themselves are increasingly data-driven, with enormous quantities of sensory and telemetry data generated by a car on each lap of a race. Teams also gather and analyse data from other teams' activities and performances, and they invest heavily in the very latest track and weather information. The vast amounts of data used to inform real-time decision-making and post-race analysis require both sophisticated electronic systems and reliable communications, particularly when considering that much of this analysis is routinely carried out many thousands of miles away from the race track at the team's base location.

Not exclusively to Mercedes, and indeed by no means exclusive to motorsport, much is made of the influence and importance of leadership in respect to team performance. This is something which both reflects and reinforces the notion that leadership can make or break resilience in an organization. However, this is more than simply an exercise in drawing convenient analogies between F1 teams and other types of business organization in the hope that connections and similarities reveal themselves. There is something undeniably simple about a racing team, and there is also something about the size, complexity, profile and pressure of F1 which probably amplifies the impact of leadership, and teamworking for that matter.

From managing internal rivalry and conflicts, to setting of team objectives, the use of mindfulness techniques, and the development of an open and trusting culture, much has been made of Wolff's management style. Interviews with and articles about Wolff regularly touch upon different aspects of leadership, as one would imagine, with many of these being the things one might expect from any CEO or COO: character and motivation, playing to your strengths, emotional connections, celebrating success, empowering those around you, and the need to learn from failure.[15] On a personal level, one of the more interesting quotes from Wolff (in an interview with UBS) relates to what he sees as clarity around tolerance for risk, meaning that he does not see himself as taking risks – his exposure is understood and accepted at all times.[16]

However, it is worth emphasizing at this point that resilience capability should not be too closely connected with a particular personality or style of leadership and nor should commentators be attempting to explain success by constant reference to some 'essential ingredient', be that the most charismatic leader or even the most talented racing driver. The true value of referencing the on-track success of the Mercedes team is about two different aspects or leadership considerations. Firstly, the importance of leadership and the impact which individuals can undoubtedly make to team performance, whilst always acknowledging the interplay with many other elements relevant to the organization. Secondly, how individual leadership tenure contributes to the long-term success of the organization, and the features and characteristics which allow it to remain competitive into the future.

The danger for any organization is that a preoccupation with a particular leader or personality will tend to reduce the importance of the whole-team effort to that of an individual performance, which by its very nature has no 'long term' associated with it – it only has relevance or meaning for as long as the individual endures, and the tenure of leaders is showing a shortening trend. Rather than challenging our definition of resilience, the inherent nature of 'personality' or leadership when considered in relation to that provided by a single individual should simply encourage us not to place too much emphasis on it when considering resilience capability as I have defined it here. This is not to deny the sometimes massive impact which force of personality can exert on organizational performance, but capability must reflect the sustainable nature of the leadership dividend being enjoyed at any particular moment in time.

In the case of Mercedes, and any other organization in a similar position, it may even be suggested that where considered to be a dominant influencer on performance, due to the individual(s) involved, we may have uncovered a potentially non-resilient characteristic – something which potentially works counter to the characteristics and behaviours associated with resilient organizations. After all, if everything about resilience capability – strength, competitiveness, re-shaping and growth – is potentially jeopardized by the leader being no longer available, then this is obviously not resilience in action. Furthermore, for any framework or model to provide value in assessing resilience capability, it must have the flexibility to cope with the inevitably skewed and ever-changing balance of characteristics within the organization.

F1 is clearly and genuinely a data-driven environment, from simulations and product development to the execution of in-race strategy and even the detail of how the race action is broadcast, minute by minute. To remain competitive, F1 teams use vast quantities of data to drive innovation and inform decision-making. Much of this is done at pace and through rapid cycles, with numerous new products released into an operational environment often within days of initial concept design work. F1 cars carry an assortment of data collection devices, measuring a wide variety of conditions from tyre temperature and air flows to driver behaviour, and this is used in real time to develop and adjust the strategy for each race and to optimize vehicle performance. Data is also used to identify improvement opportunities and to drive efficiencies within in-race processes, most famously perhaps in relation to speed with which pit stops are now performed.

How data is referenced as a characteristic of a resilient organization is extremely important. It doesn't need to have its own discrete 'category' in terms of how we seek to assess and examine resilience.

However, organizations need to be able to 'position' and consider it effectively and consistently and they also need to be able to assign an appropriate level of significance to it – significance, that is, very much within the context of their own unique organizational circumstances. As illustrated by this particular case study, the ability to collect, communicate and analyse large quantities of data is a critical aspect of F1 and the ability of individual teams to compete effectively, far more so perhaps than in some other organizations.

Case study 3: The re-invention of retail by Alibaba and others

If we were required to hand out prizes to the most effective disruptive force within a commercial sector, then we would probably award one to e-commerce. In common with other similar disruptive forces, historians will pinpoint specific phases and developments as online retail activity exploded on to the scene, charting the detail of local connectivity, the use of alternative payment mechanisms and the migration to mobile technologies. Linked by reference to the general changes in the sector, this case study is intended to highlight how companies like Alibaba are applying technology in order to deliver a growth strategy through re-inventing the retail experience. Emphasizing that the phrase 'business as usual' has probably never been so misplaced as it currently is for retail, the following quote brilliantly captures how recent developments are being viewed and reported:

> E-commerce is rapidly evolving into New Retail. The boundary between offline and online commerce disappears as we focus on fulfilling the personalized needs of each customer. New Retail is a critical chapter in the comeback story of physical retail, and the evolving narrative of the digitization of all retail.[17]

The emerging retail environment is one in which physical outlets can continue as being essential to a company's overall strategy, just as the application of new technology at the user interface remains vital. Businesses such as Alibaba are not just investing in an ever more sophisticated online marketplace, but are actively seeking to recreate the customer experience at a 'bricks-and-mortar' level, albeit in ways that the management of HoF may never have considered. For example, the potential for robotic shopping assistants and for payments to be taken in such a way as to remove the need for queues have all been commented upon extensively.

That e-commerce has changed the retail landscape is clearly not in any doubt, and nor is the ongoing and rapid development of technologies associated with the buying of goods and services. Growth potential and the ability of the market to support new start-ups is not just about the need to predict future trends, although we can highlight a number of these with some degree of certainty: the application of augmented reality (AR) or product visualization to enhance the user (shopper) experience by, for example, maximizing the camera functionality on mobile devices seems like an obvious bet, particularly with the constant improvements in fixed and mobile connectivity. Similarly, the expansion of automated online assistants (chatbots) and voice control appears inevitable, and not just for simple queries, bookings or payment commands.

It appears that Alibaba and others are seeking to influence the market in new ways, such as through the expansion of web-only brands, responding to an increased interest and ability of manufacturers to sell direct to consumers and to the demand from consumers for same-day delivery. The move to new physical shopping experiences, which could be described as digital-led or custom-shopping, is also recognition that e-commerce isn't always able to match the physical experience afforded by bricks-and-mortar. For Alibaba, this is not simply about opening a traditional store to complement its online presence. From a resilience perspective, this is about awareness and being able to innovate from a position of strength. It's also about creating value from data, the commercial acumen necessary to exploit new markets and the speed with which new products and services (and facilities) are made available to consumers.

The size and influence of some of the commercial organizations which are behind the New Retail revolution is immense, and routinely commented upon.[18] Amazon, for example, now accounts for £4 of every £100 spent by UK consumers, with total online retail spend accounting for 17 per cent of the total in 2018. In the United States, Amazon was responsible for an estimated 50 per cent of the growth in online sales in 2016, which was 10 times higher than the combined growth reported by the eight largest 'traditional' retail businesses. Much of Amazon's revenue comes from electronic products and merchandise and digital media content. It boasts over 300 million customer accounts, enjoys significant cash reserves, has over 300,000 employees and is active in emerging markets, such as India, through investing in established retailers.

Alibaba is a very different business to Amazon, for example, both in respect of number of employees, operating countries and selling model; however, this has not stopped them from being constantly compared – they do also have many similarities. Alibaba's numbers are impressive: after its initial public offering (IPO) in 2014, it has grown to become one of the top 10 most valuable and biggest companies in the world. In 2018, Alibaba became the second Asian company to break the US $500 billion valuation mark and has the ninth highest global brand value. As of December 2018, Alibaba's market capitalization was reported as US $352 billion. Alibaba's share of total retail spend in China is reported to be over 11 per cent, but this jumps to an astonishing 80 per cent for online sales.

Online activity also enjoys access to a unique growth engine in the form of advertising revenues.[19] In 2018, Alibaba was able to provide access across its various marketplaces to over 650 million active shoppers in China. Although its digital advertising revenues are significantly lower than those enjoyed by Facebook or Google, it is estimated that Alibaba is now the world's third largest seller of advertising, with US $30 billion annually.

Alibaba and other pioneer organizations afford us the opportunity to consider resilience as a concept which is relevant to rapid growth and success within an emerging and rapidly changing sector. What makes this so refreshing is that it comes without needing to discuss failure or decline or to offer any comment on the company's crisis management capabilities. These organizations may promote their own agendas, for example a desire to establish a particular ethical or behavioural standard, but what makes them so valuable from the perspective of defining resilience capability is that we can simply focus on how they are helping to create new models for retail within what is an increasingly mature digital environment.

So, what differentiates companies like Alibaba and Nike and all those others which are part of the new age in retail, and how should we be employing resilience models and resilience thinking to help us make sense of it? Are these companies simply more tech-savvy and more customer-centric than retailers of old? In a 2018 article for *Harvard Business Review*, Ming Zeng discussed aspects of Alibaba's business model, and he did so from a position of significant knowledge, as he is the chairman of the Academic Council of the Alibaba Group.[20] In this article, the majority of references and indicators of success are related directly to data and to technology, and leadership is relegated to almost an after-thought. Now, this may or may not be significant, and of course it may simply be a product of how the article was edited, but it appears to present an interesting contrast to the case study provided by Mercedes. I may be reading too much into this, and particularly given that Alibaba (as indeed have Facebook and Amazon and others) has grown under the tech-stewardship and entrepreneurship of specific individuals, but this sounds like we should perhaps be looking at aspects of our resilience model other than leadership.

Awareness, however labelled or described, is widely acknowledged as a critical component of an organization's resilience capability, and it appears to have a particular relevance for environments not only where rapid and constant change are the norm, but also where entire (and extremely valuable) market segments are created, seemingly from nothing and seemingly overnight. It is also important to remember that awareness and visibility is not just limited to what is happening within the organization's wider environment – a clear understanding of internal resource availability or geographical limitations, for example, may be just as relevant. Furthermore, a focus on awareness both inside and outside of the organization should not be taken to imply that a passive approach is either more likely or more appropriate. If the examples of internet and e-commerce companies demonstrate one thing it is that existing environments are not just exerting shaping forces on the organization; whole environments are themselves being actively created and formed.

There is also a narrative within the story of organizations like Alibaba which speaks to an enhanced appetite for risk exposure and how this translates into product and service innovation. The creation of a new app or new payment system, however, cannot be easily compared to historical service delivery via a physical store or classic human interface. Return on digital innovation investment can be rapid and customers are increasingly remaining online, turning to social media to share their service experiences in real time. Innovation in digital services is also less dependent upon traditional and cash-/time-hungry research and development activities, although this is probably less true when extended to robotics. Even more so than concepts of awareness, innovation delivery is proving to be a complex mix of resilient characteristics, from organizational culture and risk appetite to retained knowledge and the quality of Board oversight. And, of course, recent corporate history is littered with examples of those who have failed to innovate quickly enough in the digital age – buttons versus screens being one of the best examples. Anyone remember Blackberry? And of course, Nokia's reliance on its Symbian operating system.

Case study 4: BP a decade after the explosion in the Gulf of Mexico 2010

That BP remains a major player in the global oil and gas industry is a demonstration of its resilience, and as introduced in Chapter 3, this is largely in spite of the way certain aspects of the crisis response were initially handled. The events in the Gulf of Mexico in April 2010 which led to the fire and explosion on the Deepwater Horizon drilling rig are well documented, including the corporate failings which led to the loss of life and the subsequent environmental disaster.[21] Prior to 2010, and of huge significance from a resilience perspective, BP had a less than favourable safety record – this was not the company's first major accident involving multiple fatalities – and for some commentators, the company's appetite for safety risk was of particular note.[22] A report into the 2005 Texas City disaster at a BP facility which killed 15 workers concluded there had been 'apparent complacency toward serious safety risk'.[23]

In the immediate aftermath of the 2010 incident, and even before the full extent of BP's liabilities were understood, many analysts and others were openly questioning the company's ability to respond and also therefore questioning the long-term viability of its business. For some, BP's apparent lack of flexibility had been underlined by moves away from alternative energy in the years immediately before the accident – there was a clear sense that the company remained dependent on oil and this allowed stakeholders to openly debate its commitment to a low carbon future.

A decade later, and in reporting its results for the second quarter of 2019 BP quoted a US $2.8 billion profit but confirmed that it was still in the process of funding the US $65 billion Gulf of Mexico compensation bill.[24] Its own report narrative spoke positively about investments in high-growth assets and business expansion across a number of market areas, and the company openly advertised itself as now providing genuine 'low carbon leadership'. During the preceding 10 years, BP sold off over US $60 billion of assets and also sought to redress some of the apparent organizational and cultural weaknesses identified in the aftermath of the accident – what a *Financial Times* (FT) article described as:

> A tumultuous process… (and) a rebuilding process that has only recently begun to restore a sense of normality to the company.[25]

There is a lot which is highly relevant, both from BP's 'starting point' at the time of the accident and also from its journey of recovery. In the same FT article from 2018, BP's chairman, Carl-Henric Svanberg, proclaimed that, 'We have been able to bring back BP to the size and strength it was before the [Gulf of Mexico] accident.' A year earlier, its CEO, Bob Dudley, stated that, 'This year has felt like a turning point. We're never going to feel complacent. But it feels like we are now dealing with the same problems that everyone else has.'[26] Those monitoring and reporting on BP's business in the years since the 2010 disaster have discussed numerous aspects of its recovery, from a renewed leadership focus, re-shaping through asset and business sales, embracing digital transformation and an entrepreneurial approach, to start up new energy businesses and problem-solving.

In examining BP's resilience credentials in the run-up to 2010, specific reference should be made to the learning environment within which it found itself – an environment which was greatly influenced by the disasters of Piper Alpha in 1988 and Texas City in 2005. That learning opportunities were freely available is a simple and undeniable point, and not one limited to BP of course, but the fact that such lessons were having to be re-learned by the company in 2010, and within the context of underwater drilling activities, would surely influence any opinion regarding resilience maturity at the time. The informed analysis and reporting on each of these events points to a number of failings, many of which share similar causal factors relevant to resilience. For example, some of the learning specifically highlighted as a result of the Piper Alpha disaster included inadequate containment capabilities, multiple safety system failures, managerial failings and poor operational decision, distorted information flows and defective regulatory controls and responsibilities.[27]

As outlined in more detail in Chapter 6, the assessment of resilience capability would normally begin with an initial data inventory, however incomplete, and informed by whatever pre-existing knowledge and understanding the assessor might have – this is simply a common-sense, quantitative exercise aimed at establishing a meaningful baseline from which to test and probe further. In common with many projects, being able to confirm a starting position is of particular importance, and it would be relatively straightforward in BP's case to draw together a number of quite specific references relating to resilience capability. In an entirely fictional world where we had been invited to undertake one, I would suggest that an assessment of BP today might include the following, prompted by what appear to be relevant pointers contained within public records and reports, and commentary from industry analysts:

- Detail of how operational risks are currently being managed across joint ventures (JVs). These have accounted for a significant proportion of BP's operations in recent times and it is understood that the detail of operational responsibilities can be taken by either party, depending upon the detail of the specific contract.
- Detail of process safety 'Tier 1' incidents. However basic or blunt such metrics may be, they do still provide a consistent means of monitoring a level of safety performance over time, and of comparing performance between organizations. The numbers for Tier 1 incidents publicly reported by BP appear to show a plateau in performance at 16–20 cases per year.[28]
- Employee engagement scores. Specifically in response to BP seeking to link bonus payments to environmental (greenhouse gas emissions) performance – it is reported that some 36,000 employees have remuneration linked to a specific reduction path in such emissions.[29]
- Assurance activities and the closure of improvement actions. Following safety concerns raised in a leaked internal report from 2016, insight could potentially be gained into BP's culture and approach through analysis of closure times and the quality of verification activities, particularly for more significant improvement actions.[30]
- Analysis in respect of digital transformation efforts. This could include detail of the company's digital strategy and the extent to which, for example, new technologies are being employed to manage risk in operational environments.
- Evidence which could demonstrate the effectiveness of management training. BP is reported to have invested in training programmes designed specifically to improve the quality of decision-making at management and leadership levels.

This initial shopping list is, of course, rather speculative and its true value to an assessment of resilience would only become apparent *in situ*. However, the example of BP should provide a useful illustration for the practitioner in how such an assessment could be fashioned, at least at an elementary level, in any organization. Many of BP's operations are highly complex and take place in extreme environmental conditions. As evidenced by the events of 2010, failure at an operational level can have catastrophic consequences. However, BP appears to have succeeded in moving on and its public agenda is very much one of new projects and growth and a focus on what it referred to in its own Energy Outlook report as 'one of the biggest challenges of our time... the need to meet rising energy demand whilst at the same time reducing carbon emissions'.[31]

The company's share price rose 30 per cent in the 12 months to 2018, and it is active in the mergers and acquisitions (M&A) market and divesting with a stated policy to focus on high-growth assets. New projects include expansion of Trinidad gas production and a floating liquefied natural gas (LNG) platform off the coast of Africa. It also announced it was exploring a new petrochemical facility in Turkey, and a new exploration licence adjacent to the giant Khazzan gas project in Oman. The true value of the post-2010 BP story is to re-emphasize the meaning of resilience and to demonstrate that the characteristics of strength and growth are perhaps best illustrated by reference to success, rather than failure. There is also enormous value in being able to focus on specific aspects of organizational activity, be that safety, supply chain or compliance, as a means of exploring resilience capability – reference contained within a broad definition is one thing, but being able to consider it in relation to an actual organization is quite another.

In this regard, we should also anticipate how future case study examples might develop. The crisis which developed for Boeing following the loss of two newly-launched 737 MAX aircraft and the deaths of over 300 people in late 2018 and early 2019 suggests a number of similarities with the BP event: for example, the mounting financial impacts, a regulatory regime which will be for ever changed and an initial corporate response which was widely criticized for being slow and uncaring. How this particular example works out remains to be seen, but it is clear that organizations continue to suffer from major events. No corporate entity is immune, impacts can be significant and drawn out, and none should be considered too big to fail.

Case study 5: The impact of the WannaCry virus in 2017

We should never tire of explaining resilience in crisis-event terms and seeking to emphasize important distinctions where they apply, and of course correcting misconceptions where they arise. Crucially, resilience is not an event-focused concept, although an organization's ability to deal successfully with a crisis is likely to have a significant bearing on its long-term growth prospects and even its viability. As with the example provided by BP, the spread of the WannaCry virus in May 2017 does indeed constitute a specific crisis event, and again this is not presented as a case study in crisis management or crisis communications. Rather, it constitutes a study in failure – that is, failure to understand and manage strategic risks in a responsible manner – which left a federation of healthcare organizations in the UK vulnerable to attack.

WannaCry, which spread to more than 150 countries in a worldwide ransomware outbreak beginning on 12 May 2017, was the biggest cyber-attack to have hit the UK's National Health Service (NHS) to date. More than a third of local organizations, which have the status of 'Trusts', in England were disrupted by the ransomware, according to the UK parliamentary agency, the National Audit Office (NAO).[32] Nearly 7,000 medical appointments were cancelled as a result of the attack, and although the impacts were particularly acute for the NHS, the attack was estimated to have affected more than 200,000 computers globally before it was fully contained, with total damages ranging from hundreds of millions to billions of dollars. Security experts believed, from preliminary evaluation at least, that the attack originated from North Korea or agencies working for the country.[33]

As we have noted already, resilience is effectively a function of the organization's risk management approach and specifically of its success in managing strategic-level risks. As such, the organization's understanding of vulnerability and exposure is of central importance. The NAO's report into the WannaCry attack highlighted two specific aspects of risk which are expanded upon below. Firstly, warnings were received about the likelihood of cyber-attacks affecting healthcare systems a year earlier, in 2016, and although actions were underway, the NHS did not formally respond with a report of its own into how cyber-risks were being addressed until after the attack, in July 2017. Secondly, central NHS bodies, within what was a large and complex federated model, did not know what level of cyber-preparedness existed at a local level, and were seemingly incapable or unwilling to enforce an effective control framework.

The NHS's own 'lessons learned' report in February 2018 accepted that the threat of cyber-attack had not been adequately considered before the attack, evidenced by, amongst other things, a failure to effectively implement previously published data control standards or the operating system fix (or 'patch') published by Microsoft two months before the attack.[34] Indeed, warnings about the need to migrate to more robust operating systems were first published in 2014. Leadership responsibilities and the provision of specialist resources were identified as being areas requiring improvement and, specifically, a requirement to review cyber-related risks at Board level. The 2018 internal report also documented a programme of cyber-security assessments undertaken across a range of NHS organizations in the wake of the attack, and highlighted some of the preventative measures taken as a result. It contained a number of specific recommendations in this area, including the assessment of 'cyber-security'.

That the NHS proved to be particularly vulnerable to this attack, running unpatched or unsupported operating systems and with insufficient firewalls facing the internet, may have come as a surprise to many IT professionals. But this was the reality at the time in the NHS, summarized by the NAO report as a failure to 'maintain good cyber-security practices'. This level of vulnerability would obviously influence any assessment of resilience capability in 2017, as would the fact that it was also not the first time that NHS organizations had been subject to cyber-attack.

The information received by the NHS in 2016, prior to the attack, appears to have described the risks associated with cyber-attack in some detail, highlighting not only the potential loss or compromise of patient data but also loss of access to critical data by NHS staff.

Although the NAO report positions risk management as a leadership responsibility, the narrative in this area is noticeably light on detail compared with some of the technical information associated with operating systems and the like.

As both reports highlight, the threat associated with cyber-attack is very real for all organizations, and it is hardly surprising therefore that other large organizations have reported WannaCry attacks since 2017, including US plane maker Boeing. What might be particularly concerning for leadership in the NHS, and provide us with insight into how effectively the ongoing risks are being managed, are the continuing reports which point to remaining vulnerabilities and a lack of preparedness. For example, in 2018 a group of UK parliamentarians (MPs) issued a report through the influential Public Accounts Committee which claimed the NHS had taken insufficient action to protect patient services from cyber-attack.[35] Research published in 2019 by Imperial College London also claimed that 'more investment is urgently needed' within the NHS to tackle the evolving cyber-threat.[36]

The need for central government departments and NHS management to obtain meaningful assurance regarding the effectiveness of cyber-controls formed the backdrop to a number of specific recommendations within the NAO's report. This situation appears to have been confirmed by information presented to MPs in 2018 suggesting that all 200 local NHS organizations (Trusts), out of a total of 236, had (at that point) failed to achieve a satisfactory grade from a formal cyber-assessment.[37] The fact that more effective assurance was highlighted as a requirement should not come as a surprise to anyone who recognizes the disconnect between senior management and operational realities being shown in reports. After all, it's a very common lesson to learn.

That the patch which would have prevented operating system vulnerability was actually available prior to the attack might appear to provide us with a simple and instant remedy. Reports into the event have also highlighted key elements of the organization's response which could have made a significant difference to how patient services were actually impacted. However, what helps us to understand resilience in this and other similar cases is not usually found within the detail of the event. The risk environment for organizations is hugely complex and fast-moving, and the willingness and ability of the organization to seek assurances about how it is managing those risks is a critical factor in considering resilience capability.

From a distance, it is impossible for us to know just how the assessment of cyber-threats was treated at the time, or whether the NHS knew but simply didn't care that its vulnerability to attack had never been properly quantified. It is also impossible for us to know just how much progress has been made in this regard since 2017. As we highlight in Chapter 6, assurance should not be too concerned with which risks the organization wishes to embrace, but rather the way in which that embrace is understood and executed. It is not our job to sit in judgement about how the NHS sought to prioritize cyber-risks at the time of the attack, but our assessment of their resilience capability should reflect the fact that the organization was simply not in a position to plan and execute its activities effectively and efficiently due to a lack of critical risk information and understanding.

Case study 6: The continued resilience of London's transport network

Critical infrastructure makes our daily lives possible and is essential for society to operate. Whilst they remain identifiable as discrete sectors or activities, these networks are usually interconnected and involve some type of partnership arrangement between public- and private-sector organizations, and a regulatory and funding model involving central or local government. In a similar way to climate risks and supply chains, the term 'resilience' is often associated, albeit in a very narrow sense, directly with these networks and assets. The context within which almost every organization operates confirms a complex and deep dependency on critical infrastructures which provide, amongst other things, transport, banking, power, water, communications and healthcare provision. This dependency is reflected in the increased focus on urban resilience, as with the publication by BSI of their new guidance document in 2019.[38]

Disruption of services, even for a very limited time, can have a significant impact on economic activity and social wellbeing, which accounts for the priority which is afforded to it by governments across the world. Due largely to the way in which they are constructed, accessed and operated, transport networks are particularly vulnerable to such disruption. A broad and varied sector in itself, threats to transport infrastructure range from asset failures and human error through to deliberate acts of sabotage or terrorism. It is within urban centres that the interconnectedness of transport infrastructure takes on a heightened degree of significance, and as such the network in London provides us with an attractive case study opportunity.

As identified in research from 2011:

> It is not surprising that terrorists have so often targeted transportation systems in their attacks.... Transportation systems are especially vulnerable. In particular, mass transit modes concentrate large numbers of people in confined and often low-security areas. Moreover, given their network character and fundamental role in advanced regional economies, they are capable of spreading substantial economic losses to the rest of society.[39]

The need for efficient, reliable public transport is widely recognized as a key requirement for ensuring the success of urban centres, with high-profile transport projects underway in many regions across the world, including the Arabian Gulf and South Africa. The topic attracts significant attention from researchers and policy-makers alike, and there is inevitably an increasing interest in the application of new technology and the delivery of environmentally sustainable solutions. Many cities and urban centres, although each with its own unique set of circumstances and constraints, are effectively seeking to address very similar challenges – namely, how to improve connectivity, accessibility, reliability and environmental performance, whilst targeting development in specific areas and for specific events and providing value for investors and taxpayers.

London's transport network continues to attract significant investment, ever since the very specific focus of supporting the 2012 Olympic Games, and its legacy is a long and significant one, with some of the underground rail system dating back to the 1860s. The controlling body, Transport for London (TfL), runs most of London's public transport services and is widely credited with establishing a truly integrated multi-modal transport network – one which services up to 30 million passenger journeys each day for a rapidly growing city of nearly 9 million people. TfL enjoys a significant degree of control and authority across the various aspects of transport infrastructure and service delivery. As such, it was a significant contributor to London's integrated infrastructure plan which runs through to 2050 and which draws together multiple other elements, including energy and housing.[40]

For those looking in London's direction in order to identify some of the critical requirements for cities and urban centres in general, integrated planning and funding certainty are probably high on the list. There is a clarity of vision in respect of transport planning, the detail of which is captured within a range of formal documents and reports. For example, the Mayor's Transport Strategy document (2018) proclaims, 'the success of London's future transport system relies upon reducing Londoners' dependency on cars in favour of increased walking, cycling and public transport use', and stipulates a key aim being for '80 per cent of all trips in London to be made on foot, by cycle or using public transport by 2041'.[41] Other specific areas of London's strength include the following:

- Span of control. TfL is responsible for multiple aspects of transportation in the capital, from congestion charging for private motorists and traffic signalling, through to cycle hire and the regulation of taxis and mini-cabs.
- Ticketing. Smart ticketing and cashless payments are now well established and the further potential to harness available technologies to enable more integrating ticketing has been recognized and informs strategy.

- Political leadership. The TfL Board, which has a multi-billion pound annual budget, is chaired by the elected Mayor of London. Successive administrations have been able to point to the delivery of long-term projects, for example the Crossrail (Elizabeth Line) project, as evidence of how the network is being managed for the long-term benefit of its citizens.
- Integrated delivery. Even though privately operated, many services are delivered with the support of TfL in respect of revenues, for example, and most are branded uniformly using TfL's official logo, known as the 'roundel'.

In some way or other, the ability of London's transport network to withstand a shock is probably tested on a regular basis, from protestors on the rail track or equipment failure through to unplanned road closures or industrial action by staff. However, the terrorist attacks which targeted underground trains and a bus on 7 July 2005, with the loss of 52 lives, is of particular relevance to us here. The impact and the response were both of significant scale. Central London transport systems were thrown into chaos, with many bus services halted until 4pm and the underground being completely closed down until the following morning. Disruption lasted several weeks. The ambulance service dispatched 200 vehicles and 400 staff across five sites in response to the attacks, with over 400 patients being delivered to seven hospitals within the first three hours.

Some degree of network or service disruption is inevitable, particularly given the type and scale of the event, and of course the terrorist attack in 2005 was certainly not the first. As noted in the Multi-Agency Debrief from London Resilience in 2006:

> The challenge is achieving the right balance between running a mass public transit system that keeps London moving whilst introducing proportionate security measures that deter and prevent terrorist attacks.[42]

In seeking to understand underlying resilience capability, one of the more interesting insights following the attacks related to the psychological effects on transport users. There was an immediate estimated drop of more than 2 million passenger journeys following the attacks and subsequent line and station closures, and subsequent modelling has been used to estimate the effect of 'fear' in reducing passenger journeys, and in the decisions to use alternative modes of transport. In taking passenger survey data from 11 to 13 days after the attacks, a 2009 research report concluded that, 'Overall, approximately 31 per cent of the sample reported substantial stress symptoms, and 32 per cent reported that once the London transport system had returned to normal, they intended to travel less'.[43] In following up these results, it was noted in the report that:

> People's sense of safety whilst travelling had significantly improved, with 19 per cent of respondents in 2005 feeling very unsafe whilst travelling, compared to just 12 per cent in 2006. Similarly, whilst 30 per cent of respondents originally said they intended to travel less often, significantly fewer (19 per cent) reported actually travelling less often in 2006 as a result of the bombings.[44]

Looking back on the events of 2005, researchers and commentators have highlighted a number of key learning points which are of particular relevance to our consideration of resilience capability. As described within a research paper from 2017, a number of 'key resilience drivers' were identified in respect of TfL:[45]

- preparing for the 2012 Olympics and terrorism in general;
- planning for population growth and decarbonization;
- increased flooding and heat risks from climate change;
- recognition of ageing infrastructure.

Within the same paper, a number of successes were identified:

- creating a culture of resilience across many agencies;
- providing online data to travellers;
- encouraging 'multi-modalism' and redundancy across rail, bus and bike transport;
- use of parking charges and congestion pricing.

Just as disruption is an inevitable consequence of such an attack, so too are the presence of learning points. In a 10-year anniversary piece, a BBC article identified the following lessons which it believed had been successfully acted upon:[46]

- introduction of new radio systems, with no gaps in coverage, and the advent of central broadcast messages;
- a centralized command centre for the British Transport Police and others, rather than in different buildings across London;
- TfL command structures aligned to those of the emergency services (ie Gold, Silver);
- many more training exercises;
- a single marked rendezvous point outside each underground station.

Conclusion

It might sound like rather an obvious conclusion to draw, but case studies only yield value if the audience is able to truly appreciate their relevance. The case studies offered here serve to promote two separate points – not only to provide specific learning which can be absorbed, applied and shared, one organization to another, but also to reinforce the broad and strategic definition built for organizational resilience in Chapter 3. Careful selection of case study material also allows us to focus on specific elements of resilience capability. For example, when considering an organization which may have been undone by a specific event, the audience should be considering aspects such as the organization's control environment, and whether specific controls were absent or simply not operating as intended. Similarly:

- What flags or indicators might management have been aware of?
- What assurance could or should have been provided to seniors in respect of the management of risk?

- What were the obvious weaknesses in management's responses, and what might the response have looked like?

Whilst a case study's relevance to our definition of resilience is often quite obvious, some of the learning points can prove to be a little more subtle and therefore require care to ensure any lessons are unpicked correctly. Thankfully, this task is made all the easier through the exploration of the ORCM in Chapter 5. Individual case studies may well provide an opportunity to look more broadly across a sector in order to identify learning, as with the winners and losers in the fast-changing world of retail. One of our other case studies, provided by Mercedes F1 team, also serves as an introduction to what else can be learned from industry-wide process, systems and approaches.

Motorsport, and in particular F1, has been the subject of analysis and learning for organizations for some time. As reinforced with the example of Mercedes, a resilient organization is one which focuses on those characteristics and capabilities which help it to compete and which understands how they contribute to building resilience. A resilient organization is also one which can learn, and we also considered the relevance of data to the team's success. Data can, and perhaps should, be considered an asset, and as such it is the health and integrity of that asset which is key to its usability. It is also something which is relevant to skills such as project management and information sharing, and not as simply a resource consideration.

In an article published by Cranfield School of Management, F1 is held up as a beacon of good management practice: 'Formula One racing teams are living examples of how this kind of highly adaptable, high-performance operation can work'.[47] The article speaks specifically to the learning culture at an industry or sector level and emphasizes the general applicability of points to other organizations. What also makes the article particularly relevant is the reference to its own research-based 'performance pyramid', the detail of which maps neatly across to elements within the ORCM.

I must admit to usually feeling a little sceptical in relation to case study examples presented in text, regardless of how or why they might be considered to qualify as such. This probably stems from some early management research and training I undertook, which drew on material from the work by Tom Peters. This experience left me believing that the relevance of case study material is often so transitory in nature, that it is almost too risky to even consider advertising. Obviously, I have mellowed a little on that belief. Tom Peters is an author and consultant, who became one of the best known and most influential management gurus of the 1980s and 1990s, and one of the principal criticisms of his work is that many of those large and conventional businesses which he first celebrated in the early 1980s were seen to be struggling several years later.

So, does it matter that success, however it is defined and in support of whatever theory or position the author wishes to adopt, can be short-lived? Well, yes and no. It is hardly surprising that organizations are regularly found wanting as conditions change around them – after all, we see this on a regular basis – and whilst this absolutely provides a commentary on the limitations of an organization's resilience capability, the conditions and arrangements under which it once succeeded should be examined with great care and attention and whatever learning can be gleaned should be considered as the most valuable of commodities.

As it happens, many of the elements which Peters reflected upon over the years and through his various books, such as leadership and service excellence, do indeed chime with our understanding of resilience capability and should therefore not be overlooked or forgotten. And as an historical analysis and source of learning, these references should actually be cherished. One final point regarding Peters' work: the range of ideas and positions which he has focused on, from individualism to corporate strength, has parallels with some of the alternative perspectives taken in respect of resilience. For example, there are certainly those who would have us believe that organizations amount to little more than a collection of individuals, and it is the aggregated resilience of some or all of these characters which determines that of the organization.

Case studies are provided in order to help us consider resilience – what it means and what a resilient organization looks like. Between the case study examples provided by BP and Alibaba, I believe the chapter captures much of what is particularly valuable. BP has a long history and prior to the crisis for which it was accountable in 2010 it was widely recognized as one of the major players in the global oil and gas markets. The resilience of BP is evidenced that after funding a bill of some £47 billion, and seeing its reputation tested in the most extraordinary way, particularly in the United States, it remains one of the major players in that same market. In reference to the disaster, and to its chairman, the *Financial Times* described the situation as follows: 'Mr Svanberg's survival, and the company's recovery, have become a source of lessons on resilience and redemption in business life'.[48] Alibaba is at the forefront of change within the retail sector. The creation of the online marketplace has changed the internet shopping experience to something far removed from simply being able to access a company's offering via a mobile device rather than in a shop environment. Alibaba is not only a big part of that revolution, it is also seeking to re-invent the sector in new and exciting ways – a world of robotic shopping assistants and augmented reality (AR) in dressing rooms and one in which there are no queues, as payments are taken automatically once you leave the store.

Staying with the question of 'What does resilience look like?', Chapter 5 will allow us to consider resilience capability through the lens provided by the Organizational Resilience Capability Model (ORCM), which I designed in 2018. From here it will then be possible to consider how resilience can be measured and reported.

Endnotes

1 GSM Arena (2015) The rise, dominance, and epic fall: a brief look at Nokia's history, 12 August. Available from: www.gsmarena.com/the_rise_dominance_and_epic_fall_a_brief_look_at_nokias_history-blog-13460.php (archived at https://perma.cc/K4PP-MA4D); Medium (2018) Why did Nokia fail and what can you learn from it? 24 July. Available from: medium.com/multiplier-magazine/why-did-nokia-fail-81110d981787 (archived at https://perma.cc/GHY4-WT3K)

2 Byanyima, W (2019) We must learn and change after Haiti sexual abuse scandal – Oxfam chief, *World Economic Forum*, 14 June. Available from:

www.weforum.org/agenda/2019/06/facing-hard-truths-to-tackle-the-causes-of-sexual-abuse/ (archived at https://perma.cc/NL8C-LELV)

3 Corporate description referenced on the Eastman Kodak website. Available from: www.kodak.com/GB/en/corp/company/default.htm (archived at https://perma.cc/GL8X-3RUM)

4 Butler, S (2018) House of Fraser owed creditors close to £1bn when it collapsed, *Guardian*, 17 August. Available from: www.theguardian.com/business/2018/aug/17/house-of-fraser-debts-suppliers-nearly-1bn-when-it-collapsed (archived at https://perma.cc/FQ2C-ZPN3)

5 Nazir, S (2019) House of Fraser collapse adversely affects Oasis, *Retail Gazette*, 10 April. Available from: www.retailgazette.co.uk/blog/2019/04/house-fraser-collapse-adversely-affects-oasis-among-others/ (archived at https://perma.cc/FX8Z-TV27)

6 Reuters (2019) Britain's Mulberry hurt by House of Fraser collapse, 19 June. Available from: www.reuters.com/article/us-mulberry-group-results/britains-mulberry-hurt-by-house-of-fraser-collapse-idUSKCN1TK0IY (archived at https://perma.cc/HZ22-2QUG)

7 BBC News (2004) Record Christmas for online shops, 19 January. Available from: news.bbc.co.uk/1/hi/business/3410721.stm (archived at https://perma.cc/5SXY-HQRW)

8 Plummer, R (2018) House of Fraser: Five things that went wrong, *BBC News*, 10 August. Available from: www.bbc.co.uk/news/business-45127423 (archived at https://perma.cc/V5DQ-KP3S)

9 Turner, K (2018) The five ways Boohoo has nailed Insta-fashion, *Telegraph*, 26 September. www.telegraph.co.uk/fashion/brands/five-ways-boohoo-has-nailed-insta-fashion-generation/ (archived at https://perma.cc/Z2G7-3SF2)

10 Nyenwa, T (2019) Under the influence: The lightning-quick rise of Insta fashion brand Boohoo, *The New European*, 5 October. Available from: www.theneweuropean.co.uk/top-stories/rise-of-instagram-fashion-brand-boohoo-1-6304397 (archived at https://perma.cc/B8LG-M3VB)

11 Azajna-Hopgood, A (2019) Mulberry swings to £5m loss after House of Fraser collapse, *Retail Gazette*, 19 June. Available from: www.retailgazette.co.uk/blog/2019/06/mulberry-swings-5m-loss-house-fraser-collapse/ (archived at https://perma.cc/C8TN-YZGX)

12 Denton, J (2019) Marks & Spencer suffers another round of falling food and clothing sales as boss admits its culture is 'siloed, slow, and hierarchical', *This is Money*, 7 January. Available from: www.thisismoney.co.uk/money/news/article-6362253/Marks-Spencer-boss-admits-companys-culture-siloed-slow-hierarchical.html (archived at https://perma.cc/E6NC-ZHE6)

13 Sky News (2018) M&S says it requires 'significant further change' as sales fall, 7 November. Available from: news.sky.com/story/ms-significant-further-change-required-as-sales-fall-11546880 (archived at https://perma.cc/47AN-RZKV)

14 Butler, S (2019) Cheap hoodies in shabby stores: House of Fraser after a year of Ashley, *Guardian*, 10 August. Available from: www.theguardian.com/business/2019/aug/10/house-of-fraser-year-of-mike-ashley (archived at https://perma.cc/QE2T-PQCF)

15 Finding Mastery (2017) Toto Wolff: Risk, Innovation, Winning, 073, 26 April. Available from: findingmastery.net/toto-wolff/ (archived at https://perma.cc/D2Q2-8YX5); Benson, A (2019) Formula 1: How Toto Wolff made Mercedes one of sport's greatest teams, *BBC News*, 9 July. Available from: www.bbc.co.uk/sport/formula1/48911849 (archived at https://perma.cc/MS2D-R5XC)

16 UBS Formula 1 (2016) Defining Success by Toto Wolff – Head of Mercedes Benz Motorsport, 29 April. Available from: www.youtube.com/watch?v=amP-F6ZfDbE (archived at https://perma.cc/2S9P-LQB7)

17 Bird, J (2018) Alibaba's 'New Retail' revolution: What is it, and is it genuinely new?, *Forbes*, 18 November. Available from: www.forbes.com/sites/jonbird1/2018/11/18/alibabas-new-retail-revolution-what-is-it-and-is-it-genuinely-new/#432d04366ad1 (archived at https://perma.cc/8PPH-K7D8)

18 Achim, A (2019) Amazon vs. Alibaba: Everything you need to know about the two biggest e-tailers, *Jing Daily*, 12 September. Available from: jingdaily.com/amazon-vs-alibaba-everything-you-need-to-know-about-the-two-biggest-e-tailers/ (archived at https://perma.cc/JMH6-WHB8); *Repricer Express*, Amazon vs Alibaba – Who is Winning? Available from: www.repricerexpress.com/amazon-vs-alibaba-winning/ (archived at https://perma.cc/57VC-KPM2)

19 Gupta, N (2019) How big is Alibaba's advertising revenue?, *Market Realist*, 22 May. Available from: marketrealist.com/2019/05/how-big-is-alibabas-advertising-revenue/ (archived at https://perma.cc/4FXQ-2Z97)

20 Zeng, M (2018) Alibaba and the Future of Business, *Harvard Business Review*, September–October 2018 Issue. Available from: hbr.org/2018/09/alibaba-and-the-future-of-business (archived at https://perma.cc/3WZA-2MXK)

21 Steffy, L (2014) BP found grossly negligent in Deepwater Horizon disaster, *Forbes*, 4 September. Available from: www.forbes.com/sites/lorensteffy/2014/09/04/bp-found-grossly-negligent-in-deepwater-horizon-disaster/#5d01d1307516 (archived at https://perma.cc/55F6-GFH7); US Chemical Safety and Hazard Investigation Board (2016) Investigation Report Executive Summary Report No. 2010-10-I-OS Drilling Rig Explosion And Fire At The Macondo Well. Available from: www.csb.gov/macondo-blowout-and-explosion/ (archived at https://perma.cc/3HV2-GSQT)

22 Seba, E and Nichols, B (2007) Panel finds safety issues at all BP's US refineries, *Reuters*, 21 January. Available from: www.reuters.com/article/us-bp-investigation-idUSN1618277920070116 (archived at https://perma.cc/NZ2R-S3Q2); Greene-Blose, J (2015) Deepwater horizon: lessons in probabilities. Paper presented at PMI® Global Congress 2015 – EMEA: Project Management Institute. Available from: www.pmi.org/learning/library/comparison-risk-events-with-risk-management-9919 (archived at https://perma.cc/7ZP5-ZM5K)

23 US Chemical Safety and Hazard Investigation Board (2007) The Report of the BP US Refineries Independent Safety Review Panel, January. Available from: www.csb.gov/assets/1/20/baker_panel_report1.pdf?13842 (archived at https://perma.cc/GU5X-4Q5M)

24 BP (2019) Second quarter and half year (results) 2019, BP corporate website, 30 July. Available from: www.bp.com/en/global/corporate/news-and-insights/press-releases/second-quarter-2019-results.html (archived at https://perma.cc/UK5R-NXH3)

25 Ward, A (2018) BP: rebuilding trust after a disaster, *Financial Times*, 29 April. Available from: www.ft.com/content/3e09d84a-489f-11e8-8ee8-cae73aab7ccb (archived at https://perma.cc/96G6-A7TP)

26 Calcuttawala, Z (2017) BP CEO: 2017 was a 'turning point' for the company, Oil Price website, 20 December. Available from: oilprice.com/Latest-Energy-News/World-News/BP-CEO-2017-Was-A-Turning-Point-For-The-Company.html (archived at https://perma.cc/8EFX-M686)

27 Woolfson, C (2013) The oil industry has yet to learn lessons of Piper Alpha, *The Conversation*, 2 July. Available from: theconversation.com/the-oil-industry-has-yet-to-learn-lessons-of-piper-alpha-15635 (archived at https://perma.cc/ST8S-YJXN); Harris, A (2013) Piper Alpha 25 years on: have we learned the lessons?, *Engineering and Technology*, 15 July. Available from: eandt.theiet.org/content/articles/2013/07/piper-alpha-25-years-on-have-we-learned-the-lessons/ (archived at https://perma.cc/HS88-QKGR)

28 BP corporate website, safety data. Available from: www.bp.com/en/global/corporate/sustainability/performance-data/safety-data.html (archived at https://perma.cc/7FJ8-L7S5)

29 BP corporate website (nd) Reducing emissions in our operations. Available from: www.bp.com/en/global/corporate/sustainability/climate-change/reducing-emissions.html (archived at https://perma.cc/8463-KZDZ)

30 Carrington, D (2016) Leaked BP report reveals serious near-miss accidents, *Guardian*, 13 December. Available from: www.theguardian.com/environment/2016/dec/13/bp-near-misses-reveal-lack-safety-monitoring-refinery-oil-sites (archived at https://perma.cc/KVS3-KNBL)

31 BP (2019) *BP Energy Outlook*, 2019 edition. Available from: www.bp.com/content/dam/bp/business-sites/en/global/corporate/pdfs/energy-economics/energy-outlook/bp-energy-outlook-2019.pdf (archived at https://perma.cc/QPE4-A4TU)

32 National Audit Office (2018) Investigation: WannaCry cyber attack and the NHS. Available from: www.nao.org.uk/wp-content/uploads/2017/10/Investigation-WannaCry-cyber-attack-and-the-NHS.pdf (archived at https://perma.cc/WWV6-NC3N)

33 Wikipedia reference to 'WannaCry ransomware attack'. Available from: en.wikipedia.org/wiki/WannaCry_ransomware_attack; *BBC News* (2017) Cyber-attack: Europol says it was unprecedented in scale. Available from: www.bbc.co.uk/news/world-europe-39907965 (archived at https://perma.cc/G5Z4-NBX7)

34 Department of Health and Social Care (2018) *Lessons learned review of the WannaCry Ransomware Cyber Attack*. Available from: www.england.nhs.uk/wp-content/uploads/2018/02/lessons-learned-review-wannacry-ransomware-cyber-attack-cio-review.pdf (archived at https://perma.cc/K626-L284)

35 House of Commons Committee of Public Accounts (2018) *Cyber-attack on the NHS*. Available from: publications.parliament.uk/pa/cm201719/cmselect/cmpubacc/787/787.pdf (archived at https://perma.cc/5JBG-NHRU)

36 Wighton, K (2019) NHS must take urgent steps to defend against hackers, says White Paper, Imperial College London, 2 July. Available from: www.imperial.ac.uk/news/191854/nhs-must-take-urgent-steps-defend/ (archived at https://perma.cc/ZH6V-UH47)

37 Hall, K (2018) Vast majority of NHS trusts have failed cyber-security assessment, Brit MPs told, *The Register*, 6 February. Available from: www.theregister.co.uk/2018/02/06/200_hospitals_failed_cyber_security_assessment/ (archived at https://perma.cc/RK4B-2X3N)

38 British Standards Institution (2019) BS 67000:2019 City resilience: Guide. Available from: www.bsigroup.com/en-GB/standards/Information-about-standards/bs-670002019-city-resilience.-guide/ (archived at https://perma.cc/UEZ3-FLPK)

39 Cox, A, Prager, F and Rose, A (2011) *Transportation Security and the Role of Resilience: A foundation for operational metrics*. Available from: www.sciencedirect.com/science/article/abs/pii/S0967070X10001137 (archived at https://perma.cc/YF9X-3W3G)

40 Mayor of London (2015) *London Infrastructure Plan 2050 Update*. Available from: www.london.gov.uk/what-we-do/business-and-economy/better-infrastructure/london-infrastructure-plan-2050 (archived at https://perma.cc/34QS-66T4)

41 Mayor of London (2018) *Mayor's Transport Strategy*. Available from: www.london.gov.uk/sites/default/files/mayors-transport-strategy-2018.pdf (archived at https://perma.cc/Z5VL-3NP8)

42 London Regional Resilience Forum (2006) The Multi-Agency Debrief: Lessons identified and progress since the terrorist events of 7 July 2005. Available from: news.bbc.co.uk/1/shared/bsp/hi/pdfs/23_09_06_lrrfreport.pdf (archived at https://perma.cc/455V-3VW7)

43 Greenberg, N, Rubin, G and Wessely, S (2009) *The Psychological Consequences of the London Bombings*. Available from: www.kcl.ac.uk/kcmhr/publications/assetfiles/cbrn/Greenberg2009-psychologicalconsequencesLondonbombingsbookchapter.pdf (archived at https://perma.cc/3PCH-HHEH)

44 Greenberg, N, Rubin, G and Wessely, S (2009) *The Psychological Consequences of the London Bombings*. Available from: www.kcl.ac.uk/kcmhr/publications/assetfiles/cbrn/Greenberg2009-psychologicalconsequencesLondonbombingsbookchapter.pdf (archived at https://perma.cc/3PCH-HHEH)

45 National Academies of Sciences, Engineering, and Medicine (2017) *Improving the Resilience of Transit Systems Threatened by Natural Disasters, Volume 1: A Guide*. Available from: doi.org/10.17226/24973 (archived at https://perma.cc/GTS6-9VJ9)

46 Edwards, T (2015) 7 July bombings: Lessons for services and transport, *BBC News*, 6 July. Available from: www.bbc.co.uk/news/uk-england-london-33325579 (archived at https://perma.cc/BJ7S-CSEX); *BBC News* (2015) 7 July London bombings: 15 changes to anti-terror planning. Available from: www.bbc.co.uk/news/uk-33388286 (archived at https://perma.cc/HE9T-K23T)

47 Jenkins, M (2018) There's no putting on the brakes: Why businesses must learn to harness the power of change, Cranfield School of Management. Available from: www.cranfield.ac.uk/som/thought-leadership-list/there-s-no-putting-on-the-brakes-why-businesses-must-learn-to-harness-the-power-of-change (archived at https://perma.cc/UN6U-B9UV), with extracts from Jenkins, M, Pasternak, K and West, R (2016) *Performance at the Limit: Business Lessons from Formula 1 Motor Racing*

48 Ward, A (2018) BP: Rebuilding trust after a disaster, *Financial Times*, 29 April. Available from: www.ft.com/content/3e09d84a-489f-11e8-8ee8-cae73aab7ccb (archived at https://perma.cc/96G6-A7TP)

5

The Organizational Resilience Capability Model® (ORCM)

Organizational resilience in an increasingly complex and rapidly changing world requires an intuitive and agile assessment approach. Through self-assessment, application of the ORCM can help practitioners develop an in-depth understanding of resilience within the context of their own organization. In doing so, the model also provides the structures necessary to engage with senior management in developing meaningful and effective strategies for achieving greater resilience.

This chapter introduces the capability model itself, the ORCM, and provides a detailed explanation of its structure and content. Each element and attribute are defined, and the principles of maturity modelling explored, with the detail relevant to executing a self-assessment exercise and subsequent reporting carried over to Chapter 6.

The ORCM assessment model allows the practitioner to present the current contribution and/or maturity of each resilience element within the context of an overall 'score', and to examine the interplay of individual aspects of organizational activity and performance. The model drives the action planning process for organizations by highlighting the known improvement and development capacity of each defining feature and the contribution of each behavioural element.

The ORCM encourages a multi-dimensional approach to the study of resilience. Firstly, it focuses upon influencing factors in order to provide the basis upon which the organization can undertake a detailed assessment and develop a best-fit approach. These factors reflect many of the same elements identifiable in respect of personal resilience, ie health, strength, fitness and personality, and as such some may initially be viewed as enablers and others, potentially, as blockers or inhibiters.

Secondly, the model is also summarized by reference to resilience outcomes and behaviours, such as those described by direction, awareness and learning. Rather than assuming that certain outcomes or behaviours are necessarily more important or appropriate than others, assessment will allow the organization to focus on making informed decisions about the specific resilience stance it wishes to take.

The ORCM is independent of the type, significance or velocity of challenges being faced by the organization, in that these aspects are already 'baked in' to the model. It can be applied equally well regardless of organizational size, complexity or operating model and is also capable of demonstrating significant flexibility, in that novel ideas or references utilized in other assessment models can be included or highlighted. The ORCM is therefore applicable in both regulated and non-regulated environments, and can be employed across large, complex organizations just as successfully as in small start-ups or community-based projects.

Apologies for employing such a well-used analogy, but when considering the ORCM and the assessment and reporting of resilience capability, practitioners may wish to keep in mind the similarities with driving a vehicle. Like our organization, the driver of the vehicle operates within the parameters defined by, amongst other things, their skills, physical make-up and mental wellbeing. The driver also exhibits certain behaviours, chooses a particular course of action and makes decisions which influence outcomes in respect of the route, destination and time of arrival.

Driving a vehicle involves the dynamic and complex interplay of these two distinct components – characteristics (ie both enablers and inhibiters) and behaviours (leading to outcomes) – but of course none of this takes place in isolation. We also therefore have to consider the context within which the journey takes place – ie the quality of the vehicle, the prevailing driving conditions and its overall purpose. Resilience is concerned with what it takes to successfully forge a path through a changing, unpredictable and often hostile environment, and the way in which this is applied to driving a vehicle has many parallels for us as we consider its application at an organizational level.

This and the following chapter focus on the ORCM and how it can be applied to assess and guide resilience efforts, building upon the definitions, benefits and case studies introduced previously. The ORCM is certainly not the only capability or maturity model which exists, indeed there are quite a number, and for completeness a brief introduction to some of those other models and sources of information which the practitioner may find useful is provided in Chapter 7.

The resilience maturity scale

The ORCM is presented in Figure 5.1 and has the maturity scale shown diagonally, increasing left to right. In itself there is perhaps nothing remarkable about the use of a multi-step maturity scale, but the reader should make note of the following points: firstly, the absence of any obvious 'scoring'; and secondly the clear and somewhat informal language used to label each step. I have also resisted the temptation to overlay an additional list of descriptors: alternative labels aligned to a particular translation of the activity. Hopefully this results in a scale which remains clear and simple and which can be applied with flexibility.

The ORCM is deliberately not mechanistic or overly prescriptive. Scoring is implicit within the model as the fundamental assessment of capability is intended to be contextual as well as absolute. Assessment would likely be both complicated and restricted if each step was expressed in numerical terms and may also create a distraction for both practitioner and the senior managers being asked to consider it.

As outlined in Chapter 6, assessment relies on a significant element of qualitative evaluation, and this is reflected in the absence of a dominant score or grading or rating scale. It is equally important to

FIGURE 5.1 The Organizational Resilience Capability Model® (ORCM)

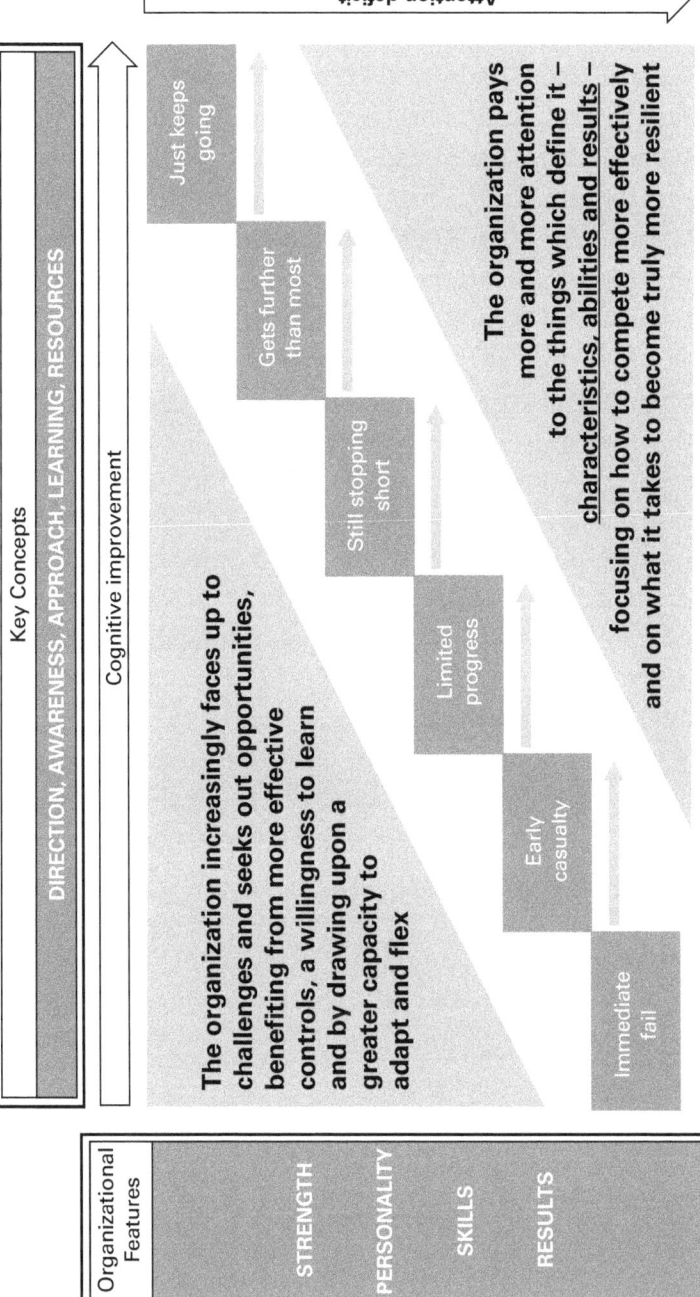

avoid anything which can result in behaviours or activities being driven by what are simply arbitrary boundaries or divisions between one grade or score and another.

Graduated and stepped, in common with standard maturity thinking, the ORCM outlines a series of phases consistent with the development of resilience capability. Each step is defined in the following sections without the introduction of new or obscure terms which might then create obstacles to understanding. Although flexible and adaptable, maturity is well defined and is expressed both clearly and succinctly within the following narrative.

As already outlined, organizational resilience is defined by the notion of success (in achieving stated objectives) and not just of persistence or longevity. However, the language of the maturity scale is deliberately oriented towards the latter. This is done both to aid understanding and to avoid the trap or disconnect which can occur when considering these potentially distinct aspects of resilience. The maturity steps are defined in a manner which minimizes any assessment appearing to be fixed or final or which is limited in time or devoid of context.

The notion that the organization is healthy and posting successes, not simply functioning, remains central to our understanding of resilience, but for the sake of simplicity, the maturity scale assumes that the enduring nature of the organization is of primary importance – after all, the ability to endure suggests that the organization is either having to deliver on a range of objectives and is doing so consistently, or has discovered a way of bypassing traditional measures of success. As can be seen below, the full description of each maturity step remains well balanced and consistent with our definitions for resilience introduced in Chapter 2.

The steps in the maturity scale include, in ascending order: Immediate Fail, Early Casualty, Limited Progress, Still Stopping Short, Gets Further Than Most and Just Keeps Going, and these are each described below.

Step 1: Immediate Fail

This describes an organization which is completely unable to respond to a change event or crisis, probably having been unsighted in the first instance, with failure as the inevitable and immediate consequence. The organization is likely to display an absence of meaningful control frameworks or structures and be woefully under-resourced and unprepared. There is nothing in the organization's make-up which would suggest a capability to positively influence its environment. Note: failure in this context is most likely to be absolute and permanent – we are not pointing simply to failure of an individual objective or target, but rather to an extinction event for the organization.

To employ a sporting analogy this time, if faced with an opponent, the organization would only have the most basic of reflex responses or instincts to rely upon. If forced to move or change direction, the organization would quickly become disoriented, confused and left behind or knocked out.

Step 2: Early Casualty

The organization is quickly overwhelmed by changes in its environment. It is unable to resist pressure or make the necessary adjustments and has no real capacity to learn from previous events. Following a short period of obvious pain or loss, the organization's existing arrangements and structures prove to be completely inadequate, and any early enthusiasm or demand for its products or services quickly evaporates. By maintaining a degree of activity for only a short period, the best the organization can hope for is perhaps to be absorbed in some way by a rival so as to prevent failure from being complete.

The organization is unable to get out of the way quickly enough or make any sustained progress. It can only take a couple of blows or defeats before it finally collapses or gives up. It only really knows one way of doing things and has limited stamina, poor technique and a pretty hopeless sense of direction. Simply avoiding the 'wooden spoon' or booby prize is probably a realistic objective and all that can be expected.

Step 3: Limited Progress

The organization demonstrates some ability to understand and influence its environment, although limitations and vulnerabilities are easily exposed. Movement, albeit slow, is guided by conventions and norms, elementary and potentially outdated skills, a reliance on established relationships or spare capacity and an aversion to innovation and risk exposure.

The organization makes some impact on its chosen markets and may even register some notable successes before it, and its brand, eventually disappears from view. The organization operates in the absence of a genuine growth strategy and shows no real ambition for expansion or development.

The organization can survive for a time and might even be prompted to try a new approach or land a few blows of its own but does so clumsily and does not present a credible threat to those around it. The organization might possess some natural ability but its desire and motivation are questionable, and it never looks like winning the contest or indeed progressing beyond the preliminary rounds.

Step 4: Still Stopping Short

The organization demonstrates an ability to learn and to anticipate change before being forced to accept it. Effective change management techniques are deployed, and the organization adopts a flexible approach in many situations and has an emerging clarity around its appetite for taking risks. In an almost predictable manner, it eventually reaches a point beyond which it can no longer operate effectively with the changing demands of the environment or is undone by a particular situation for which it is unprepared and from which it simply cannot recover.

The organization has a brand which is recognizable but perhaps no longer relevant, and it may now be synonymous with the event which led to its demise. Where it continues to trade, it often does so on the back of past successes or some residual loyalty.

The organization can consider itself, on occasion at least, to be a genuine player and one which can compete with the best when conditions prove to be favourable. But this is not a sustainable long-term position and will see the organization failing to progress due ultimately to lack of fitness or technique or that one big knockout blow which appeared to catch it off-guard. Fans have grown accustomed to an empty trophy cabinet, but many can still remember those triumphant nights from 20 or 30 years ago.

Step 5: Gets Further Than Most

The organization wields considerable influence and is capable of delivering transformational change and dealing with significant challenges. It may even be a benchmark performer in a certain area and has developed an enviable stock of skills and behaviours to help it prosper and do well.

The organization has a definite longevity to it, is well established in its core markets and has a proud history of product or service innovation and development. It routinely establishes new commercial relationships or partners with other organizations through sponsorship or licensing deals. However, concerns may have been raised about it not always achieving its true potential, and sometimes appearing to lag behind rivals.

The organization is recognized for its strength, depth, fitness and agility and routinely seeks out and adopts a novel stance. It is well organized and resourceful and features regularly on the podium or in the semi-final draw. It has a large and loyal fan base who expect to be winning something and it should never be ruled out of contention. The organization can be its own worst enemy and complacency and not taking its rivals seriously enough is probably the biggest danger.

Step 6: Just Keeps Going

The organization is constantly re-inventing itself and is defined by being 'always ahead of the curve'. It relishes uncertainty, is supremely creative, and it possesses an uncanny ability to turn a negative event into a positive outcome or a commercial success. The organization possesses boundless energy and always seems to be in the right spot. It makes adjustments with great speed and can absorb virtually anything that is thrown at it, absorbing rivals or managing to trump the competition with its own perspective on an already successful idea.

The organization has a long and illustrious history and has a brand which is synonymous with product and service excellence. It is immediately recognizable and is often used as a generic term to describe any brand in a particular market or one which dominates within a particular region or industry sector.

The organization has won pretty much everything there is going and continues to do so with monotonous regularity – the only surprise is if it's ever beaten into second place. The organization boasts the best facilities and attendance records and its staff are highly sought after by opponents.

The features contained within the ORCM

The ORCM is essentially a two-dimensional maturity model, and on the left vertical axis (Figure 5.1) can be seen a set of organizational 'features' or characteristics. It is these which fundamentally define the organization and it is these characteristics, abilities and results which the organization is seen to pay more and more attention to as it focuses on how to compete more effectively and on what it takes to become truly more resilient.

The linkages here to personal and employee resilience are strong and deliberately made. Much of the thinking and language associated with the set of features is derived from that used in the description and study of personal resilience. Similarly, the language of physical structures (ie assets and networks) is also clearly relevant, particularly for (but certainly not limited to) infrastructure organizations.

The set of features provides both the context against which maturity assessments are undertaken and also describes the relevance of the organization's various characteristics. In improving resilience capability and in progressing up and along the maturity scale, the organization is becoming increasingly aware of those characteristics, how each relates to the organization's own unique circumstances and is thereby seen to be addressing any deficits in its collective attention.

One common criticism levelled at maturity models is that they tend to underplay the significance of competence and performance. An important aspect of the set of features within the ORCM is that it explicitly calls out both the skills and the results which the organization has acquired and achieved, thus recognizing their significance in the overall assessment of resilience. It is also worth noting that the relative importance of individual features can change over time, as indeed can their make-up. Features can also change independently of other attributes, such as culture, which we will turn our attention to later in this chapter, and can vary enormously in how they respond to internal and external influences and in how easy or difficult they are to change.

During the assessment of resilience capability, care should be taken to avoid 'double counting' of individual features as they can often be considered as components of more than one set or category. Whilst it is more important to ensure that the features are comprehensive and complete, any duplication can create an unnecessary bias within the model and may therefore skew the assessment outcome or result. For example, regardless of its relative potency, 'brand' and 'brand loyalty' need to be considered as part of the set of features. However, within the definitions listed below, brand is captured as a RESULT, but it could also be considered as a STRENGTH or even as part of the organization's PERSONALITY.

When applying an assessment approach using the ORCM, and as outlined in Chapter 6, the set of features described below will be considered both in terms of its contribution to current levels of resilience and also in respect of the potential which exist for further improvement. The concept of 'potential' in this context would obviously vary according to the culture, nature and strategic objectives of the organization in question. Due to the nature of the features, it is likely that the organization would rely primarily on quantitative assessment techniques to support its assessment efforts and would therefore draw upon information and data available through IT systems and other records and reports.

The defined set of features within the ORCM include STRENGTH, PERSONALITY, SKILLS and RESULTS, and these are described as follows.

Strength

For most organizations and in most circumstances, it is probably helpful to apply the meaning of 'strength' quite literally and in a rather traditional way; for example, as a measure of volume or to signify industrial muscle, but also to mean robustness and 'strength in the face of adversity'.

Within the set of features, 'strength' may be defined and influenced by organizational size and complexity, redundancy and spare capacity, flexibility in design or processing, the quality of assets and data, resilient characteristics of staff, financial and other reserves, the effectiveness of networks, dependencies and other soft structures, historical issues and events or the detail of formal improvement programmes.

An alternative but complementary summary for this set of features would also refer to 'health', again to be taken quite literally, which is a concept not just limited to personal resilience in either a physical or wellbeing sense, as it is also frequently used in respect of an organization's physical assets, data sets and cash flows. By way of further illustration, organizations which have invested heavily in something which is of particular relevance to them, be that physical assets, IT infrastructure or engineering staff, should absolutely highlight this as a key strength (assuming that is in fact the result of the investment) within the set of features. Doing so recognizes its contribution to the organization's overall resilience stance and is precisely what the ORCM is intended to do.

Much like individuals, organizations are usually quite adept at pinpointing their strengths, and so the detail presented here as part of this particular feature-set is intended to give some structure to allow exactly that. The generic references allow us to highlight those strengths which we believe are particularly relevant to the development of resilience capability, and it is by referring to these that the organization can identify those within which it wishes to work.

A quick word about 'networks', which are pretty much universally acknowledged as one of the keys to developing resilience capability. Networks are included as a 'strength' within the ORCM but they also appear elsewhere within the model, specifically in relation to 'learning' and 'resources'. As a 'strength', any assessment is able to refer to their presence and potential as part of the organization's core or defining characteristics. References to networks within 'learning' and 'resources' are more associated with behaviours and how the organization seeks to deliver on its long-term aims and ambitions.

Note: other characteristics which may be considered as strengths, such as technical skills, are covered separately below.

Personality

'Personality' can be a somewhat abstract concept and applying personality traits in the context of organizations and resilience can prove particularly difficult to digest. However, we can again rely on the linkage to personal resilience to help make sense of this, and in particular the references to 'proactive personality' and its association with resilient behaviours:

> In organizations, proactive personality disposes individuals to change-oriented behaviours, and has been positively related to initiative in career management, seeking support from others at work, and leveraging workplace resources.[1]

In taking a lead from the above reference, personality in the context of the ORCM may be defined and influenced by commercial legacy, degree of regulation and external interference, staff loyalty, engagement and turnover, the position, maturity and conditions within which the organization's markets, ownership and funding can be viewed, and by the behaviours exhibited across the industry or the organization's peer group.

To reinforce the point around positivity, employee resilience can be defined as follows:

> The capacity of employees, facilitated and supported by the organization, to utilize resources to positively cope, adapt and thrive in response to changing work circumstances.[2]

The inclusion of 'personality' within the ORCM allows us to assess the organization's distinctive character and therefore to highlight what its disposition might be and what further potential there might be for development in this regard. It is also recognition that a forward-leaning organization, and one which fully expects to make changes on a routine basis, is likely to exhibit greater resilience than one which does not.

Skills

It should not be surprising to find 'skills' identified and listed as part of the features and characteristics within the ORCM. However, the list of skills which may provide contributory support for an organization's resilience can be rather long, and therefore potentially unwieldy and difficult to unpick. The requirement for some skills will, of course, be greater than for others within each organizational setting. The generic list presented here may appear to be rather technical in nature but it does have the advantage of pointing to a selection of management disciplines from which many resilience practitioners are drawn and within which the term 'resilience' is often employed.

Although I rely heavily throughout this text on the parallels between organizational and personal resilience, it is important to differentiate at this particular point. The skills listed below as part of the ORCM are those relevant to organizational resilience and are not those ordinarily associated with the development and maintenance of resilience at a personal level. The latter tends to encompass notions such as positive self-image and empathy, and again being wary not to double-count organizational features, it is suggested that the resilient qualities of staff are reflected under 'strengths', as outlined above.

The list of skills within the ORCM can be defined as:

- crisis response and incident management;
- performance improvement;
- management of project delivery;
- information sharing;
- decision-making;
- risk management;
- change management;
- monitoring and reporting;
- commercial acumen;
- asset and facilities management;
- financial control and governance;
- health and safety;
- security; and
- supply chain management.

Results

The 'results' which the organization can point to are probably the most straightforward feature of the ORCM and also one of the easiest to deal with from an assessment perspective. Potentially, those results could have enormous significance for the organization in relation to its resilience capability and it is much more than simply believing that past performance might be a good indicator of what might happen in the future. Results influence a wide range of things, from being able to attract high-calibre staff to the cost of an overdraft, but perhaps most significantly they will likely have a significant influence over customers, regulators and supply partners and the decisions which they make and which will therefore directly affect the organization's future.

Nevertheless, a number of alternative resilience models do appear to examine capability within something of a vacuum and without due consideration to those historical pointers which may be highly relevant. It is also important to highlight that the reference to 'results' within the ORCM should not be confused with an overall 'measure of success' or the outcome of some resilience indexing or assessment. The reference to results is about how past achievements position or equip the organization – it is about situational positioning and what this means is required going forward.

The list of results within the ORCM includes:

- brand loyalty;
- measures of product or service excellence;
- the quality of relationships;
- market position;
- levels of compliance;
- certification successes;
- service availability and continuity of operations;
- operational efficiencies;
- capital costs;
- growth indicators;
- sales or attendance figures;
- profit margins;
- safety performance; and
- ethical or sustainability indices.

Paradoxically, and something for organizations and practitioners to be aware of, this is not about a rush to measure and report or about the need to create a new resilience register. So as to underscore the inherent flexibility and adaptability of the ORCM, this is about the organization selecting those results or indicators which have particular relevance and doing so in a manner consistent with the principles of resilience described within these pages. For example, it would be highly unusual, at least for most established organizations, if many of the results most relevant to resilience were not already captured and reported in some form or other.

Attention deficit

The notion of a 'deficit' is intended to supplement the four features or characteristics outlined above and is included in order to draw attention to the idea that as the organization gives more consideration to those things which define it, so its understanding of resilience capability, and therefore how to enhance it, should increase. In reality, of course, it is more than simply the organization paying attention, it is about understanding how to maximize potential and where changes and improvements need to be made.

However, an increase in attention and therefore awareness is not to be confused with increased internal regulation or control. Paying more attention to the organization's core characteristics allows for improved understanding of what it takes to be more resilient and is not directly related to the number or type of restrictions or compensatory measures which are in place. An increase in awareness also ensures that the consequences of the organization's decisions can be appreciated in a meaningful context and acts to discourage activity which may be disproportionate or ineffective.

To illustrate the point, let us consider the potential need for investment in communications infrastructure. Any such decision is likely to take account of numerous factors, and for the resilient organization this isn't simply about assessing the reliability of competing solutions or mapping maintenance costs across the life cycle of a new asset. Rather, this is about an awareness and understanding of how a particular asset is likely to affect the organization's capability now and into the future. And this is a future which the organization expects to be defined by increasing change and uncertainty, and one in which technological change in particular is likely to continue at an exponential rate.

Understanding the contribution and potential associated with each of the organization's characteristics is the basis for informed decision-making and it constitutes a significant element of the assessment process outlined in Chapter 6. The organization will need to consider both the contribution and potential for each of the characteristics outlined above and do this within the context of the massive and ongoing change which is almost universally predicted.

In early 2019, *Forbes* magazine ran an article on the growth and impact of AI.[3] It reported that by 2030 the contribution of AI to the global economy could be as much as US $15.7 trillion, and quoted a PwC report referring to this as 'the biggest commercial opportunity in today's fast changing economy'. The resilient organization would expect to be at the forefront of this change and profiting from taking a proactive stance. This would only be achieved through paying close attention to those characteristics which define it and through seeking to understand the potential which exists within that future context.

The concepts contained within the ORCM

As outlined above, the ORCM is a two-dimensional maturity model, with organizational 'features' or characteristics on the left vertical axis of Figure 5.1 and with 'concepts', behaviours and activities on the horizontal axis. Whilst it is the set of features which fundamentally defines organizational parameters, it is the concepts and behaviours which detail the organization's willingness to learn and point to its capacity to adapt and flex. It is mainly within these behaviours and activities that we see a degree of consistency across the various definitions for organizational resilience and also across the other models and frameworks which exist.

Increases in resilience capability are unlikely to be achieved by the organization simply allowing things to happen or feeling that it has unlocked some hidden potential somewhere. Resilience is achieved not through passive behaviours but rather by the organization increasingly facing up to the challenges that it faces and through actively seeking out opportunities for development and growth. In doing so, the organization will learn how to benefit from more effective controls and better understand the value associated with mutual aid and external networks, to name just two of the concepts described below.

Given that 'leadership' is frequently given headline status in much resilience literature, it may be somewhat surprising to see it shown within the ORCM as part of other concepts rather than as a concept or category in its own right. This is for two reasons. Firstly, the labels for the ORCM concepts have been chosen deliberately to align to a 'journey' analogy or to that akin to driving a vehicle, as described at the beginning of this chapter. Actually, a number of different analogies could have been selected, but having the analogy to fall back on helps us to maintain consistency across and between the various concepts within the ORCM and also across the set of features. Using this approach, leadership is not viewed as a discrete behaviour or activity but rather one which has a significant influence across a number of related areas.

Secondly, I believe there is a danger of presenting leadership as being something which is more important to resilience capability than it actually is, and I say this not because the right leadership behaviours and activities are not critical, but rather because resilience always needs to be considered as a whole-organization concept. If we present leadership as being first amongst a number of resilience requirements, as some approaches do, then we run the dual risk of supporting personality cults within the organization and negating the vital contribution of all those within the organization who do not qualify for inclusion in the leadership cadre or for the leadership label.

The broad application and relevance of leadership is highlighted within Chapter 3 and there are several points within the ORCM concepts where leadership has a particular significance. Perhaps the two concepts where leadership activity can be most easily identified and understood relate to the setting of strategic direction and the allocation of resources. Much of this of course has to do with the exercising of authority and the clear association across the organization between visible action and a named individual (leader). The role of leadership in the general approach which the organization adopts to various things is of no less significance although how obvious that might be and how easy it is to identify and assess might prove to be a little more problematic.

As also referenced within Chapter 3, the ORCM contains a number of 'bridging concepts': notions or elements relevant to resilience which can be considered as either features (ie the vertical axis) or concepts, behaviours and activities (ie the horizontal axis). This is not intended to confuse but rather to recognize the interplay between the two dimensions within the model – it reflects both the importance of organizational features and those associated with behaviours, activities and outcomes. Examples of these bridging concepts are drawn out below, but as a reminder, 'compliance' is one such concept. Using this example, an organization may have a particular sensitivity to rules and regulations and may therefore consider itself to be compliance-minded. However, the organization's level of compliance, its *actual* compliance performance, is picked up separately in the ORCM. This point simply reflects the distinction between compliant behaviours and attitudes on the one hand, and compliant results on the other.

When applying an assessment approach using the ORCM, and as set out in Chapter 6, the concepts described below will usually be considered against a series of benchmark statements – positional accounts of what constitutes resilient behaviours and outcomes. In contrast to the assessment of organizational features outlined earlier in this chapter, the use of qualitative techniques is far more prevalent. A typical assessment of behaviours and outcomes would therefore usually rely on interviews or focus groups and observations drawn from evidential reviews in order to obtain the required level of insight.

The defined concepts within the ORCM include DIRECTION, AWARENESS, APPROACH, LEARNING and RESOURCES.

Direction

In referring to what resilient organizations do, the following quote nicely summarizes the main components of what is defined here as 'direction':

> They exist in a constant state of transformation and reset goals every few years. Every time they do, they set a clear time-bound vision and communicate it regularly. Information is disseminated quickly, and they involve as many people as possible in mission planning.[4]

For it to be meaningful, direction must be something which can be described or articulated, and this is also something which must be possible at any chosen moment in time as direction can change and can do so very quickly. In describing direction, it is also important to be able to differentiate between orientation and movement or progress – to be set on a particular course is certainly not the same as being able to evidence that any such instruction is either understood or being followed, or indeed that it has any true value potential.

One of the reasons why our chosen assessment methodology is so important is because of these potential differences between the intended direction and that which is experienced, and of course if these differences exist, they may not be consistent across all parts of the organization. Such differences may simply be the result of a lag between action or instruction and an actual, observable change. Other differences might suggest that actions or instructions have simply not been effective:

> Leaders are the stewards of organizational energy [resilience]… they inspire or demoralize others, first by how effectively they manage their own energy and next by how well they manage, focus, invest and renew the collective energy [resilience] of those they lead.[5]

Within the ORCM, direction is defined by reference to vision, leadership and planning. Direction does not have to be intentional, even though much of the literature in this field implies that it is, and as the above quote reminds us, direction is usually something which needs to be considered broadly and not just in relation to individual leaders. In setting direction for the organization, and in maintaining it, the influence of leadership on direction may well be enormous, but it is unlikely to be the only factor we need to consider.

The role of the Board provides us with another example of a 'bridging concept' and also provides us with a possibly less familiar way of thinking about the organizational elements of direction and leadership. The Board's role is something which can be treated as either a 'feature' or a 'concept' or both. This can be useful as it provides some additional latitude and flexibility in respect of how it is measured.

The Board provides 'direction' in the form of guidance and insight through capturing risk appetite and has a role in crisis prevention.

As such, the Board also accounts for 'skills' in respect of responding to a crisis, although admittedly for most organizations it is not always clear what that role is or should be in any given situation. Regardless of what form the Board takes within an organization, it usually assumes responsibility for assuring business viability, a crisis typically being something which almost inevitably calls that viability into question:

> The critical factor is the Board's remit to look at difficult issues and risks and to challenge the executive on how they are being managed, with the goal to prevent a crisis.[6]

As practitioners, and in preparing for our assessment of resilience capability, we would expect the Board to have detailed knowledge and understanding of the organization's current direction of travel and what is needed to deliver on its future vision. We would also expect the Board to have set about ensuring that the organization can be maintained going forward, and amongst other things, has taken appropriate measures to protect itself from harm.

Awareness

Within the ORCM, the concept of 'awareness' has a particular depth to it and is broadly defined by reference to sightedness, context, orientation, contacts, information, environment and conditions (past, present and future). The depth is recognition that, unlike 'direction', there is a particular focus on learning from past events and understanding their meaning for the organization; from a directional perspective the route the organization took in arriving at its current position (ie the historical viewpoint) is often of little practical importance when undertaking an assessment of current capabilities.

Readers may be familiar with 'situational awareness' as a concept either from management literature or from the study of safety behaviours, human factors or through the science of psychology. It has provided a focus for the study of organizational resilience for a number of years and, for example, was part of the thinking captured by Resilient Organisations from New Zealand even before the study was given additional impetus following the Christchurch earthquakes of 2010–11:

> Situation awareness is a measure of an organization's understanding and perception of its entire operating environment. This includes: the ability to look forward for opportunities as well as potential crises, the ability to identify crises and their consequences accurately, an enhanced understanding of the trigger factors for crises, an increased awareness of the resources available both internally and externally, a better understanding of minimum operating requirements from a recovery perspective, and an enhanced awareness of expectations, obligations and limitations in relation to the community of stakeholders, both internally (staff) and externally (customers, suppliers, consultants etc).[7]

Denyer's '4Sight model' of organizational resilience provides an excellent introduction to the depth of the awareness concept, picking out what are referred to as core processes: foresight, insight, oversight and hindsight. For example:

> Foresight will help people in your organization to be mentally prepared for uncertainty and change. Foresight also needs an inward focus to help your people anticipate and notice problems, errors and issues within the organization that could grow into significant incidents.[8]

Awareness often has a currency attached to it and is usually defined as a prerequisite for effective decision-making and, for example, the safe operation of a machine or system. From an ORCM perspective the timeframe which the organization adopts is also of major importance. As mentioned in Chapter 3, the organization's horizons need to be sufficiently expansive so as to create a landscape view which shows up those strategic threats and opportunities which will ultimately result in beneficial product or service and market decisions being enacted.

Predictably, awareness is also about the collection, analysis and dissemination of complex information. Looking at this, as we must, through a whole-organization lens, this is not something limited to senior management and how well a handful of people understand the detail of what is around them. If organizations hold information away from staff and prevent them from seeing it, and if we set only modest ambitions for ourselves in respect of sharing and comprehension, they effectively set a ceiling on their resilient capability.

One final aspect of awareness, and something again which speaks to its depth from an ORCM perspective, is the importance of self-awareness. In this sense, self-awareness is less to do with an individual's emotional intelligence or the detail of personal transactions and more to do with an appreciation of how organizational behaviours and outcomes are actually constructed. Much of what passes for 'organizational' or 'organization-wide', be that behaviour or outcomes, does so only because it has achieved some invisible and undefined critical mass – and much of this relies upon it having been reported, either internally or externally.

Misreporting of behaviours or outcomes, and dare I say 'fake news', is not a sustainable position, and therefore any attempt to deliberately falsify information within the organization or present things dishonestly will eventually be reported as such. Leaders who lack this depth of self-awareness will probably be completely unaware of the disconnect between what they say and how others receive it and report it on to others.

Approach

The concept of 'approach' is probably the broadest which is defined as part of the ORCM and contains a number of significant topic areas. I have already touched upon a number of these areas within Chapter 3 and the focus within this chapter is on several of the elements which collectively describe the organization's way of dealing with the challenges it faces. For completeness, the organization's 'approach' can be defined as incorporating its values, appetite, mindedness, expression, culture, collaboration, decision-making and change readiness, amongst other things.

The notion of 'appetite' can be applied across numerous areas of business activity, but we are perhaps most familiar with it being applied to the management of risks. Whilst the organization's appetite for risk may or may not be clearly defined and well understood, it serves to operate as a way of self-regulating behaviours and activities, and as such, has a significant influence on resilience capability.

However, it is important that we do not limit our interpretation of risk appetite as only being an output or written statement; it is in fact descriptive of a whole strategic-level process. As such, this process should be defined and consistently applied. It should allow for the organization's risk profile to be considered and for the Board to gain assurance that emerging risks are properly understood. Not only does this process need to facilitate strategic decision-making, it also needs to be capable of translation and application by operational management, enabling them to seize opportunities and avoid any unnecessary or undesirable exposure.

The organization's appetite needs to be set in the context of what risk the organization can actually absorb or tolerate, something which is particularly relevant in a crisis situation. Even if references in some quarters have been dropped, for example within ISO 31000 (Risk Management Guidelines), understanding of appetite remains foundational for undertaking assessments of risk and implementation of risk management processes.

The way in which the organization approaches others will speak volumes to how it views its neighbours, supply partners and peers and to the value it attaches to the idea of an inclusive and supportive network environment. In fact, so important is the need for a collaborative approach and an appreciation of the wider context within which the organization operates, that its absence should effectively preclude any meaningful claim of resilience.

Collaborative networks can be identified and understood in relation to specific physical or environmental locations or they can be defined by the industry or support system across which they operate. Urban and city environments attract a considerable amount of interest in this regard due not just to the sheer volume of investment and specific high-profile events such as super storm Sandy in 2012, but also to the increased realization of their significance:

> Businesses, governments and civil society are just beginning to discover where there is mutual gain to be found from collaboration on resilience.

> A basic strategic framework for collaboration on resilience is emerging that combines well-founded principles for successful collaboration among business, government and civil society with a structured approach to action on the building blocks for resilience. Clearing a pathway to a collaborative resilience agenda will now depend on the sectors coming together to work on well-defined, practical problems that they can experiment with and learn from.[9]

Interestingly, the role which organizations adopt, or are expected to adopt, in respect of these collaborative endeavours is not always clear. For example, the guide to city resilience published in 2019 by the British Standards Institution (BSI), BS 67000, presents organizations as one element within a collective which includes communities, government and citizens, and does so without always calling out the point that the city's infrastructure is likely to rely on the resilience of individual organizations more so than the other way around.

It is also difficult to overstate the importance of the interrelated topics of culture and values. One rather neat way of considering their significance is in relation to what is termed 'mindedness'. The concept of safety, be that personal or societal, speaks to a duty of care which the organization has with regard to its operations and activities. Outside of closed, authoritarian societies, a disregard for safety is simply not a sustainable position and is something scrutinized by Boards and shareholders of most organizations:

> A strong core purpose and shared values have been identified as central to organizational resilience.[10]

The way in which safety is considered by an organization will be reflected within the adequacy and suitability of the control measures in place and by the behaviours evident in meetings, on site, and importantly within some of those peripheral activities which take place outside of the day-to-day. For an organization to think of itself as genuinely safety-minded, it probably has to pass a number of tests, one of the simplest being the quality of its incident investigations. The rigour and commitment with which these investigations are undertaken is a function of the attitudes of all those involved and often reflects poorly on those with accountability for the risks taken on their behalf at operational levels.

Learning

Resilient organizations, either directly or by implication, will often find themselves also described as learning organizations: that is, ones which facilitate and promote learning, and which can point to learning as one of the reasons for their enduring success. In the context of the ORCM, 'learning' can incorporate cognition, knowledge management, application, sharing, transparency, recognition, reinforcement and experience. Several aspects of learning were considered within Chapter 3, including knowledge management processes and the learning of lessons, and in this chapter, we will begin by extending the application of 'collaboration' outlined above:

> The most resilient organizations are eager to learn from their own and others' experiences to minimize problems and grasp opportunities. Peer-to-peer networking and knowledge sharing are vital, for example when they seek to invest in new areas, introduce innovative products and processes or penetrate new and unfamiliar markets.[11]

The quote from BSI serves to attach and emphasize the value-proposition for collaborative endeavours beyond that of incident response. In this context, collaboration is described as almost the inevitable consequence of adopting a proactive stance and of seeking to exploit opportunities. Plus, there is nothing muscular, macho or sinister implied – nothing to suggest that a 'dark side' exists, although we know that it does as evidenced by the announcement in April 2019 by the European Commission that car makers may have acted to delay the introduction of new technology between 2006–2014.[12]

Turning the notion of collaboration inward, there is much support for the principle as a means of creating competitive advantage for the organization through focusing on mutual support and encouragement and on information transparency – employee to employee. The traditional rationale for collaboration has relied on the promise of cost reduction (through reduced duplication of effort) and the desire to promote new ways of working. The scale and complexity of the modern technological environment and the speed with which it changes provides a whole new justification for efforts in this field.

Integral to the process and practice of learning are the ways in which knowledge is managed; however, for resilience purposes it is more important that this is relevant than it is to trouble ourselves too much about how learning might actually have come about. If we anchor our thinking with a useful definition of what constitutes organizational resilience, then determining relevance should be relatively straightforward. It is from this proactive standpoint that the particular significance of newly created knowledge becomes apparent.

Much in the same way that resilience can be created or destroyed, so organizations can elect to adopt a range of positions with regard to learning. Investment is required to understand learning preferences and to preserve knowledge during periods of change; mechanisms and touch-points for information and data need to be constantly assessed to ensure they remain relevant, as do the physical and non-physical structures within which employees interact; 'celebrating success' ceases to be a vacuous, albeit subtle, exercise in trying to convince the wider organization that senior management were involved somehow and instead becomes a genuine opportunity to understand how the success came about and how it can be repeated.

Communications is highly relevant to learning capabilities as an enabler or inhibiter and also as part of establishing how technology is employed across the organization and what this means for learning outcomes. We are accustomed to thinking about communications specifically in relation to how much better the learning experience would have been if only the messaging were easier to digest, and very often this is associated with a particular internal product or campaign. The actual value derived from campaigns is often inferred or indeed not properly measured at all, but for the resilient organization the notion of creating a campaign in order to satisfy some rudimentary legislative obligation would certainly not sit well, regardless of how effectively it could be delivered.

A final word in this section is reserved for machine-learning and AI. Whilst in one sense the march of the machine and of technology is simply another aspect of our rapidly changing landscapes, it does have a particular relevance to learning as we will no longer be limited in our thinking to employees and to human requirements and considerations. However, the way in which organizations are most likely to approach this is in relation to what AI developments mean for newly acquired skills in the workforce or in trying to plan for future information access when governance and ethical considerations in this area remain extremely immature.

Resources

As a concept, 'resources' is less bound by behavioural considerations than some others but is no less important in describing those aspects of resilience capability which sit outside of the organization's core characteristics or feature-set. The description of resources includes funding, support, networks, relationships, mutual aid, access, availability, community and inclusivity.

Mutual aid agreements (MAAs), which have enormous potential in this area for many organizations, are defined as being a voluntary reciprocal exchange of resources and services for mutual benefit – organizations join together, usually in a material sense, in order to assist one another and often in response to a particular event or challenge:

> There is no alternative to MAAs that will enable the achievement of similar levels of resilience, other than those that require significant additional cost.[13]

Many essential services across the world are underpinned by such agreements, often delivered through some formality and with regulatory and/or governmental support. The provision of assistance and the idea of a reliable support network is clearly not restricted to emergency situations, and the output or result of such collaborative efforts can be seen across a wide range of endeavours from airline operations to academic research projects. Such arrangements will obviously differ in their longevity and in the number of organizations involved, and some will be driven by the desire to access information or reduce costs and others by the wish to promote a brand or gain a foothold in new territories:

> Successful brand collaboration depends on both brands being able to benefit from the existing market of the other, or from gaps in the market that can be filled, through a collaborative relationship that competitors will find hard to replicate. Think Nike and Apple.[14]

Access to funding is a critical element across all organizations and in respect of building an enduring enterprise the funding of small companies has a unique significance as they may be ineligible for mainstream lending products. Research suggests that financing for start-ups and established small and medium-sized businesses remained uneven in the 10 years or so following the financial crisis.[15] Whilst there is significant interest in other aspects of resilience funding, for example in respect of climate change and urbanization, the requirements associated with growth funding appear to receive little attention, at least at 'headline' level. However, anecdotal evidence would suggest that small businesses are particularly adept at innovating their way around budget constraints, for example through the adoption of digital solutions and relying on social media to enhance branding.

Does anyone remember a world before social media? Most of us have lived through a genuine revolution in communications and information technology and the experience has not always been one which we have understood or indeed always found enjoyable. However, its significance for resilience is as undeniable as it is profound. From a community perspective, the explosion of digital technologies has created massive connective potential and for many organizations this has proved the catalyst for re-examining their place within that community and how that can best be exploited.

Implications for organizations go beyond thinking about community simply as something which can be mobilized in hard times or as a proxy for MAAs. The level of ongoing engagement and trust established with communities will have implications for many day-to-day requirements in addition to local service provision, access to support from experts, ex-employees, citizen groups or alternative resources and supply networks. Organizations need to be at the forefront of social media and the use of digital technologies, and they need to be seen to be innovating in areas such as voice-enabled apps and chatbots, 5G mobile and the use of Blockchain for applications beyond cryptocurrency.

The elephant in the room

Put simply, Board members can stop worrying about resilience if they have a product or service which nobody wants or has interest in. In such circumstances, the detail of how we think about resilience becomes largely irrelevant as the organization would simply lack any foundation upon which it *could* endure or succeed. Paradoxically, the quality of an organization's offering is so fundamental to its enduring success that it can almost get forgotten about when considering the detail contained within the ORCM. As we have seen already, the model works for different types of organization by allowing a significant degree of flexibility in how it is applied and by covering critical aspects of organizational performance in a variety of ways. This allows each organization to successfully consider the ORCM in relation to its own unique requirements and circumstances.

Returning to product and service quality, there are several elements within the ORCM which allow practitioners to include it within an assessment, thereby ensuring that is does not get missed. For example, the following elements may be considered for inclusion:

- Most obviously, product and service detail can be included as part of the RESULTS (ie reliability, satisfaction scores, brand recognition, sales volumes, social media measures) highlighted as one of the organization's characteristics or features.
- Specific aspects of the ORCM can be applied in order to create a focus around service or product excellence, much in the same way that one would seek to draw out 'asset quality' if this was being approached from the perspective of a network infrastructure organization. This can be done by applying ORCM elements such

as innovation, change readiness and project management to the way in which products and services are developed, and can therefore be reflected within the elements of PERSONALITY and/or SKILLS.

- From a behaviours perspective, customer obsession can definitely be viewed as a value and can therefore be highlighted as part of the assessment questions around the organization's APPROACH. For example, how well is the 'customer journey' defined and used, and has a clear customer strategy been agreed?
- Compliance with regulatory and statutory requirements for products and services is another important element of an organization's RESULTS and speaks directly to quality requirements.

The archives are not short of examples suggesting less than optimal product or service experiences, and in relation to just one industry sector we can highlight how customers abandoned Nokia and Blackberry, or how Apple sought to reduce the speed of some older devices without telling their customers. Perhaps one of the best examples in recent years of a product which simply could not be sold was the Samsung Note 7. The market leader, Samsung launched its new device in 2016, with pre-order levels so high that initial supply shortages appeared to be the only issue for the technology giant to contend with. By October of that year, the phone had been recalled, following failed attempts to rectify the quality problems associated with its battery, and production was permanently ceased. The phone's successor, the Note 8, was ultimately released in 2017.

Conclusion

The ORCM provides practitioners with a powerful and highly adaptable framework through which to consider resilience within the unique setting of their own organization. It addresses both the core characteristics of the organization together with the behaviours and outcomes with which it is associated. It is also capable of reflecting elements of interest to the practitioner adopted from other resilience models. The language used within the ORCM is straightforward, as exemplified by the labels used in the maturity scale, and it shares many elements common to the study of personal resilience. To allow for clarity of meaning, the structure also encourages easy analogies such as those relating to undertaking a journey or sporting endeavour.

Within the maturity scale, readers will note that the wording is light on some of the language of success seen in a number of resilience definitions, which often imply a gain, growth, achievement or other benefit outcome for the organization. This is deliberate, as the assumed objective for the organization is to still be around in 12 months', or 24 months' or 10 years' time. The maturity language used in the scale is therefore more 'persistent' or 'endurance' oriented than it is 'thrive', and it is intentionally not 'victorious'.

Everyday operations and activities suggest specific elements or concepts which can be readily mapped to the ORCM, and this is illustrated above in relation to product and service excellence. Other models and approaches to organizational resilience highlight elements such as leadership, collaboration, personal resilience and supply chain resilience as being of particular significance. Through being multi-dimensional, the ORCM is able to cater not just for specific organizational circumstances, but also for elements which are in fact key enablers for the nine features and concepts documented here.

Two final points of note. Firstly, personal resilience is not simply employed as a useful analogy; having the right staff should be an essential part of any organization's consideration of resilience capability. Some claim that it is somehow the 'missing ingredient' which unlocks our understanding of organizational resilience, and whilst this may be true in respect of other models, we can say that it is already baked into the structure of the ORCM. Personal resilience can be drawn out within the organization's STRENGTH and its contribution to behaviours and outcomes is reflected within a number of the ORCM concepts. It is not the missing ingredient that many claim it to be; rather it is something specific for practitioners to consider as they seek to apply the model in a way which makes sense to them.

Secondly, and ahead of the detail within the following chapters which speak to assessment and implementation, it is at this point that we should unpick one of the potential shortcomings in how organizations may seek to apply the ORCM. To avoid the trap or disconnect which can occur when focusing on the language of the ORCM maturity scales, ie 'survive' versus 'thrive' or 'prosper', we need to ensure that we avoid seeing any assessment as fixed, final or out of context. The same would apply to a health assessment which we might subject ourselves to. Understanding the progress which may have been made and/or what objectives or targets are relevant is vitally important, as is the recognition that the organization's feature-set will change over time. As such, practitioners should be prepared to adapt their application of the ORCM as circumstances and resilience capability change.

Endnotes

1 Nguyen, Q, Kuntz, J, Näswall, K and Malinen, S (2016) Employee resilience and leadership styles: The moderating role of proactive personality and optimism, *New Zealand Journal of Psychology*, 45 (2), August, referencing Ashford and Black (1996); Seibert, Crant and Kraimer (1999); Thompson (2005). Available from: www.psychology.org.nz/wp-content/uploads/Employee-resilience-and-leadership-styles.pdf (archived at https://perma.cc/GF2Y-CMTK)

2 Nguyen, Q, Kuntz, J, Näswall, K and Malinen, S (2016) Employee resilience and leadership styles: The moderating role of proactive personality and optimism, *New Zealand Journal of Psychology*, 45 (2), August, referencing Ashford and Black (1996); Seibert, Crant and Kraimer (1999); Thompson (2005). Available from: www.psychology.org.nz/wp-content/uploads/Employee-resilience-and-leadership-styles.pdf (archived at https://perma.cc/GF2Y-CMTK)

3 Holmes, F (2019) AI will add $15 trillion to the world economy by 2030, *Forbes*, 26 February. Available from: www.forbes.com/sites/greatspeculations/2019/02/25/ai-will-add-15-trillion-to-the-world-economy-by-2030/#68f8c05b1852 (archived at https://perma.cc/3RXW-GE85)

4 Gleeson, B (2017) How leaders build the resilient organizations of tomorrow: A Navy SEAL's perspective, *Forbes*, 17 August. Available from: www.forbes.com/sites/brentgleeson/2017/08/17/how-leaders-build-the-resilient-organizations-of-tomorrow-a-navy-seals-perspective/#4821de9f1ba8 (archived at https://perma.cc/6XBP-PWLW)

5 Affinity Health at Work (2011) *Developing Resilience: An evidence-based guide for practitioners*, referencing Loehr and Schwartz (2003). Available from: www.cipd.co.uk/Images/developing-resilience_2011-evidence-based_tcm18-10079.pdf (archived at https://perma.cc/8HCF-6QG2)

6 Deloitte (2019) *Stepping In: The board's role in crisis management*. Available from: www2.deloitte.com/uk/en/pages/risk/articles/the-boards-role-in-a-crisis.html (archived at https://perma.cc/285Z-B2UY)

7 Resilient Organisations (2007) *Resilience Management: A framework for assessing and improving the resilience of organisations*, research report 2007/01. Available from: ir.canterbury.ac.nz/handle/10092/2810 (archived at https://perma.cc/8WYN-4W3Z)

8 Denyer, D (2017) *Organizational Resilience: A summary of academic evidence, business insights and new thinking*. Available from: www.cranfield.ac.uk/som/case-studies/organizational-resilience-a-summary-of-academic-evidence-business-insights-and-new-thinking (archived at https://perma.cc/F8R6-TXY8)

9 Smith, M (2016) *Collaboration for Resilience: How collaboration among business, government and NGOs could be the key to living with turbulence and change in the 21st century*. IUCN, Gland, Switzerland. Available from: portals.iucn.org/library/sites/library/files/documents/2016-047.pdf (archived at https://perma.cc/V563-9G6X)

10 Lucy, D and Shepherd, C (2018) *Organisational Resilience: Developing change-readiness*, Roffey Park Institute. Available from: www.roffeypark.com/wp-content/uploads2/Organisational-Resilience-Developing-Change-Readiness-Reduced-Size.pdf (archived at https://perma.cc/E8FU-28PY)

11 British Standards Institution (nd) *Organisational Resilience: Harnessing experience, embracing opportunity*. Available from: www.bsigroup.com/globalassets/LocalFiles/pt-BR/organizational-resilience/Org-Resilience-Exec-summary2--FINAL-25Nov15.pdf (archived at https://perma.cc/FQT4-H5B2)

12 European Commission (2019) Antitrust: Commission sends statement of objections to BMW, Daimler and VW for restricting competition on emission cleaning technology. Available from: ec.europa.eu/commission/presscorner/detail/en/IP_19_2008 (archived at https://perma.cc/7HFN-R5QP)

13 European Union Agency for Network and Information Security (ENISA) (2013) *Mutual Aid for Resilient Infrastructure in Europe*. Available from: www.enisa.europa.eu/topics/critical-information-infrastructures-and-services/cii/mutual-aid-assistance/mutual-aid-for-resilient-infrastructure-in-europe (archived at https://perma.cc/LM69-SBGX)

14 Coleman, A (2017) What are the benefits of collaboration for big brands? Virgin. Available from: www.virgin.com/entrepreneur/what-are-benefits-collaboration-big-brands (archived at https://perma.cc/88FQ-LSVC)

15 OECD (2018) *Financing SMEs and Entrepreneurs 2018: An OECD scoreboard*. Available from: www.oecd.org/cfe/smes/Highlights-Financing-SMEs-and-Entrepreneurs-2018.pdf (archived at https://perma.cc/A2GS-LGUM)

6

Assessment and reporting

Resilience is neither an abstract concept nor something which lacks an obvious pathway from theory through to practical application. Resilience capabilities are eminently measurable and must therefore lend themselves to assessment and comparison. Thankfully, for many organizations, structures and processes already exist through which management and the Board are routinely provided with information from profitability and employee engagement to carbon emissions, control effectiveness and societal contributions. It is also the case that many of the points highlighted below in relation to the ORCM are equally applicable, regardless of which assessment framework the organization chooses to adopt.

Fundamentally, the ORCM is designed to be a self-assessment tool, and as such, practitioners should not assume that external assistance is necessarily required when assessing and reporting on resilience capability. External assistance may well come with a catch, or two: the providers of such services are likely to have their own proprietary models which they will be keen for the organization to adopt; and even if conversant with resilience, these third parties will not be intimately familiar with the ORCM. Either way, self-assessment or assessed by an external provider, the organization will definitely need to have one essential element in place. In order to bring the ORCM to life – in order to actually apply the model and framework – practitioners will need a methodology for undertaking and completing the assessment as well as a strategy which clearly positions the work and which provides sufficient context for the rest of the organization to allow for meaningful reporting.

The structure of the ORCM, relying as it does on two distinct aspects of capability – characteristics and behaviours – requires information to be drawn from a number of sources across the organization. Some of this will likely already be available, and some will have to be newly sourced. Likewise, some of the information will be quantitative in nature and some will require qualitative efforts, and care will certainly be required to ensure that information is not only accurate and representative but is also presented correctly against the detail of the model. Upon receiving outputs from any assessment, senior management and the Board will be just as keen to confirm that subject matter experts (SMEs) have been able to confirm the meaning of the analysis as they will be to understand how the ORCM is constructed and how it relates to their particular organization.

Once a clear strategy for assessment has been defined, particular attention should be given to how the features and concepts within the ORCM are to be applied and to how the assessment process will actually operate. Rather than defining an inflexible set of requirements for each level of maturity, which can appear rather prohibitive, the ORCM describes various levels of performance or outcomes which can then be understood in the context of influencing factors and behaviours and activities. The detail in this chapter also provides a variety of questions against which the relevance of each application can be judged.

Finally, it is worth emphasizing the whole-organization aspect of the ORCM and the implications this has for assessment and reporting. Unlike some other disciplines, and this is a comment particularly relevant to standard-compliant approaches to business continuity, safety or security, it is neither meaningful nor appropriate to seek a limited scope for the ORCM assessment and reporting activity. However tempting it might be to apply the assessment to a regional operation or a particular product group, for example, it should be understood that decisions about such things are nearly always taken within the context of the wider organization and the contribution they make to its success and longevity. As such, assessments of resilience capability should be similarly constructed.

This chapter provides practitioners with advice on selecting an appropriate assessment strategy, explains the steps and sequencing involved in a typical assessment process, introduces practical advice on information gathering and also provides suggested scripts for completing qualitative assessment with groups or individuals. It also covers the crucial aspect of reporting and the reporting process, including the various considerations which can shape the report and some of the options for presenting conclusions and maturity information.

The provision of assurance

Organizational resilience is an exercise in the management of strategic risks, and as such it is right that we present the outputs from any assessment under the banner of 'assurance'. Admittedly, in some organizations this might present the practitioner with something of a challenge even before they have started. It is an unfortunate reality that assurance and the management and reporting of risk will often not have realized its full potential within an organization and will therefore not be perceived by senior management as being particularly helpful to them. It is in this regard that it is also helpful to separate the words from the actions. How many senior managers actively seek assurance across the risks they are exposed to and for which they have accountability, and do so without attempting to influence the colour of any resulting report for fear of how it might appear? In my experience the answer to that question would be very few.

The risk environment, as we know, is a dynamic one. Risk appetite has usually been seen as reflecting the organization's willingness to pursue potential loss, ie how comfortable the organization is with a particular level of exposure. Furthermore, risk appetite has traditionally been a strategic, top-down concept, it being the absence of clarity and information from the Board which often makes it an operational issue rather a strategic one.

Assurance should not be too concerned with which risks the organization wishes to embrace, but rather the way in which that embrace is understood and executed. Senior management and the Board need to understand whether the arrangements they have overseen are consistent with their ambition for and attitude to such exposure, and they need to understand where the pinch-points are and what might trip them up. Fundamentally, they need to understand if they are likely to achieve the risk orientation they actually desire.

The reality for many organizations is that assurance is rarely strategic in nature, and the tragedy is that so much time and resource is invested in the testing of individual components and often in a way which appears to the rest of the organization to be disjointed and poorly timed. Every assurance plan, and each assignment within it, should be explicitly informed by the Board's appetite for risk, and it should be equally clear how each assignment helps the Board to answer those strategic questions set out above.

Assurance planners will often claim to oversee a risk-based programme of activity, informed by some sort of mapping of assurance to business risk or process. The detail of any such claim, and how it might affect the assessment of resilience, is of some importance as much will depend upon which risk categories the organization believes it should be seeking assurance on and the way in which the programme is used to reflect what is an increasingly complex and rapidly changing risk environment. Using mapping information, it may therefore be possible to identify assurance activity which relates to the 'features' and 'concepts' contained within the ORCM. However, placing reliance on such work to inform an assessment of resilience across the organization requires enormous care. For example, even if some read-across was evident between individual elements, it would prove quite challenging to generate a strategic opinion on exposure based on what might be a largely operational assurance programme.

The detail of assurance provision within many organizations follows a well-established model commonly referred to as 'Three Lines of Defence' – a giveaway perhaps to the dominant posture within the profession, that being rather a defensive one. This model provides a convenient separation between the prevailing responsibilities for assurance activity, the degree to which such activity could be considered as independent and also an indication of who the intended audience usually is. In respect of the ORCM, we should expect our assessment to form part of the 'third line', ie assurance activity which is clearly independent of those responsible for the management of risks and which is intended for Board-level recipients. At a practical level, the whole-organization approach effectively precludes it from being viewed as anything other than third line.

This conclusion brings us nicely to the main question to be addressed within this section, which is: Who should actually be undertaking the assessment activity against the ORCM? As practitioners, are we to undertake it ourselves under some mandate agreed with the Audit Committee or do we agree a programme of work with the established Internal Audit department and have them deliver the work under our guidance or supervision? The answers, of course, depend very much on the governance arrangements already in place and the availability of appropriately skilled and knowledgeable resources. And, as with the organization's favoured assessment strategy, which we will come to next, much also depends on the available budget.

Although it is certainly not without its challenges, as alluded to earlier, one of the neatest solutions may be to carry out any assessment separate to the established assurance programmes within the organization, and to do so utilizing some element of external specialist resource. Just as the application of the ORCM should be tailored to reflect the details and circumstances within which the organization operates, so too the provision of assessment activity. Whatever course is chosen, practitioners will need to be able to explain how the requirements for the assessment came to light and how it supports, supplements or supersedes other assessments which the Board has sight of. In particular, practitioners should be prepared to explain how it maps to related areas of risk such as regulatory compliance, security, safety and business continuity.

Selecting the correct assessment strategy

Whilst it is easy to assume that the objectives for any assessment activity are already defined and understood, it is worth confirming what these might actually be, and as practitioners we need to ensure they are aligned with those sponsoring our efforts at the most senior level. Most importantly perhaps, we need to consider the whole-organization aspect of resilience, and in this regard, it might be helpful to think of the task in terms of organizational *health*. Although this term is now employed as a proxy for resilience by at least one of the major consultancy companies, possibly to attempt some differentiation in the marketplace, it can provide a useful reference and analogy for us as we consider assessment.

Health can be broken down into numerous parts, as it is applied on a personal level, but it is as a holistic concept that it takes on another, more significant level of meaning. Whilst the reader is not about to be taken on a detailed exploration of an alternative, medically-oriented model, it is worth registering the reference to health and the point that the objective of the assessment should be to understand all aspects of health across all aspects of the organization; therefore a strategy is required which reflects this. Even with a clear, whole-organization objective, practitioners may still come under pressure to limit their focus of attention or to discount certain activities, business units or even regions.

One of the most important elements of any assessment strategy relates to the type of assessment the organization is seeking to deliver, and this will depend very much upon the understanding and application of the ORCM, time pressures and access to resources and what information sources are available and appropriate to use. As outlined in Chapter 5, the ORCM is intended to be a flexible and adaptable tool, and one which allows organizations to draw out specific elements which may be of particular importance; for example, due to local or industry-specific factors. Without the constraints of pre-defined data tables or spreadsheets, the ORCM can be tailored to individual circumstances, and although maturity scoring is implicit, the model's clearly defined framework allows outputs to be remain meaningful and recognizable and therefore consistent from one organization to another. In seeking to apply the ORCM for assessment purposes, practitioners may wish to consider the following points:

- the organization's digital development and how this influences the volume of, and access to, information;
- the ability to place reliance on assurances received about the accuracy of the organization's data;
- the presence of regulatory reporting mechanisms and whether this is perceived as being a positive or negative influence on assessment activities;
- use of e-learning across the organization and other engagement methods, including surveys and the use of in-house social media;
- the nature of change activities or major initiatives, together with commercial pressures or structural issues affecting ownership and financing;
- the organizational make-up in respect of how growth and/or acquisition may have created obvious sub-cultures or differences in approach.

Before any assessment is actually started, a full review of the ORCM should be undertaken with the aim of confirming what it is within each of the combined features and concepts which should be focused upon. Importantly, this is not about trying to pre-empt which aspects *can* actually be measured, and nor is it about introducing a convenient weighting in order to satisfy pressures internal to the organization. Each of the features and concepts outlined within the ORCM must be considered as part of determining resilience capability and maturity within the organization, but the application of each must be reflective of the organization's reality. As practitioners, our role is to guide the development and implementation of assessment strategy; we must see the ORCM through an organization-specific lens whilst interpreting it in a way which is both consistent with theory, defendable and coherent.

Outside of the detail within the ORCM, each of the above considerations is likely to inform the assessment approach and be particularly important in respect of the timescales involved, which itself will be influenced in some way by the resources available. In large, complex organizations, short duration assessments of this type are only usually possible with a considerable degree of pre-planning, choreography and concurrent working by a team of assessment staff. A shorter duration does have the advantage that assessment results are less likely to be affected by specific events and any 'interference' with normal operations can be minimized.

Much will also depend on ready access to reliable information, and the nature of the ORCM requires this information to be both qualitative and quantitative. Strategy will need to be informed by the organization's information and data landscape and by whether the overall objectives for the work include establishing mechanisms which will allow for resilience capability to be monitored and assessed on an ongoing basis. Although this latter point is something we will revisit in Chapter 8, it is likely to have a significant impact on the overall approach as it makes the difference between information identification and collection being an ad hoc, and potentially rather unpredictable exercise, versus something much more routine and stable and which requires the design and implementation of an enduring process.

As noted in more detail below, a number of data collection techniques will usually be required to support an organization-wide assessment and some of these will employ established sources, such as ERP systems and customer feedback analysis. Others will necessarily involve the introduction of novel and bespoke methods, such as focus groups and interviews. In general terms, the different dimensions of the ORCM lend themselves to different data collection techniques. The features or characteristics, defined as representing the organization's STRENGTH, PERSONALITY, SKILLS and RESULTS, often align with data which is already analysed and reported in some form, for example through annual accounts, or data which can be readily accessed through electronic or other means.

The concepts or behaviours identified within the ORCM, defined as the organization's DIRECTION, AWARENESS, APPROACH, LEARNING and RESOURCES tend to be more qualitative in nature and therefore often require the use of new and deliberate techniques aimed at addressing resilience-type issues. The assessment strategy will clearly need to establish the extent to which qualitative data is sought within different parts of the organization and to the techniques which are to be employed. Whichever approach is decided upon, it should be remembered that assurance is an evidenced-based exercise, and just because interview or other similar techniques may not be immediately associated with 'data' in the same way as other techniques, an appropriate level of rigour and validation should still apply for it to be of legitimate use.

Planning and the assessment process

Defining an assessment process allows strategy to be translated into a series of explicit steps which can then be used to form the basis of a timed project or assignment. As presented in Figure 6.1, the assessment process should specify not only the key elements of the assessment but also the overall sequence of events. As with any assessment process, the description can also be extended to include detail of information sources, product or service categories, named teams and locations, etc, together with the anticipated nature of the analysis and reporting.

FIGURE 6.1 Generic assessment and reporting process

Information – Qualitative
(Interpretation of observations, descriptions and quotations, relying on discussions, interviews and documents)

Information – Quantitative
(Emphasis on measurement, using data available in systems and supplemented with questionnaires or tests)

Validation
(Review with SMEs seeking to ensure relevance and suitability of information and confirming interpretation)

Reporting
(Summary of measurement and analysis, together with conclusions, opinions and recommendations)

The process outlined in Figure 6.1 is necessarily a rather simplified one and is only intended to be illustrative. Whilst recognizing the distinction between qualitative and quantitative techniques, data collection and validation activities are often somewhat iterative in nature, rather than being sequential as shown. For example, it is highly likely that the initial planning work for the assessment will require some degree of information review, identification of potential data sources, and discussion with SMEs or those responsible for performance reporting, and much of this initial work will probably be quantitative.

Given the strategic nature of the exercise, the link to assessment strategy should be clear, and this is often best achieved through establishing Board-level sponsorship and direction for the assessment project or assignment and ensuring that appropriate governance arrangements are clearly established at the outset. Importantly, the intention here is to provide the Board with the necessary assurances around what is likely to be a new endeavour, and which might ultimately be highlighting some significant issues for members to consider. Planned and delivered according to some elementary project management rules should provide assurances around how the assessment has been conducted, who has been involved and what oversight and challenge has been provided in respect of the information used and the opinions presented. As a minimum, the Board deserve to understand how the assessment will be undertaken in a timely, cost-effective and accurate way, and they deserve to have these points revisited and confirmed as part of the final report.

Following such an approach may also make it more likely that the assessment is undertaken outside of the established assurance programmes within the organization and underlines the notion that perhaps the assessment deserves to be treated differently, and ultimately reported separately. Formal project governance encourages authority to be clearly established and a defined plan of action to be followed. It also allows for progress and outputs to be verified independently and for key review points or stage-gates to be introduced, specifically for validation activities. Independent oversight of the project will encourage an objective and flexible stance to be adopted.

Each assessment will have its own characteristics within the unique context of the organization, and this will be true whether delivered through self-assessment or by a third party. One common consideration will be the need to share objectives and expectations with the wider organization and to communicate progress and, ultimately, findings. At a minimum this would include those directly involved in the provision or validation of data and information, and most organizations would be expected to share more widely, at least at a senior management level. Two specific aspects of the assessment will drive much of the communication volume, these being the presence of any particular challenges, for example recent incidents or near-term changes, and the likely use of qualitative techniques requiring wider staff participation, for example through the use of focus groups.

One particular group for which the process will have a significant impact, both in terms of engagement and the need for communications, will be the subject matter experts (SMEs) upon which any information validation is likely to depend. The opinions, conclusions and any recommendations which result from the assessment activity will be built upon the information drawn from the organization and it is the validity of this information which the SMEs should be invited to consider, rather than necessarily how the detail of the ORCM is being interpreted or applied. For this purpose, SMEs can typically be engaged either at project reviews or on a more ad hoc basis. In establishing the project's authority, consideration should be given to not only how the SMEs are to be used but also to potential time commitments and whether this creates any particular vulnerability or failure points for the project.

Perhaps the most significant single consideration in respect of the assessment process is the ready availability of data, and in particular how much new data might be required for the assessment to have meaning. Every organization will have data, and some will have vast quantities of it, but guided by the organization's chosen assessment strategy and the detail of how it intends to apply the ORCM, time and effort will be needed to confirm the detail of this situation. Some new data may need to come from novel sources, and some may be in the form of proxies – that is, a data set intended to be representative of something within the ORCM, usually in the form of a more convenient and cost-effective substitute for what the model initially suggests.

Practitioners may find that for quantitative data in particular, assessment planning is dominated by analysis of reports and frequent exchanges with SMEs across the organization regarding cycle times and access. For qualitative data, planning is likely to involve some fundamental decisions about how and from whom it can be obtained, but also about how the assessment and reporting against the ORCM will be informed by its collection and analysis. The value of qualitative input cannot be overstated, and practitioners should ensure that sufficient space and attention is given to it.

There is also an interesting paradox here, and potential danger for the organization, as whilst qualitative input may appear to be more difficult to land given that it often requires an additional level of creative input, in many respects it is actually easier and requires less overall investment, particularly from a third-party perspective. Arranging a series of one-to-one interviews with managers and presenting the results as a meaningful assessment of resilience capability is much easier than finding out what is actually happening in practice, and the Board should be alive to this risk when confirming assessment strategy and the accompanying budget.

Using the ORCM as the basis for the assessment requires an approach which minimizes the risk of a report which simply presents a picture of what management would like to happen. However, access to senior management during the assessment is likely to prove a significant challenge and some may remain reluctant to engage until the reporting phase, by which point of course it is too late for them to provide any meaningful or productive input. Whilst this is not something unique to assessments of resilience, it nevertheless represents one of the biggest challenges for practitioners and is something which should be highlighted and addressed as soon as possible during the planning process.

Finally, as detailed later in this chapter, the process should detail how the assessment outcomes and conclusions are to be delivered to management and in what format. The detail of the reporting activity should not be left in any way unclear and early consideration should be given to the following points:

- What is the intended audience for the report, and will this include groups or individuals external to the organization?
- What opportunities exist for dialogue and exchange and at what stages will management have the chance to review and challenge the report's findings?
- Will the report follow the format of other assurance reports and will the Executive Summary be reported separately?
- Is it the intention to publish management's review comments separately to the assessor's opinions or will it be presented as an agreed position?
- Will qualitative information be attributed to named individuals or work groups?

The reporting phase of the process emphasizes two important aspects of assessment. Firstly, the expectation should be that the report stimulates a response of some sort from management – that is, it should be the beginning of something. (Improvement planning and how outputs from the assessment process can be taken forward is covered in Chapter 8.) Secondly, practitioners should not expect the assessment process to remain fixed. As with any process, the organization should be seeking to learn from the experience and to make improvements to it. Over time it is quite likely, for example, that the suite of quantitative data measures will change or that some qualitative techniques will prove to be more relevant and informative than others. Assuming that the assessment of resilience capability is not simply to be a one-off exercise, future reporting should clearly highlight any changes to the assessment process or significant changes to data sources, etc, in order that appropriate adjustments can be made to the commentary.

Data gathering and analysis

As referenced above, data gathering and analysis is likely to be iterative in nature, and indeed the defined process should always remain flexible enough to accommodate potential changes to the way in which data is made available and utilized during the course of the assessment. Much of the quantitative data is likely to require a request being made to the relevant part of the organization, unless of course it is readily available or can be secured independently in some way by the assessment team. Quantitative data can also be generated through focus groups and structured interviews, for example – techniques more often associated with qualitative data gathering.

Many organizations are able to provide significant volumes of measurable data through routine, day-to-day operations and much of this is increasingly digitized and systems-based. As part of establishing what the information landscape will eventually look like, specific types or data groups will need to be identified together with the timing or cycle with which they are associated. Similarly, access requirements will need to be confirmed, and as referred to previously, it may also need to be understood if data can be accessed going forward on a routine basis to facilitate future monitoring and assessment.

If not already done so, assessment activities will typically establish a suite of measures relevant to the ORCM for which routine data is available, and these will often form the basis for initial collection efforts. Any data requests made into the organization will need to be well informed and clearly described so as to avoid unnecessary delays or the inclusion of potentially misleading data. Once analysed, it would be expected that this information is subject to some form of clarification and challenge before it goes forward to reporting, and that subsequent changes or additions are made to the measures and/or to the analysis.

The requirement and application of qualitative data is particularly important for ORCM-related assessment, and as primary techniques in this regard, focus groups and interviews can also provide excellent opportunities to verify the meaning which is applied to quantitative data. Observations generated during the assessment through reviews of documents and other records should be captured, together with statements made and opinions expressed by those invited to contribute. Both as data collection techniques, and as opportunities to seek clarification in support of other analysis, interviews and group discussions should be deliberately guided. As with any voluntary exercise, engagement with the organization's employees needs to be relevant and time efficient, whilst at the same time the precise detail of the ORCM might not need to be explained, as it may simply present an unnecessary level of complexity and serve no valuable purpose in drawing out usable information.

Regardless of source or type, assessment data will need to be both comprehensive and representative of the organization's scope of activities. Whilst this may appear to be a rather obvious point, it can present particular challenges for the assessment when gaps or inconsistencies appear. Simply being unable to bridge a gap in the assessment, and thereby potentially leaving little or no useful data against which to assess specific aspects of any model or script, is not uncommon. In the absence of any suitable proxies or qualitative indicators, practitioners will be required to make judgements both in respect of the significance of such gaps in allowing conclusions to be drawn against the ORCM, and also whether the presence of the gaps themselves are potentially indicative of the organization's resilience capability.

Where gaps appear due to inconsistent measurement or reporting across the organization, the assessment picture might be a little more difficult to determine and as practitioners we should be alive to the potential drain on assessment time and resources which might result in seeking to understand the underlying causes in every case. For example, gaps or inconsistencies may be the result of cultural differences, be that local or national, or due to the relative maturity of systemization in one part of the organization versus another. Validation through SMEs and focus groups or interviews may assist in at least being able to point to some understanding as to cause, although again those receiving the final report will expect the authors to have accounted clearly for their significance.

Where contradictory qualitative data is presented, this is perhaps a little more straightforward, and is often evidenced as a difference of opinion or a variation in observed behaviours or control implementation and effectiveness. Such variation would normally be referred to as inconsistency and therefore as something likely to present a limitation in respect of resilience capability and reported as such.

However, there is potentially a difficult balance to be drawn between what on the one hand might appear to be overly optimistic or even extreme indicators, and on the other to simply be realistic insights to true capability in an otherwise understated organizational culture.

Wherever focus groups are employed, particular care should be taken to understand, recognize and manage the dynamics within them. As referenced above, clear guidance is necessary for the support of qualitative techniques and one reason for this is to ensure that any group opinions are not distorted or hijacked by the eloquence and personality of the ill-informed. It is important to clearly establish the aims of focus group work as it is not always obvious to participants whether those aims are to build a consensus or collective view or to simply ensure that a common understanding can be reached on the points raised. Taking the latter approach, which would usually be the most appropriate for assessment purposes, group discussion of a particular topic can often be beneficial in allowing ideas to develop and individuals to gain insight and understanding which they might not otherwise have enjoyed.

The practitioner's ability to identify emerging themes and draw meaningful conclusions from the available data is a function of the quality of the analysis, including access to measures for addressing the inherent weakness of relying on snapshot data and thereby encouraging interpretation of data as part of a broad range of evidence. In addition to considering the relationship between data and individual elements of the ORCM, and of course how these are being addressed, analysis of data should also consider any differences within the data sets and changes within the data as observed over time. Practitioners should also be concerned with practical considerations, such as how data is stored, and the analytical skills required by the assessment team.

In most situations it would appear likely that a satisfactory assessment could be undertaken without reliance on analytical software or advanced techniques, and there are two main reasons for suggesting this. Firstly, most of the heavy lifting, from a data perspective, is probably done already, as quantitative data can often be drawn from existing reports or submissions. Secondly, whilst the detail would be dependent very much on local circumstances, volume data is not necessarily required for this type of assessment activity and information for a number of the ORCM's features and characteristics can be drawn from relatively modest data quantities. For example, even in large complex organizations it is unlikely that significant data volumes would be required to account for previous historical issues or events, or the provision of finance.

Linked very much to the above, a final word about data assurance. Whilst we should always aim to work with assured data, this is obviously not always going to be possible, and herein lies an important point regarding the responsibilities of the assessment team. As practitioner and/or assessor, the responsibility is one of process and reporting accuracy – you are not responsible for the accuracy or timeliness of the actual data. This means that any conclusion or recommendation should be clearly informed by what assurances it has been possible to obtain about the data used, and being able to reference the exact source of any data used is a vital element of that equation, just as much as is the validation provided by SMEs.

Assessment practices relevant to the 'concepts' contained within the ORCM

The concepts contained within the ORCM relate to behaviours and activities – very much the 'how' and 'who' in relation to the provision of resilience capability. As such, qualitative data-gathering techniques can prove to be particularly useful and practitioners are usually keen to identify scripted questions or statements which can help to provide structure to such things in order to collect as much measurable data in these areas as possible.

The questions below could equally be reproduced as a series of statements and each suggests a heightened level of performance across the various concepts, qualities or behaviours referenced within the ORCM. They are written deliberately to emphasize practice and reality within the organization and to avoid the trap of too much credit being given to the sophistication of, for example, control design or simply to what may have been intended. Practitioners may wish to supplement or tailor these statements to reflect local conditions, but in doing so care should be taken to retain the bar at the highest conceivable level. After all, these statements are intended to reflect a significant resilience capability.

In seeking to generate quantitative data from interviews or focus groups, decisions need to be made regarding the coding systems for capturing answers and feedback. A simple scale is usually sufficient providing it allows participants to indicate their level of comfort or agreement with the statement or question posed. For example, participants would be expected to contribute effectively with a numeric scale of 1–10, providing it was clear which end of the scale related to 'strongly agree', for example, and that this was presented consistently across the range of statements or questions used. It might be worth avoiding an obvious mid-point in any scale, so as to deny participants the option of not committing either way.

The following represents a list of questions which could be useful in generating information for the assessment, probably in a focus group environment, although care should be taken to ensure they do not generate confusion for participants by seeming to combine more than one point. The statements below may therefore need to be split out.

DIRECTION

- Does the organization provide clear, visible and effective leadership, direction and coordination in relation to change and to potentially disruptive events?
- Does the organization genuinely embrace risk by preparing staff to react positively to threats as opportunities and does the organization communicate strategies designed to ensure that maximum value is delivered from each opportunity?
- Do leaders consistently challenge complacency, promote vigilance and embrace the need for continual improvement?

AWARENESS

- Does the organization effectively anticipate the needs of its customers and other stakeholders and do senior management demonstrate a deep understanding of the commercial landscape?
- Does the organization understand its performance in the context of its peers and is comprehensive, real-time intelligence constantly made available to decision-makers?
- Do senior management have confidence that strategic and operational risks are being managed in line with their appetite and expectations, and do they have an intimate knowledge of any gaps and control weaknesses?

APPROACH

- Do managers demonstrate a detailed understanding of change and a ready appreciation as to what is expected from each area and level within the organization before, during and after change activities?
- Are change activities comprehensively described in advance, and do staff recognize their own heightened levels of change readiness?
- Do leaders openly welcome change and demonstrate and communicate a genuine desire for the organization to flourish and prosper within a changing environment?
- Is the organization defined by collaborative leadership and is sufficient deference shown to experts when preparing for and responding to specific events?
- Is the organization's appetite for risk clear and consistently understood at all levels?
- Is openness actively promoted and are concerns raised routinely by employees through a variety of methods and celebrated as evidence of that openness?

LEARNING

- Are near misses seized upon by management as genuine learning opportunities, and can reporting of performance be demonstrated to be open, accurate and transparent?
- Is learning actively shared across industry-level networks, and are improvements quantified and reported?
- Are the tools and techniques necessary to support learning promoted and monitored at an individual, function and organizational level?
- Are individuals rewarded for ensuring that learning is truly embedded within the organization?
- Do decision-makers routinely draw upon learning from previous events including projects and crisis events?
- Is it clearly defined and understood how knowledge can be obtained, organized and retrieved?
- Is knowledge transfer actively monitored and reported and are targets set for its improvement?

RESOURCES

- Does the provision of dedicated learning resources have the highest priority?
- Does the organization enjoy benefits and tangible commercial advantage from its community presence?
- Is the organization actively engaged with mutual aid programmes at an industry, region and local level?
- Has the organization enjoyed success with its funding strategies?
- Is the organization yielding significant benefits, such as revenue growth or cost reduction, from its strategic partnerships?
- Is the organization growing its collaborative network across an increasingly diverse set of industries?
- Does the organization's brand enable it to be recognized as an employer of choice and does it have a track record of attracting and holding top talent?

Before we leave the topic of focus groups, it is worth sharing some of the important considerations regarding their set-up and operation, some of which we have touched upon already.

REINFORCING THE OBJECTIVES

Each session should begin with a discussion about the topic, including some example definitions, together with confirmation of the objectives. The topic should be compared with other topics, to help delegates differentiate, and at least one case study should be referenced. If the objective is to test and gather information, rather than build a consensual position, this should be clearly stated and referred to during the session as required.

GROUP SIZE AND MAKE-UP

There is a balance to be struck between having too few participants, which can make it difficult to generate discussion, and too many, which can make the interactions difficult to manage. Between 7 and 12 is probably the ideal number. Knowing who is represented within the session is just as important as who is not. The assessment strategy should include how the participant population is to be generated and from which parts of the organization. Similarly, having all the participants for a particular session drawn from the same area of the organization will doubtless create a different dynamic than if the session was 'mixed' in some way.

THE NUMBER OF QUESTIONS

The number of questions or statements presented to participants must make sense when set against the objectives for the session. Whilst there is no set number of questions, each session should aim to cover a minimum (eg 15) and some flexibility should be built in to ensure potential data-gathering opportunities are not wasted.

UNDERSTANDING THE QUESTIONS

Time should be taken during the session to explain and illustrate each question to ensure a consistent understanding. Remember that in most instances the aim will be to obtain information and feedback at an individual level and not to seek a 'group view' or consensus.

SCHEDULING OF SESSIONS

In establishing strategy for the assessment, senior management should demonstrate some sensitivity to how group sessions, and therefore wider participation in the assessment, might be received, particularly if there is potential for conflict or disruption following exercises viewed as similar, for example employee surveys.

Applying capacity measures to the 'features' within the ORCM

The detail of the ORCM's features tends to be more 'mechanical' in nature than those contained within the concepts. As reflected in Figure 6.2 and Figure 6.3 in the following section, the nature of the feature-set within the ORCM, coupled with the likely use of the organization's existing performance data, lends itself to the assessment and reporting of capacity or potential – that is, an indication of where the organization believes additional resilience capability can be drawn from. This may actually relate to capacity or potential in respect of a particular part of the organization or a particular service line, but fundamentally this is about features within the ORCM and the perceived gap between current performance and what the organization has reason to believe is achievable.

Whilst this approach offers a very useful way of expressing resilience capability and of providing indicators of future improvement activity, it does come with a couple of specific challenges. Firstly, in contrast to the assessment of many features within the capability model, and therefore somewhat ironically, any notion of capacity or potential tends to be rather subjective and therefore constructed from qualitative data. Attempting to determine the degree to which individual characteristics (such as project or crisis management skills, the speed of response or availability of operational assets) can be enhanced can prove to be extremely difficult, particularly given the absence of a reliable measure or gauge.

Subjectivity can be reduced if performance or capability in some aspects has slipped back, and therefore indicators can at least point to a previous, measurable level. Having a baseline or historical reference can certainly help in being able to provide a sense of scale for the audience of the report. As with all qualitative data, there is also a reliance upon verification through SMEs and focus groups – in fact, any indication of potential capability is most likely to come via the SMEs in the first instance.

The second challenge in seeking to apply indicators of potential resilience capability is that detail tends not to be costed or prioritized. Unless the review and reporting process is highly iterative, and therefore potentially quite lengthy, it is unlikely that indicators will actually form part of agreed improvement or investment activity and therefore the likelihood of such potential being delivered remains largely unknown. Together with the absence of any formal mapping of capability against stated risk appetite, and unless addressed within the report's narrative or via the review process, this can result in gaps being presented somewhat 'cold' to the audience and can therefore lack impact, or even prompt a negative reaction.

Options for reporting

Reporting is hugely important to the success of any assessment activity and deserves early and measured consideration as part of determining strategy for the overall exercise. Perhaps the most important aspect of resilience reporting is recognition that it rarely takes place in a vacuum – the Board and senior management in many organizations can give the impression of being overwhelmed by the volume of information they receive and the trend appears to be for increased standardization and brevity of not only reporting but also the meetings in which reports are considered. A number of these reports, although in reality probably a small proportion, are likely to be providing assurance to senior management across a particular exposure, sensitivity or category of risk.

It is also worth emphasizing that reporting should always be considered as a process rather than simply a specific documented output; reporting constitutes a distinct phase of the assessment cycle and itself usually consists of discussions, drafts, reviews, re-drafts and presentations, the delivery of which can often take several weeks. Sponsorship of the exercise and any independent reviews during the course of the assessment carry responsibilities and also present opportunities in this regard. The role of sponsor has a number of responsibilities associated with it and one of those should be to assist with reporting by facilitating discussions with senior colleagues on the detail and by seeking to raise awareness and understanding of the subject.

Reporting activity can be influenced by a host of elements from within the organization. For example, some of those involved during the course of the assessment as reviewers, or those with a risk or assurance background, can often prove to be useful during the reporting phase in providing feedback on the wording of opinions and the detail of any recommendations. Reporting of resilience capability can be considered challenging in a number of ways, particularly when it involves introducing a senior audience to a new way of considering risk and capability, and for some of course resilience may be a completely new concept. Although resilience capability in the organization never really advances significantly just by us having delivered an assessment, as practitioners, we should remember that we are the providers of information and insight, and the various pointers listed below are worthy of consideration in addressing these challenges, although the relevance of each will obviously depend on local circumstances.

External context

Reception may be improved and some of the initial challenges or questions pre-empted through providing senior management with external context for the assessment. This may simply be a case of repeating information presented as part of the initial business case and can be readily achieved with reference to freely available studies and articles, many of which reflect the opinions and resilience-related concerns of executives in other organizations.

Objectives and scope

The scope and purpose of the assessment should be stated early, clearly and often during the reporting phase. Just as important as what the report covers will be the detail of what it does not, and what the next steps are intended to be. As an exercise in expectation management, the audience should also understand the extent of the report in respect of recommendations or even the inclusion of agreed actions.

The ORCM approach

Similarly, the unique perspective of resilience captured within the ORCM should be stated and re-stated, drawing the distinction with other concepts the audience may be more familiar with. Employed repeatedly, reference phrases taken from the definition detail in Chapter 2 might be particularly helpful, such as 'resilience is not an event-focused concept like business continuity or crisis management', and 'resilience is about strength, competitiveness, re-shaping and growth'.

The assessment process

The unique elements of the assessment may need to be spelled out, particularly in relation to the governance arrangements in place and also the detail of validation and reporting. Amongst the senior management audience practitioners should expect interest to be shown in who amongst their peer group has had early sight of the report findings and how reliance is being placed on other work with which they may already be familiar. Practitioners may wish to include reference to how effective they believe the assessment process was and how it could be improved in the future.

Opinion-based or information-only

As perhaps one of the most fundamental considerations, and something which should absolutely have been clarified from the outset, senior management can approve an assessment exercise which results in an opinion-based report, or one which is based only on reflecting data analysis. Opinions are not necessary in a report and nor are recommendations, and an information-only approach, highlighting gaps and relative positioning, can certainly appear less threatening. If opinions are to be included, it should be clear to the audience whether this represents an agreed position with management or if alternative or contrary opinions have been expressed and what they might be.

Format and style

Whatever information is reported, it should be presented in a way which is not only easily digestible in a documented format, but also one which can be extracted and presented in other media, and potentially for other audiences. As illustrated below, a variety of graphics can be used to summarize and present findings against the ORCM, and these can be extended (as 'infographics') to explain and support the detail outlined above. The use of radar diagrams or charts is a standard way of presenting a potentially complex and detailed output, such as maturity assessments, and one which senior management should be familiar with from other sources and across other disciplines.

Caveats

However much care is taken in setting the context for the reporting, the introduction of some clear caveats or health warnings can often prove to be a good idea. For example, it may be helpful to highlight potential limitations in the assessment by reference to activities or elements which were not included, for whatever reason, or to explain issues associated with missing or potentially unreliable data. Similarly, those familiar with receiving audit reports will understand the need for cautionary statements, explaining that any conclusions are only as accurate as the data made available, and may not be representative of current or future conditions, etc.

Solutions and recommendations

Practitioners may expect senior management to appreciate receiving solutions to gaps or weaknesses identified, even if the reporting is officially light on opinions or recommendations. Expectations in this regard should probably be identified early in the reporting process, and any potential solutions referenced directly against the detail contained within the ORCM should appear objective and informed.

Q&A

Delivering a formal report of optimal length and detail for any audience is a common challenge and one which often feels all the more acute when the audience is the Board or executive management of the organization. One approach which avoids the need to include volumes of detailed information involves a summary report supplemented with a series of points or questions and answers. This detail can obviously be informed during the initial exchanges with management during the report phase and it can prove to be a valuable way of helping the audience appreciate the richness of the outputs and findings without the need to read through page upon page of narrative.

Data balance

Qualitative elements of the report can be extremely powerful, particularly when paired with more measurable data. The quotes, references and observations captured during the assessment can form part of the reporting narrative and individual elements highlighted in order to create additional emphasis. Qualitative elements are also just as portable as the facts and figures and should not be confined to the formal documented report.

Wider reporting

Dissemination of reporting information is very much a matter for senior management, but practitioners should seek to enable it by delivering appropriately formatted documents and ensuring the use of graphics and narrative which could be applied or extended to a wider audience.

Scoring, charts, infographics and grading

As a natural extension to the review of reporting possibilities outlined above, practitioners have a responsibility to present key assessment detail and findings in a meaningful and engaging manner to their audience. The organization's data can be easily graphed, and many reports now employ infographics or a reportage/journalistic style as a way of seeking to maximize speed of understanding, particularly for new concepts, patterns of data, scale comparisons or trends. The detail of exactly how data and the individual elements of the ORCM are reported, as with everything else, should be informed by organizational norms and practices.

Component models such as the ORCM, and particularly those which adopt a clear scale, lend themselves to a particular style of summary graphic, as presented below. The first of these (Figure 6.2) is commonly referred to as a 'radar' or 'spider/web' diagram, which allows both scale and comparison to be presented at a summary level across numerous variables within the same illustration. Trend or benchmark information can also be included, together with pointers or references for particular gaps or recommendations included within the wider report. With some care in the use of colour and shading, radar diagrams can also present model data across numerous 'layers', which might, for example, reflect previous analysis or elements of the wider organization, such as legal entities, product groups or service territories.

The scoring in Figure 6.2, which is entirely illustrative, utilizes a 6-point scale for both concepts and features of the ORCM, based on the practitioner's interpretation of maturity definitions and content outlined within Chapter 5 and the additional assessment guidance provided above. A gap is highlighted between actual and potential measures for the feature-set simply by the use of different colours or line styles.

FIGURE 6.2   Typical 'radar' reporting chart

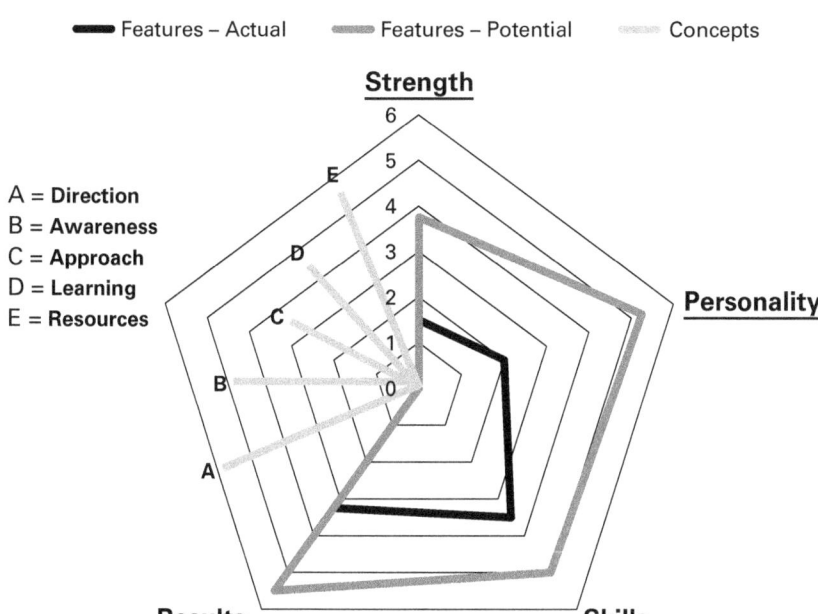

Whilst traditional bar charts and those employing 'sliders', such as presented in Figure 6.3, are perhaps a little more limited in respect of the amount of data which can easily be communicated, they can sometimes be easier to digest due to their simplicity. One of the disadvantages of a radar diagram is that linear patterns can be presented using very different results, as can be seen for the ORCM's concept scores in Figure 6.2. Linear patterns are very easy to detect, but where they are simply the unintended consequence of the diagram's structure, they can lead to key messages being missed or distorted.

The scoring in Figure 6.3 utilizes a 'low–medium–high' scale for the ORCM's features and a continuous, sliding scale for the concepts. The potential for improvement in resilience capability is referred to in the diagram as 'known capacity', which may or may not be appropriate depending on the circumstances of the assessment, and utilizes an arrow/bar to indicate relative scale. The diagram also presents an indicative 'state' of resilience capability, shown as 'limited progress', more of which below.

FIGURE 6.3 Linear/bar reporting chart

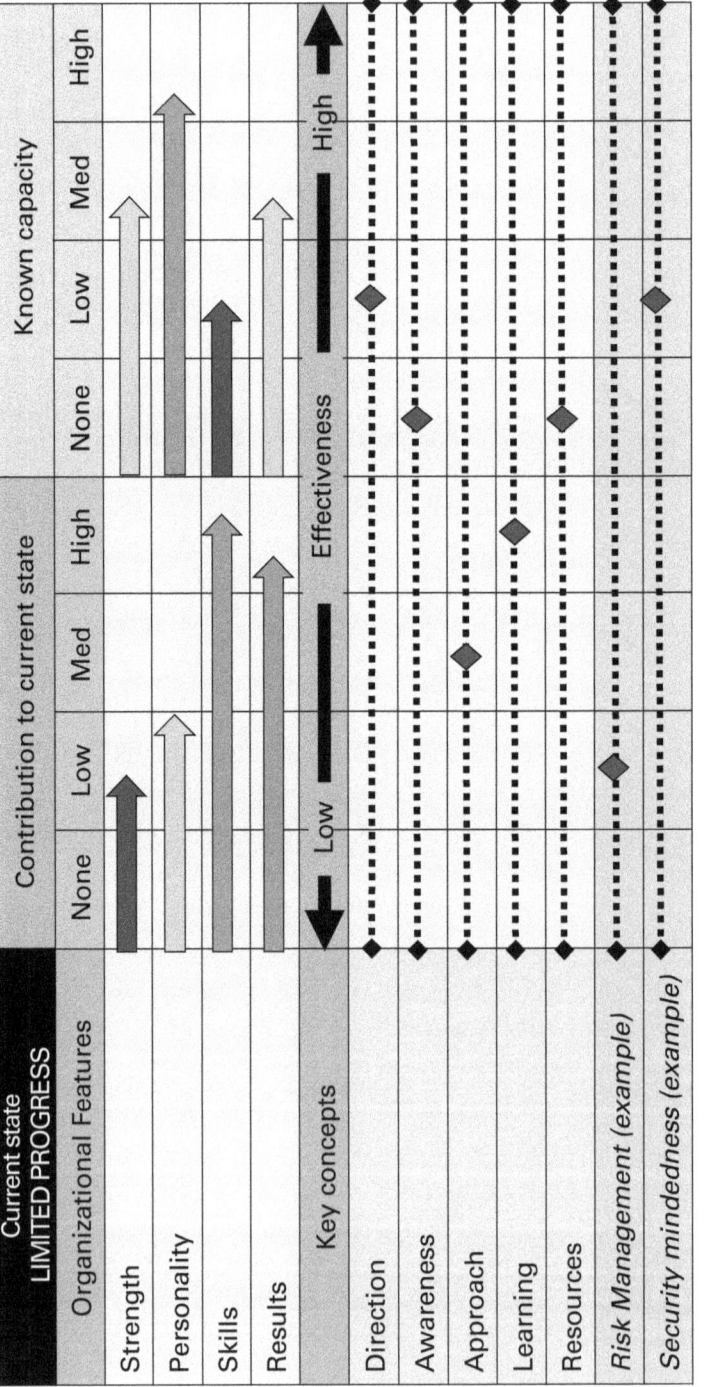

Figure 6.3 introduces aspects or detail which the organization has elected to highlight for specific attention – in this case, risk management and security mindedness. Although these two elements are already captured with the model – risk management most commonly as a SKILL and security mindedness as an APPROACH – it is quite legitimate to also show them as separate entries, assuming a local need to do so, although some additional narrative explanation might be considered helpful in such circumstances.

As referred to previously, the ORCM seeks to avoid creating a numerical framework within which to consider and assign overall maturity for the organization. Not only does this allow flexibility in application, without undermining the detail of the assessment against the feature-set and the various concepts, it also avoids the unhealthy preoccupation with labels or grades which can bedevil any assessment report. The descriptors provided for the ORCM's maturity scale in Chapter 5 are clear and indeed rather colourful; however, the organization may be advised to concentrate exclusively on the detail of the assessment and not to assign a maturity label or overall capability statement.

Even if no overall maturity label or grade is applied to the assessment result or the report, practitioners are encouraged to employ the language of the maturity scale in articulating the organization's relative position as part of the summary narrative or opinion presented to the Board or senior management. Even in organizational environments which display some sensitivity to 'bad news', the quality and integrity of the assessment activity and of the wider assurance process is undermined if senior management are not presented with informed judgements and opinions.

Benchmarking performance

Whilst it can be considered an integral part of the improvement cycle, and therefore to be covered further in Chapter 8, our assessment and reporting activities should be considerate of benchmarking and the need to highlight the positioning of resilience capability within an external context. There is, perhaps, an inevitability about senior managers seeking to understand performance in relation to other similar organizations, or organizations operating within a similar environment, but this can prove to be an extremely challenging requirement, particularly with a concept which carries so many different interpretations and opinions.

Just as our examination and understanding of organizational resilience draws upon multiple sources, so should our approach to benchmarking of capability. For many organizations, it appears unlikely that any single source or approach would yield sufficient information to satisfy the Board or executive management in this regard. As a consequence, our focus should be on the value to be derived from external comparisons and in seeking information in those areas where our assessment against the ORCM suggests the organization has the most to learn. In doing so, the detail of the model or approach which may have been used by those other organizations then becomes less important.

There is a further challenge in that self-assessment results are notoriously difficult to validate and whilst we might have reasonable confidence in our own assessment, relying solely on a capability index provided by a third party or on aggregated or anonymized survey information can make for an unrewarding exercise. The ORCM describes the subject matter of resilience and introduces its constituent parts, and our assessment should have identified gaps and weaknesses in respect of what it takes to build an enduring and successful organization. Understandably, senior management wish to be well informed with insights and examples: reference points to help them make sense of the ORCM and their own relative maturity.

Whilst on the one hand benchmarking can easily be over-complicated, on the other organizations can land on something which is overly simplistic, and which offers unnecessarily restricted vision. With this in mind, practitioners may wish to consider the following approaches.

Case study references

These are some of the most powerful external references which can be employed, and they often have the advantage of being well known to a wider audience. Open source information routinely provides a degree of detail and commentary in respect of what went well or what went badly wrong for the organization in question, and this can be mapped to the ORCM in order to help management understand it more easily and appreciate its potential. Being selective about the case study example might also allow practitioners to highlight those which have a particular relevance to their own organization's capability assessment or operating environment.

Other models and indices

The purpose of benchmarking should not be to invent a league table supported by questionable data. Rather, it should be to facilitate a better understanding of what enduring success looks like, and to identify practices and sources of learning from which the organization can benefit. Practitioners should therefore seek to digest as much external performance information as possible and from as many different sources as possible, always mindful of the quality of that information and the basis upon which it is being published. Such information is notoriously difficult to validate and many organizations will have submitted inflated assessments of their own capability in the past if they thought the results might reflect favourably for them.

Elements of resilience

Having pressed the notion repeatedly within these pages that resilience is an organization-wide concept, the reader might be surprised if I now promote discrete elements of that picture as a way of enabling performance to be benchmarked. This is purely a practical consideration and not one which should change our understanding of the wider concept. The simple fact is that if potentially valuable resilience information comes to light against a narrow interpretation of what is important, for example only covering supply chain or technological resilience, then we should consider using it for comparative purposes. Narrow it may be, but providing that it genuinely constitutes an element of what we understand as resilience, it should be possible to map it against the ORCM and therefore to draw value from it.

Industry peers

Practitioners may conclude that comparisons at an industry level are largely irrelevant, but this can be a mistake for a couple of reasons. Firstly, by definition, these are the very organizations with which you are competing and therefore comparative performance has a unique significance. It is a market-specific view which can allow the organization to best prioritize its improvement efforts. Secondly, performance information can often be more easily accessed via the shared interfaces, larger staff pool and industry forums which are in place, and the meaning or application of such information can often be easier if organizations are using common terminology, for example. The principal challenge for benchmarking is not in finding organizations which use the same assessment or performance model, or which share exactly the same understanding of what it means to be resilient, but rather access to meaningful and trusted performance information, and it is here that many industry groups win out.

Conclusion

Any robust, well-defined maturity model should allow for improvement steps to be thought through and considered – that is, the model should facilitate assessments which provide some indication not only of what current performance looks like but also what is required to move the performance dial forward. Central to the success of any such endeavour is a meaningful assessment and reporting strategy and the understanding and confidence necessary to convert that strategy into an effective assessment plan.

The most appropriate strategy for undertaking an assessment of resilience capability can only be determined through some knowledge of the organization, and in particular its governance, assurance and risk management arrangements. Without a clear mandate and agreement on how an organization-wide assessment of resilience capability fits within existing governance arrangements, it is hard to see how this could qualify as a coherent strategy. Equally important will be the organization's culture and management's expectations and understanding of the topic. Similarly, the strategy must make sense in relation to the organization's size and complexity, the nature of its products or services and the location of its employees and other assets.

The use of detailed calculations and spreadsheets to determine maturity can appear overkill for many organizations and can easily create a preoccupation with the scale or the demarcation between maturity steps; it can all appear to be both arbitrary and at the same time rather too rigid and detailed. As outlined in the previous chapter, the ORCM is intended to be applied in a flexible manner using language which can be easily understood. In a similar way, assessment is presented here in a way which is straightforward and designed to complement existing risk assurance activity within the organization. The detail of how assessment results are ultimately reported is very much down to the individual practitioner and to the guidance provided to him or her by the organization's leadership.

As with any maturity model which relates, for example, to project management, business continuity or the provision of IT services, the ORCM should not be used to suggest any form of guarantee or that applying it for assessment purposes in itself builds capability in this area. Whether applied to the organization directly or to its supply partners, care should also be taken not to suggest that reported increases in maturity necessarily equate to improvements in service quality, greater standardization, reduced development times or savings for customers.

Self-assessment can often prove to be the most effective and efficient mechanism in helping the organization to understand its resilience potential and in drawing attention to those improvement opportunities which are available, and a number of external sources suggest the detail of assessment mechanisms in support of their proprietary resilience models. In addition to digesting the detail above as it applies to the ORCM, practitioners are encouraged to explore these alternative assessment sources with the aim of ensuring that strategy is well informed. High-level requirements associated with assessing resilience characteristics are listed within ISO 22316 and other sources, including the Australian Government's REAG model, for example, which contains detailed 'health-check' tools, questionnaires and even spreadsheet templates for the analysis of results.[1] A number of research studies also reference measurement of resilience maturity and capability, including 'What we know and do not know about organizational resilience', by Ruiz-Martin *et al*.[2]

Finally, it is worth reiterating the point that for the assessment itself, new mechanisms are likely to be needed in order to provide for the capture and measurement of data, particularly in relation to that which is qualitative in nature. Observations and (structured and unstructured) interviews or discussions will need to be planned and conducted, from which descriptors and messages will need to be identified and recorded and turned into meaningful data. These are important sources of information in respect of views and experiences of the organization's staff and stakeholders and are critical to delivering a comprehensive assessment across the ORCM, or indeed any such model.

Chapter 7 focuses upon the connections between resilience and other, perhaps more established organizational disciplines. It is these connections which not only provide valuable local context but which also help to explain resilience in risk terms.

Endnotes

1 Australian government website, Organisational Resilience HealthCheck. Available from: www.organisationalresilience.gov.au/HealthCheck/Pages/default.aspx (archived at https://perma.cc/MP8Y-BU32)

2 Ruiz-Martin, C, Lopez-Paredes, A and Wainer, G (2018) What we know and do not know about organizational resilience, *International Journal of Production Management and Engineering*, vol 6, 31 January. Available from: www.researchgate.net/publication/322860087_What_we_know_and_do_not_know_about_organizational_resilience (archived at https://perma.cc/SNF6-UVGQ)

7

Other key issues and ideas

This chapter explores a number of other topics relevant to the study of organizational resilience and discusses opportunities for their application with reference to some of the external information sources already identified. In order to reinforce resilience thinking, the chapter also touches upon some of the alternative resilience models and approaches which exist.

Understandably, one of the most effective ways of introducing and discussing resilience with colleagues across the organization is to do so within the context of topics they might be particularly familiar with. If done well, this can help to emphasize the organization-wide nature of resilience and to differentiate it from narrow or more technical fields of activity and event-focused concepts and ideas. However, care should be taken not to overdo the 'compare and contrast' approach – resilience is neither the same as other topics and nor is it the polar opposite of any – as we need colleagues to develop a deep understanding of their contribution in building resilience capability and how this can be best delivered.

For a number of colleagues, there is also likely to be a developmental angle to explore as we engage with the subject of resilience. Many professionals and subject matter experts (SMEs) will have a natural affinity with resilience and recognize it as affording them an opportunity to extend and build upon existing knowledge and qualifications. This is true of risk managers and compliance specialists just as much as it is of HR or IT professionals – in fact, anyone who recognizes the contribution of their particular specialism and who is keen to demonstrate a broader understanding of the organization and how to make it successful. Linking specifically to Chapter 6, there is often a discrete cadre within many organizations who are charged with assurance, audit or performance reporting activities, and these individuals can also prove to be fantastic ambassadors for resilience and will frequently recognize its developmental potential before anyone else.

The topics introduced in this chapter by way of *support* for resilience, of which I have selected five, have a particular relevance and currency. The topics are not truly technical or mechanistic, such as financing or asset/project management, for example, but each has a unique and important connection to the building of resilience capability within an organization. Two of these, namely compliance and transformation, have been touched upon already in previous chapters but their application is worthy of further examination here and is done so through the lens of 'disruptive technologies', such as artificial intelligence (AI). I have also included a section on the need for investment as part of recognizing the potential costs associated with the organization's resilience journey. The other two topics, safety and security, might appear to be very traditional and easily recognizable, but we will approach them from a largely behavioural perspective and seek to draw out the similarities with some of the concepts we have already examined in the ORCM.

For it to be meaningful, the study of organizational resilience should include and acknowledge the existence of different models and definitions, given that several exist, and each competes in some way for recognition and wider adoption. However complete or adaptable an individual model might appear to be, and given the disparate and varied nature of the subject, it makes sense to highlight example models of which practitioners may wish to make a separate study. Both of the examples provide commercial platforms for consultancy organizations, but both have a clear research basis to them. The first of these alternative models is presented by the British Standards Institution (BSI) and the UK's Cranfield School of Management, and the second is presented by Resilient Organisations, based in New Zealand.

Both of these examples, and I could have selected a number of others, offer something different to the ORCM, but these differences are largely about emphasis and perspective rather than fundamental content; the differences are more about style than about substance. Alternative perspectives offer practitioners the opportunity to think about resilience capability using different terminology from that contained within the ORCM and through applying a slightly different approach. For example, it may be that in a particular organizational setting an emphasis on adaptation and terminology which is explicitly evolutionary or Darwinian in nature carries with it a particular value. Under such circumstances, practitioners should not be afraid to borrow terms or references from these other sources if it helps to generate interest in the subject and to better inform colleagues.

Compliance in a period of technological revolution

The notion of 'compliance' is frequently introduced in a manner intended to describe something which is consistent but also rather simplistic or inflexible, and it often suffers with a poor image as a result. In some circles compliance or a compliant mindset can even be viewed as something of an insult. As referenced in previous chapters, this matters for one very important reason: the approach outlined here and around which the ORCM is constructed means that strong and effective governance, of which a compliant mindset is a critical component, is essential for building resilience capability. Furthermore, rather than providing the counter or opposite to organizational flexibility and agility, compliance and achieving a compliant position actually reduces uncertainty in a way which affords the freedom needed to properly explore opportunities and satisfy the organization's appetite for exposure.

The exciting, and somewhat daunting news for all organizations, regardless of size or complexity, is that for the near-term future they can probably forget pretty much everything they have ever learned about compliance. The reason? Buried deep within the underlying definition of compliance, literally at a foundational level, is the notion that in order to be compliant we need to understand what compliance actually looks like and the pace of regulatory and statutory change makes this an almost impossible task – simply having a compliant mindset is actually not sufficient.

Organizations exist and operate within a wider context, be that at a community level or internationally and with ties and connections which can be, for example, commercial, governmental or faith-based in nature – the detail really doesn't matter. What matters is that all these organizations are emerging from a period of relative stability during which the machinery and mechanisms of compliance were reasonably well understood, at least most the time. Even since before the financial crisis of 2008, things have felt different and increasingly so, and they have felt like we are at the beginning of some truly revolutionary change. In fact, we are probably at the beginning of several revolutionary changes, and from a compliance perspective this brings with it a particular challenge – that is, how to deal with the distortion created by so much concurrent change. Our collective sense of 'what compliance looks like' is being clouded and our clarity of focus in many areas has all but disappeared.

Examples are not difficult to find, and many relate in some way to what are described as 'disruptive technologies', but certainly not all. A growing number of norms are no longer what they were and appear to be increasingly irrelevant, replaced by uncertainty and unpredictability, and by new forces which we struggle to understand. Western European societies are being disrupted in ways not seen for two generations by migration, new security threats, economic upheaval and the rise of extreme politics; the Middle East and North Africa have been transformed as a pattern of conflict and unrest has been repeated in new countries; the potential for fresh conflict at an economic or military level is reported as a matter of routine from Central America to Asia and the Far East. Even at a micro level, our expectations and what we are seemingly prepared to accept from our political leadership is no longer even measured on the same scale as it was – the domestic political landscape from the United States to Europe is being transformed.

However, it is at the technological level that our understanding of compliance, and our approach to being compliant, is perhaps facing its most important challenge, and one which is multi-dimensional in nature. Not having the assurance that operations are compliant is bad enough, but this can often be compounded by adjustments made to operational processes in an attempt to obtain or regain a compliant position – adjustments which can often be clumsy and which can increase costs or delivery times or both, as illustrated below by Denyer and Pilbeam (2015) and by the Organisation for Economic Co-operation and Development (OECD):

> Organizational Resilience can be undermined as these factors can combine to create blind drift and organizations can sleepwalk into disaster. Once failure does occur most organizations respond by bolstering preventative control by adding new safeguards, reinforcing barriers and redoubling training efforts but rarely engage in fundamental changes to the adaptive innovation or mindful action aspects of resilience.[1]
>
> Dramatic regulatory failures tend to produce calls for more regulation, with little assessment of the underlying reasons for failure.[2]

The increasingly rapid introduction of new technologies challenges our understanding of what compliance looks like, not just because the technology itself is often so specialist and therefore beyond the comprehension of most people, but also because the processes and mechanisms within which it is applied are often opaque and so different to what we have been accustomed to. Organizations, and more importantly the legislative authorities, are having to play catch-up, repeatedly left behind by private technology companies and by those seeking to do us harm or intent on stealing from us. To compound the issue, we also know that recent controls around technology and how technology is used to create a compliant position have proven to be monumentally unsuccessful and open to widespread abuse – through data loss and exploitation, non-compliance has been evidenced in ways never seen before and in volumes which were unimaginable only a few years ago.

It is against this backdrop that we introduce 'voice' technology – voice controls and commands delivered across new and existing devices and with the creation of an entirely new interface for the user.

A recent HBR article captures the significance of voice by referring to it as a 'platform and user interface (UI) shift comparable to the web and smartphones'.[3] The advent of the voice assistant has already changed the nature of countless digital interactions and all indications are that this is just the beginning of another technological revolution involving the application of AI.

Records have long been created as a result of interactions and exchanges, but the way in which technology is now being used to interpret and create digital records from instructions that have been freely spoken introduces a significant new test for organizations. Much of what has been created and stored digitally over the last few years has been the result of manual input – of individuals, either privately or as part of an organizational process, deliberately entering and submitting specific, limited information using physical commands, and often with the added protection afforded by specific input fields and some sort of conscious review step. As acknowledged already, citizens and organizations continue to struggle with ensuring the safety and security of these records, but at least the nature of the records has previously been quite predictable and defined – defined by the data fields within the electronic systems and applications through which it was captured. And much of this data has been submitted voluntarily and deliberately, and the user may at least have had the opportunity to waive their right to limit its use. Not so, voice.

As noted in the HBR article, 'The shift to voice doesn't require any training. Users simply "speak" as they do naturally', and herein lies many of the challenges for organizations seeking to maintain or develop a compliant stance: voice technology, and to repeat the point this is a technology that most people understand very little about, potentially captures everything, and in an unfiltered way. The records we've lost to date have largely been specific and clear and deliberately captured: bank records, dates of birth, etc which were explicitly requested at some point or other during a transaction and which were provided knowingly. Voice records are potentially quite different: potentially intimate, personal, even libellous, and all captured whether unintentionally or otherwise and completely unfiltered. Records could now be based on raw transcripts of private conversations, interpreted and held as electronic information without the provider even being aware, captured at home, in car or in the office – wherever voice technology is being applied.

At an organizational level, the rapid adoption of cloud computing over recent years, coupled with the introduction of multiple and often opaque layers of control and third-party ownership, has also changed many compliance norms. Voice is most obviously promoted at this stage for its positive impact at a consumer experience level and in a domestic environment, but this will soon begin to have a much broader application and as such our compliance norms will change again. Compliance thinking will need to keep pace with the way in which new and existing devices are being used, and with technologies which rely less on instruction and physical interaction and more on behind-the-scenes interpretation.

The capability to deliver transformational change

Transformation is often suggested, implied or directly associated with organizational resilience, and we have already touched upon it in Chapter 3 in relation to the ambition which is a prerequisite of the resilience mindset. Ordinarily, transformation definitions include references to appearance or make-up (ie a profound, complete or radical change) and to strategy or performance (ie a new direction or a completely different level of effectiveness).

All of this suggests a common linkage, either directly or indirectly, to change and disruption, which in turn would suggest that some organizations will feel the need for transformation more sharply than others and also that different influences will be at play at different times – we should not expect transformation to always relate to or be limited to changes in an organization's culture. For example, 3D printing is driving the introduction of truly distributed manufacturing, the creation of new materials, and seemingly limitless applications in the field of medicine. From a system perspective, resilience can be defined as relating to:

> The magnitude of shock that the system can absorb and remain within a given state; the degree to which the system is capable of

self-organization; and the degree to which the system can build capacity for learning and adaptation.[4]

Whilst we can carry these social-ecological linkages across to an organizational level relatively easily, the proposition that 'more resilient (organizations) are able to absorb larger shocks without changing in fundamental ways', and that 'when massive transformation is inevitable, resilient (organizations) contain the components needed for renewal and reorganization', is particularly compelling.

Continuing the theme from the earlier section, a topic against which transformation is routinely applied is that of the digital economy and digital technologies. The digital world, like other resources, is a shared one. As the World Economic Forum (WEF) describes:

> This presents unprecedented opportunities and benefits in terms of infrastructure, applications, and data, but also poses a number of thorny issues and dilemmas. Existing institutions, mechanisms and models may not be able to effectively respond to the pace of change.[5]

With technology creating a massively disruptive influence and enabling a significant proportion of what is viewed in transformational terms today, it is safe to assume that future technologies will enable future transformations – that is, fundamental changes in the way organizations operate, engage and deliver value, enabled by successfully harnessing the potential of new technologies. However, from a resilience perspective, this is not just about the future of work and nor is it about who can make the most accurate predictions about the future; a technologically induced apocalypse is easy to predict, and dire, sensational predictions are notoriously difficult to counter. It is also not about transformation per se, as it is very easy to limit our thinking based on today's reality – the hysteria presented in news media around driverless vehicles being a good example.

Our interest in transformation, in this chapter at least, is based not upon what it might look like or upon the strategy which sits behind it, but rather the organization's ability to deliver it. For example, organizations need to possess a degree of fluency in the language of technology simply in order to keep abreast of the latest developments, to recognize how the opportunities can be exploited and therefore to inform strategy. But this fluency and knowledge also forms part of the organization's capability profile. Understanding how AI is being applied to knowledge-work and to activities which require thinking is just part of the requirement for organizations – delivering transformational change successfully and repeatedly is a fundamental requirement and necessity for organizations which have long-term ambitions, and as such the following should also be considerations in respect of capability:

- The risks and governance controls appropriate to data management and to extreme growth in data volumes. The WEF notes that, 'the borderless nature of digital technologies is increasingly testing the limits of existing institutions and rule-making – at both the global and national levels'.[6]
- Implementation of automated decision-making and exploiting the potential for reduced response times from sensors and data triggers.
- Redesigning tasks and workflows based around stable, high-speed connectivity and the widespread adoption of interactive technologies.
- Relationships with commercial service providers which can support design and implementation of the best digital strategies.
- Skills and awareness not just in being able to spot new trends and applications but also in being able to apply those new technologies in the workplace as intended.
- Recognizing the changed role of ICT and of needing to move beyond the traditional mindset of ICT-oriented cost reduction and process efficiency.
- New investment and project delivery timeframes which can keep pace with the innovation environment – one which saw widespread adoption of voice-command interfaces in the home only 10 years after the launch of Apple's first iPhone.
- Horizons which reflect the realities and potential of future technologies, such as future 6G networks, and which consider extreme predictions for climate change and energy provision, for example.

- Leadership and thinking which permits the development of new operating models and levels of advocacy which support the implementation of new ways of working.

Organizations should actively test their transformational capability. This is not scenario planning, but rather testing the strength and accuracy of their capability assessment around transformation and seeking to understand if the requirements for creating capability in this area are sensitive in some way, for example if the underlying assumptions about transformation drivers are changed. What if the drivers introduce not only a great sense of urgency but also one which is most apparent at a societal level? What if the revolution in technology is driven by something other than competitive advantage and insatiable consumption?

Capability gaps can be addressed through introducing specialist resources to the organization, and transformation offers a wealth of opportunities for external consultants due to its breadth, relevance and the urgency with which many organizations feel the need to act. Transformation was alive within consultancy providers in the late 1990s, but it was quite a different undertaking back then – often limited to breathing life into stalled efficiency programmes, process redesign or supporting the first attempt at introducing enterprise-wide ICT systems. Today's context is fundamentally different, as is the approach, and a brief trawl of the internet can provide some very helpful pointers for organizations considering the need for help in this area. The following provide but two examples of what can be uncovered.

In an unusually expansive website, BIE (www.bie-executive.com (archived at https://perma.cc/T83X-7ALJ)) introduces transformation by recognizing its make-up, the common drivers which sit behind it, and the steps which a successful transformation programme should contain. Amongst other resources and case study material, BIE offer insights through their own business survey, which includes: in what ways transformation buying has matured; how transformation teams are structured today; who the major sponsors and organizers are; and how businesses are engaging their employees in transformation.

The survey report quotes 'an overwhelming 80 per cent of respondents said their company was going through a transformation of some nature'.

PwC (www.pwc.com (archived at https://perma.cc/GML2-MT6P)) tread a similar path, in presenting a list of elements or principles deemed essential for any transformation to succeed, and focusing on the role of leadership in delivering that success. Perhaps one of the most useful, if not obvious, steps is referred to as 'setting up a parallel organization to run the transformation'. This recognizes that 'you need to keep doing business whilst you change your business. Don't ask managers and line workers to do both'.

From a change perspective, the decade to 2020 has had a number of distinctive characteristics. Some change has been massive and rapid, often led by private technology firms. In other areas, for example employment and financial systems, we are told to anticipate massive disruptive change which has not yet materialized, or at least not in the way we were told to expect. Many social and political norms have been disrupted as societies across the world struggle to cope with change where for decades there had only been stasis. Other areas or aspects of life appear to have stagnated or even gone backwards: our speed of travel is certainly no quicker, and we seem to struggle to re-establish certain things which we once took for granted, like reusable space craft or stable international borders. Our planet has become even more overcrowded, our natural environment is under pressure like never before, and the effects of human activity are becoming more apparent and more widely accepted.[7]

Considerations of change capability shouldn't just be concerned with the advent of machine-learning per se, and it is certainly not about insulating organizations from future change. The question is, what do organizations need to consider when they look ahead and how should they think about future developments in their social and commercial environments? This is about considering the projections regarding future developments in AI, for example, and understanding what this means for our model of organizational resilience.

To illustrate, and with reference to leadership and to PERSONALITY as defined within the ORCM, organizations should be able to demonstrate an understanding of what the following questions mean within their own unique context:

- What will be the requirements for leadership in the next 10 or 20 years?
- Will the cult of personality which pervades many organizations, and certainly not just those born of a recent entrepreneurial spirit, be more or less evident, and what does this mean for resilience capability?
- Will organizations be any more or less focused on the development of resilient traits within a small leadership cadre and on the importance of role-modelling resilient behaviours?

The relationship between resilience and safety

High reliability organizations (HROs), as defined by the UK's safety regulator, the Health and Safety Executive (HSE), are those that are able to manage and sustain almost error-free performance despite operating in hazardous conditions where the consequences of errors could be catastrophic. HROs, and the desire to become one, are important from a resilience perspective for two reasons. Firstly, and most importantly, there is need to emphasize 'culture' and to recognize that a transformation in safety culture is a common and necessary requirement for organizations wishing to break through the ceiling of traditional safety thinking and safety performance. Secondly, safety within HROs is usually considered and approached at an organizational level, which allows policy-makers access to all that is important to safety performance from asset design and equipment certification through to team behaviours and the adequacy of learning across industrial sectors. Importantly, both of these points are more widely applicable – they actually allow easy translation to organizations operating within more benign conditions.

Safety performance can be viewed as the combined result of several factors across the organization, namely availability and quality of resources, operational conditions and the nature of barriers, in addition to other elements such as human behaviour, supervision, process design and planning, etc. As detailed within a review of literature by the HSE in 2011, many of the same cultural elements and references used in respect of HROs are directly similar to those referenced in respect of resilience.[8] In reference to a model defined by Weick and Sutcliffe (2007), the review identifies two key characteristics of HROs as being 'learning orientation' and 'mindful leadership', both of which find many parallels with the detail contained within the ORCM, for example.[9] Also, as described within *Organizational Safety: From safety culture to organizational resilience* by D'Oliveira and Mário:

> Several cultural facets appear to be associated with the ability to adapt to change and disturbance, namely interpersonal relationships at work and the involvement or workers and the traditional conflict between productivity and safety.[10]

As suggested above, connections with safety performance and the work of HROs are numerous and can be examined in a variety of ways. Two such opportunities are presented by the advent of technology and what this means for performance and for organizational learning, and through the impact of risk-taking behaviours at an individual level and in respect of the organization's stated risk appetite. From a technology perspective this is certainly not about the safety of AI or about citing examples of where AI might have failed, although a huge and important topic in its own right, but rather the impact which AI can have on safety and safety performance. The prospect of supplementing or even replacing human decision-making, of correcting and compensating for human behaviours through autonomous intervention, and of harnessing the power of analytics to predict faults or unsafe outcomes is of huge significance to the resilience of organizations and therefore to societies.

AI algorithms are already being applied to safety engineering and to the design, testing and manufacturing of engineering solutions, and are pushing the boundaries of predictive maintenance. AI is also embedded within the control systems for some of our most critical infrastructure and asset networks. Traditional control systems operate using predefined parameters and are governed by operational rules which are the result of previous (human) experience. Introduce autonomous, self-learning systems and safety-critical decision-making and intervention might suddenly look altogether different.

Evidence to date from the managed, cautious and very public introduction of driverless vehicles points to an underlying distrust of autonomous systems and to the application of safety thresholds or performance criteria which are not necessarily in line with human performance, for example with regard to historical death rates for both (driverless vehicle) passengers and pedestrians. However, AI is being used successfully and more openly to introduce new levels of surveillance and revolutionizing supervisory control over worker behaviours, for example in respect of adherence to safety rules such as the wearing of protective equipment.

As an extension to detail contained within Chapter 6, the safety impact of introducing new technology can be mapped to resilience models, such as the ORCM, through the use of metrics. As part of developing and implementing a robust assurance framework, practitioners should ensure that leading indicators are reflected within their chosen suite of resilience metrics, such as those relating to alarm responses and the analysis of passive detection systems. Where such metrics are reflective of new technologies and AI, their particular relevance should be examined and understood in respect of establishing the organization's overall resilience capability. In some cases, this will highlight changes and improvements in preventative activities, and in others it will draw attention to the organization's speed of response.

Even if AI leaves the majority of hazards unchanged, which seems highly unlikely, it has the potential to fundamentally change the worker–hazard relationship, and overall safety performances as a result. Within a generation, worker–hazard relationships will no longer be described by the interpretation of information and having to make decisions within the often-pressured cycle of operational processes. Safety performance will be measured against the background of more limited human intervention and one which is focused much more on understanding, consequence analysis and policy-making. Even through a conservative lens we can see that AI has the potential to elevate humans above the hazard zone in many situations, perhaps as early as 2030.

Until recently, learning has remained a very human endeavour and failures within hazardous environments have often been associated with human factors and in the quality of that learning. The ability of organizations to learn lessons has been touched upon in previous chapters, and this topic provides a convenient link to awareness and the implementation of an effective safety culture, as alluded to above. However, the introduction of new technologies can and does have unpredictable consequences, which is one reason why the 'disruptive' tag is such an apt one. Machine-learning, by definition, removes the human element from at least part of the learning process and inevitably changes the overall cultural setting within which learning can take place. Just as importantly, we only have to consider the cliff-edge drop in general awareness in public places due to our dependency on mobile devices to understand the potential safety parallels within an organizational setting.

Within a safety context, the second opportunity to understand more about the links between safety performance and resilience, referred to above, relates to risk-taking behaviours. Until such time as human intervention is eliminated entirely, safety performance will continue to be influenced by the appropriateness of individual decision-making and by an individual's approach to risk. The approach adopted is not just relevant to the individual(s) in question, and the likelihood or otherwise of injury, but also very much to the safe delivery of operational processes and therefore to the safety of others both inside and outside of the organization. As such, assessment of resilience capability should identify safety risk-taking as a major contributory factor, as for example the ORCM achieves through reference to APPROACH within the list of behaviours and outcomes.

Just as resilience is much more than simply a set of conditions created through having a dedicated cadre of highly resilient individuals around which organizational activity is built, so too safety performance. However, understanding and ensuring that the messages around what constitutes acceptable risk-taking behaviours are effectively communicated and acted upon remains critical for all our risk-related considerations. From the perspective of safety performance, this presents a unique challenge for the organization, namely the need to understand risk-taking behaviours at an individual level, in all aspects of the individual's life, and what the implications of this might be. For example, and whilst this might only be relevant to a relatively small number of the organization's staff, ie those working in safety-critical roles, what do we really know about an individual's risk-taking behaviours and how have we reflected this within our organization and in how we deliver products and services?

Data can be sought to assist the organization in a better understanding of risk-taking behaviour. For example, if near-misses or incidents are indicative of such behaviours, then investigators should ensure that the decision-making is mapped and analysed at an individual level in order to help build as comprehensive a picture as possible. Similarly, and somewhat paradoxically perhaps, higher than normal levels of productivity or reduced cycle times might also be indicative of such behaviours if the trade-off between safety and productivity still holds true.

Understanding risk-taking and its implications for the organization is not so much about the need to create intervention strategies, based on some mechanical or arbitrary scale of sensation-seeking, for example, but is more about the value in seeking to understand and pinpoint different perceptions of risk and how this is translated into activities and behaviours which might be relevant to safety performance and therefore to resilience. As such, practitioners may wish to engage with the organization's recognized safety, employment and behavioural experts in attempting to answer the following questions:

- Is the organization able to identify risk-taking at an individual level and/or map risk-taking to existing demographic data, for example in relation to age?
- What does the organization's current risk-taking profile look like in respect of safety-critical roles and what strategies might be employed to deliver future change?

- Can the organization's pension or insurance schemes help to improve understanding and appreciation profiling techniques and how they can be applied to real-world issues?
- What are the implications for commercial risks and how might the organization's strategies for communicating wider risk appetite information need to be adapted as a result?
- Is the organization willing to undertake and/or support further research in areas such as the psychology of safety, attitudes and risk perception and the safety impact of organizational climate and culture?

Finally, practitioners should ensure that their chosen model for assessing and reporting on resilience capability adequately reflects the importance of risk-taking within a safety context. The ORCM achieves this as part of the defined list of concepts, most notably through linkages to compliance and to the category of AWARENESS. For example, whilst a compliance mindset doesn't easily translate to an understanding of recreational risk-taking or 'sensation-seeking', it might help to provide insight in respect of those individuals with poor safety records.

The importance of security

Security is an often-implied aspect of organizational resilience, with the most frequent references perhaps being to cyber- and/or information security. Those with an 'ecological' bent might consider food and water security, and others will immediately be focused on physical security. The prolonged Brexit saga in the UK during the period from 2016 to 2020 and to a lesser extent the increase in trade tensions between the United States and China, Mexico and others, has also highlighted the importance of energy and supply chain security. For many, security remains fundamentally a preventative control – a 'locking up' activity. It is perceived as simply being about closing down a particular vulnerability. As part of our examination of resilience, we will consider security from two less familiar, although critically important perspectives, namely, that of an 'insider act' (not to be confused with insider trading), and also the security of the organization's supply chain.

The UK Government's Centre for the Protection of National Infrastructure (CPNI) defines an insider as 'someone who (knowingly or unknowingly) misuses legitimate access to commit a malicious act or damage their employer'. This definition therefore covers both the intentional and unintentional act. In addition to the application of ever more sophisticated controls designed to prevent an insider from exploiting IT systems, a significant amount of attention is also being given to the behavioural aspects of insider acts and how these can be used to identify individuals and then intervene. As outlined by CPNI:

> An insider could be a full-time or part-time employee, a contractor or even a business partner. An insider could deliberately seek to join your organization to conduct an insider act, or may be triggered to act at some point during their employment. Employees may also inadvertently trigger security breaches through ignorance of rules, or deliberate non-compliance (due to pressure of work).[11]

As highlighted a number of times within this book already, resilience is not an event-focused concept, and yet it is perhaps easy to think of the insider threat only in event-related terms. Whilst practitioners should remember that the ability to respond well to a business continuity event and/or to a crisis will speak directly to the organization's short-term and long-term success, insider acts may or may not result in a specific event, or series of events, and furthermore organizations may or may not respond to them as such in any case. From a resilience perspective we are less interested in the motivations of the insider or exhibited behaviours and more interested in the effects any activity can have on the organization and the choice of controls which are available to help in mitigation.

The key for the organization is to identify high-risk activities and to adopt an appropriate and informed stance in respect of particular roles. It is also important that practitioners and security professionals recognize the specialist knowledge necessary for an effective assessment of risks, such as with the insider; for example, an appreciation of physical security threats does not in itself provide the insight and understanding necessary for managing insider-related risks. As alluded to within the CPNI definition above, insider acts can take various forms and be based upon a range of motivational factors for the individual. They can take both digital and non-digital forms and can include theft, extortion and even violence or the suspension (through some form of denial or forced interruption) of critical business processes. From a resilience perspective, and regardless of the anatomy of the act, the impact on the organization can therefore be significant.

There is a wealth of case study information relating to the insider threat which is freely available online. Although focusing on US national security issues, organizations such as the Center for Development of Security Excellence (CDSE) provide a useful resource which expose the range of insider-related activity which has come to the attention of investigators in recent years. One such example, the story which broke at Tesla in June 2018, was a little unusual for a number of reasons, whilst in other ways it appeared to be quite mainstream. It is likely that only a tiny proportion of insider acts ever come to the attention of the public, and whilst the Tesla story played out in full view of both employees and the media, it is often very difficult for those on the outside to confirm exactly what went on and why. Nevertheless, the Tesla story, as widely reported at the time and summarized below in an article by CNBC, highlighted some of the basic elements of a typical insider act, namely sabotage, access authorizations and data theft:

- Tesla CEO Elon Musk sent an e-mail to all employees on… alleging there was a saboteur within the company's ranks.
- Musk alleged this employee tweaked code on internal products and sent company data out without authorization.[12]

As with any control measure, particular care should be taken not to overstate the importance of those associated with the insider threat. Within the suite of measures employed by the organization to help assess and report on resilience capability it is normal to rely on the presence of controls associated with various aspects of security.

However, the insider threat provides a particularly good example of where controls may be ineffective and yet because they are operating as intended, undue weight is attached to them during the assurance process. An example of such a control would be 'background checking' of employees or contractors, and because of this considerations for the organization might include the following:

- The authority given to recruiting managers to potentially ignore concerns flagged through pre-employment screening, it being only the completion of, or timeframe for the screening itself which is often reported.
- The appropriateness of pre-employment screening, particularly if certain activities and roles have been identified as high risk.
- The likely limitations associated with repeat background checks for existing employees or contractors, including the challenges in being able to assess psychological aspects such as loyalty or allegiance, the need to obtain repeat consent, the challenge to employee relations when potential problems are identified and the checks only ever being valid or relevant at a particular moment in time.

With regard to supply chain security, many in the UK will remember a spike of (often violent and unlawful) protest action against suppliers and supporters of Huntington Life Sciences, much of which dates back to 2004 and before. In sticking with the animal welfare theme, 2018 saw the emergence of widespread action in protest against the damage done by the international trade in palm oil. In April 2018, protestors targeted the European offices of Unilever, with some protestors wearing orang-utan costumes. As reported by Reuters, Unilever owns many household name brands in foods, beverages, cleaning agents and personal care products and buys some 1.3 million tonnes of palm oil a year, making it, according to Greenpeace, the world's single largest buyer of the product.[13] Greenpeace claims the peatland forests of Indonesia, one of the last remaining habitats of the orang-utan, are being damaged to provide palm oil.

There is undoubtedly some degree of vulnerability associated with any activity which involves transfer, movement and exchange, but those which involve physical processes, or which lend themselves to the disruption of (often unrelated) physical processes are particularly attractive to protestors. As such, physical security considerations need to extend beyond the parameters which may initially be suggested by the organization's supply chain connections, but it is these very connections which should inform their assessment of physical security risks. It is perhaps only when protestors begin to have an impact at a community or societal level, as happened internationally in 2019 with the Extinction Rebellion movement and with anti-government demonstrations in Hong Kong, that organizations can claim the immediate security solution also sits within a wider sphere of influence.

The following quote from PwC sums up the importance of a resilient supply chain:

> Supply chains today are complex and global, and for many are regularly disrupted, often opaque and increasingly regulated. Coupled with the megatrends of accelerating urbanization, resource scarcity and the breath-taking pace of technology proliferation, supply chains continue to rapidly evolve and transform. Yet, the majority of companies do not regularly assess the resilience of their supply chain.[14]

As part of the above, organizations also seek to mitigate the potentially disruptive effects of protests and demonstrations through developing contingency plans and business continuity arrangements, learning from other, related arrangements such as those relevant to industrial action. In respect of today's global and multifarious supply chains, the threat posed by protests and demonstrations requires organizations to consider the following:

- access to, and understanding of, national or international digital solutions and intelligence, for example in respect of local social media use;
- knowledge of hard supply chain interfaces, for example those which involve national and commercial borders and/or payment triggers for duty and other taxes;
- understanding of the local and regional political and cultural situation, including access to specialist in-country knowledge, for

example through government agencies, supply partners or third-party organizations;
- dates within the commercial calendar which might attract particular attention, for example shareholder meetings, publication of results and investor presentations or contract announcements;
- adequacy and suitability of incident response arrangements, together with the impact of any ongoing incidents elsewhere within the organization.

Investing in resilience

As mentioned in the examination of the ORCM in Chapter 5, defining resilience by reference to the organization's growth and long-term success, product and service quality should always form a significant part of our thinking. Product and service quality has multiple dimensions as an indicator of resilience, for example in respect of a meaningful focus on customer service which so many organizations neglected for years, or through an organization's investment plans for replacement or upgrading of an ageing asset base. It is also evident within case study references, for example those included in Chapter 4, particularly where organizations have been undone by no longer having a product or service which is relevant or appealing.

Many articles have been written over recent years which effectively point to the neglect of customer experience within organizations and indeed across entire sectors, making the implied connection with resilience through loss of brand loyalty and failure to build a sufficiently strong reputation. Much of this suggests that Board members have actually been looking in the wrong direction and have been doing so for some time. However accurate this conclusion may be, two things are certain: firstly, customer experience is no more the 'missing link' to resilience capability than is the resilience characteristics of the organization's most senior staff; and secondly, the road to service excellence is rarely toll-free.

Of course, there is nothing unique about service excellence in terms of requiring investment, but a significant proportion of references do appear in print with little or no reference to cost or to the impact on financing. Admittedly, investment may be limited to implementing some element of behavioural change for staff but even so neither the direct nor indirect costs should ever be ignored. It is also important that suitable measures are in place prior to any investment being made in order that changes in performance or results can be properly monitored and reported, rather than costs being carved out from an existing training or marketing budget, which simply results in a lack of visibility.

Investment in resilience capability is an everyday occurrence for many organizations, but not all such activity would readily to be badged as such. Spend on cyber-security, for example, would qualify for most people as investing in resilience, as indeed would any spend directly associated with disaster-prevention or recovery infrastructure. Similarly, investment in asset renewal or upgrade programmes could easily be described in resilience terms, particularly where reliability or efficiency data for post-investment assets are already known. As a general rule, it is likely to be those investments which are less directly associated either with a specific threat or well-understood metric or target which are not always considered as enabling resilience.

Regardless of our starting point, the challenge for the organization remains being able to identify and then deliver the investment necessary to build resilience capability in the way suggested by an assessment – a challenge made all the more difficult as many of the elements which contribute to resilience are new, hard to measure or they even sit beyond the conventional boundaries of the organization. For example, the collaborative networks which are so vital to building and maintaining resilience may require some rather speculative investments on the part of the organization, particularly given the diverse nature of the communities and industry bodies or associations upon which resilience relies.

With the need to ensure clarity and consistency of measurement, practitioners are advised to consider how traditional approaches to investment can be applied to the breadth of elements which go to make up an organization's resilience capability. One such approach is introduced by a report published by The Resilience Shift in 2017, titled *Resilience Return on Investment (RROI)*, which focuses on investment calculations within engineering and infrastructure projects.[15] The value of the report, as captured within its conclusion, is to 'promote resilience engineering to integrate resilience practices into infrastructure projects', and this is something which all practitioners should be willing to embrace.

It is perhaps the discipline and the promise of a defined process for assessing the resilience value of investment which is particularly attractive in this approach, rather than some of the detail promoted within the report itself. For example, project processes are already well defined, and the skills associated with project management and delivery are already captured within the ORCM; it is their application to investment planning, from scope and business case through to implementation and optimization, which the organization needs to focus on. Similarly, we already have definitions for resilience which are holistic, and which have taken us beyond the outdated 'flex and rebound' approach – we don't need a separate definition of resilience engineering which potentially puts that into reverse.

Another aspect of investment, of course, concerns those organizations such as fund management firms and insurers which are investing in resilience as part of their core business and are selecting particular companies, sectors, strategies or causes, or which are providing products and service which are directly linked to resilience performance. In many cases, investing in resilience is simply taken to mean investments deliberately aimed at mitigating climate risks, the rationale for which might not always be consistent one organization to another. Whether as part of some voluntary sector-specific initiative or a reaction to targeted shareholder pressure, the potential for investment to act on societal-level threats is widely recognized and many large corporates have now had to explain their sustainability credentials to investors and shareholder groups for a number of years.

In another context, and again without wishing to unpick or judge the rationale, investment is simply taken to mean a donation, often given at a community or regional level and often in response to a specific disaster event or appeal. However, such investment can also be much more preventative in nature, and also quite sophisticated; for example, guidelines were published in the United States following hurricane Sandy in 2012 which identify the need for performance metrics and structured analysis in support on infrastructure decisions.[16] For any organization, and as we have already identified through the ORCM, the emphasis on community resilience is likely to yield wider and longer-term benefits beyond the relief of disaster-specific impacts.

Other models

Models and frameworks are important in allowing practitioners to interpret and apply the principles of resilience and to do so in a clear and defined manner. The lack of consistency between models, as already acknowledged, can present a major challenge for organizations looking to learn lessons and to understand more about their own particular strengths and weaknesses; however, an appreciation of alternative approaches can still prove extremely valuable. Two such approaches are highlighted here and are presented both as alternatives to the ORCM and also as complements to it – they provide an alternative perspective on organizational resilience rather than introducing something which is fundamentally or radically different or at odds with the principles I have already introduced and which are presented within the ORCM.

Before we dive into the detail of these two alternative models, it is worth acknowledging that, just as organizations mature and their understanding of what constitutes resilience capability changes over time, the models and frameworks against which capability is measured can and do change. Furthermore, change can also be apparent with regard to a commercial organization's use of its own proprietary model, for example in how assessment activity is supported or in how licensing arrangements may be used.

Internal assurance functions which operate self-assessment activities for an organization can be affected by both aspects of this change, either as they seek to adopt or mimic a model which they have been exposed to previously, or as a result of knowledge and expertise being built up within the organization over a period of time. It is perhaps the dangers associated with attempting to take on a model or framework which has been kept deliberately hidden, for example by a consultancy firm, which practitioners should be particularly sensitive to. It can be very tempting to adopt an assessment and reporting template previously used by an external expert as a means of providing the Board with what are consistent references and labels, but unless the model has been properly and openly described, and of course properly understood, any such assessment is likely to be flawed and next to impossible to deliver consistently. What might look like an attractive option may turn out to be of very limited value.

The resilience models presented by Resilient Organisations (RO)

Resilient Organisations, based in New Zealand, offers services and undertakes research in this field and does so using experts with a global reputation. The group offers access to diagnostic and benchmarking tools and provides an outline of its current resilience model and the structure which this takes through its online pages. It boasts a strong research heritage, much of which has a country-specific focus, and has a wealth of real-world experience and references to draw upon and to support how it presents organizational resilience to a wider audience.

The group's work has clearly been massively influenced by the 2010/11 earthquakes in Christchurch, as reported in the following case study. Some of the early work, published as research papers, outlined a resilience model which was clearly dynamic and still developing and one which referenced back to a series of specific events and research encounters. Now, we know that resilience is not an event-focused concept, but we must acknowledge that an organization's ability to deal successfully with emergencies and disruptive events has a significant impact on overall resilience capability. In this particular case, the anchoring of research against a specific set of events, well known and highly impactful in the region, is actually very helpful and undoubtedly lends a degree of authority and relevance to the group's approach. Research which allows us access to the detail of individual case study organizations, and which provides insight into their resilience capability or profiles is always likely to be particularly powerful.

THE CHRISTCHURCH EARTHQUAKES

On Tuesday 22 February 2011, a magnitude 6.3 earthquake caused severe damage in Christchurch and Lyttelton, in New Zealand's South Island, killing 185 people and injuring several thousand. The earthquake's epicentre was near Lyttelton, just 10 km southeast of Christchurch's central business district. It occurred nearly six months after the 4 September 2010 earthquake.

Although not as powerful as the magnitude 7.1 earthquake the previous year, this earthquake occurred on a shallow fault line that was close to the city, so the shaking was particularly destructive. The earthquake brought down many buildings damaged the previous September, especially older bricks-and-mortar buildings.

Research published by the group in 2007 referenced a number of resilience indicators, several of which were grouped under the heading of 'Adaptive Capacity', and this reference to adaptation has been something which emerges time and again since then and in many different references to organizational decision-making and capability.[17] The emphasis on decision-making, and on those making decisions, highlights the importance of culture, leadership and organizational structures and these aspects should be evident within any resilience model. References to adaptation inevitably focus attention on an organization's changed circumstances, and to the responses to those changes, and this is what makes it such an important element within a modern organizational context. Importantly, the reference to adaptation also draws attention to the organization's approach to risk and how this can be used as an indicator of capability.

Further research following the 2010/11 earthquakes resulted in a framework of 'Adaptive Resilience' being presented, which included the following summary description in highlighting why some organizations performed particularly well (relative to others) following these specific events:

> This research showed that adaptive resilience was the key to this success. This type of resilience is about what an organization actually does during a sudden upheaval. It involves adapting to a situation that is outside your experience, and often outside your plans.
>
> Adaptive resilience involves the whole organization being agile, coordinated, and learning rapidly. This type of resilience is dynamic. It continues to respond to unpredictable developments as they unfold. It is much more than just the personal resilience of individual employees.[18]

From the model, elements identified as being critical to the organization's ability to adapt include 'collaboration', 'leadership type', 'learning organization' and 'valuing employees'. Many of these elements and their constituent parts can easily be mapped to the 'concepts' listed within the ORCM, being very 'behaviour', 'people' and 'outcome' oriented. However, it should be noted that the emphasis within the RO model is quite specific and relatively narrow and is built primarily around responses to sudden or dramatic changes in the organizational environment.

For information, the current model presented via the group's website suggests resilience is defined by reference to a set of 13 indicators, the detail of which is organized around three distinct attributes – 'Leadership and Culture', 'Change Ready', and 'Networks and Relationships' – and is not presented with any direct reference to adaptation.

The organizational resilience report presented by Cranfield School of Management and BSI

Research and analysis by Professor David Denyer of Cranfield School of Management, published with BSI in 2017, presents concepts and methodologies which provide an extremely valuable insight and approach to organizational resilience. Supplemented by case study references, the true value of this type of work, besides the fact that it is easily digestible, is that it seeks to explain resilience by reference to what is actually happening within an organization – the forces, pressures and influences which need to be examined and understood in an organizational setting. These aspects of course are common, in some combination or other, within almost any organization and notions of competition and balance provide powerful ways of considering the background to resilience capability and to how it may have developed in the way that it has.

Whilst not always applicable as an assessment tool, this work is undoubtedly useful in bringing the key concepts of resilience to life and also in explaining why the different aspects of an assessment framework are present. Whilst many organizations and practitioners will not necessarily recognize the 'evolution of thinking' described in the report, either conceptually or as a reflection of their own experiences or individual journeys, the idea of managing conflict or tension with an organization, and the need to establish an effective working balance as it seeks to manage and deliver on its strategic objectives, is a compelling and natural one. As the report identifies, some sort of balance must be established, however imperfectly, as 'it should be noted that a preoccupation with one particular dimension could create blind spots that can impair Organizational Resilience'.[19]

The report describes an organization which is balancing its approach across two simple axes –referred to as 'progressive' versus 'defensive', and 'consistency' versus 'flexibility' – managing the tensions which inevitably exist therein whilst guarding against the erosion of performance over time. For each of the four dimensions listed, the report provides a summary description and also highlights some of the potential issues associated with each. For example, in referring to a 'defensive' approach or perspective – what the report refers to as 'preventative control' – organizational losses are minimized, value is preserved and standardization, stability and compliance are flagged as key concerns. Whilst recognizing that organizational resilience requires the application of control and compliance, the report suggests that weaknesses of this singular focus would include lack of flexibility and agility.

The report also introduces a specific methodology which describes key practices which help to explain how organizations have achieved resilience capability – the '4Sight' methodology. This methodology outlines what could be described as processes or approaches for managing activity within the organization, much in the same way that one may adopt a high-level project methodology to manage the creation and delivery of a new product to market.

The 4Sight methodology is defined by reference to four individual processes, namely, 'foresight', 'insight', 'oversight' and 'hindsight', which capture a range of aspects such as horizon scanning, risk management, employee engagement, governance and organizational learning. Collectively, these processes can also be used to test and challenge the organization's approach to specific threats and opportunities at a strategic level and are described in the report as follows:

> The four processes of the 4Sight model enable an organization to respond to and create disruptions and opportunities. Creative responses to emerging threats and opportunities can only be achieved by stimulating innovative ideas and new ways of working, drawing on multiple perspectives and interdisciplinary teams, or co-creating with customers and consumers.

Conclusion

Organizational resilience is one of those concepts which needs to be well grounded, and when it comes to introducing it, context and positioning is everything. Some of this grounding can be found, for example, within the case study examples in Chapter 4, but being able to relate resilience capability to emerging technologies or to well-established disciplines such as safety is particularly powerful. One of the reasons for this is that such references allow the practitioner to better signpost the organization's unique resilience journey rather than having to rely solely on a predefined and generic model or framework.

Much in the same way as a weak assessment process, real-world application of resilience theory, or rather its absence, presents the practitioner with one of their most important potential obstacles to progress. Within any organizational setting, not only will emerging technologies have already made an impact, but a clear strategy may already have emerged – the same will be true for safety and security – and this simply cannot be discounted when thinking through what is needed to enhance future resilience capability. Similarly, compliance will undoubtedly feature in almost any organizational setting, and for some of course this may be significant enough to overshadow many other influences and drivers.

The message for practitioners from this chapter is that key aspects of organizational activity should not only be mapped to the ORCM or other resilience models and applied in the context of a capability assessment, but also dissected to some degree in order that further value can be extracted for improvement planning purposes. For example, we have already identified in Chapter 5 how compliance can be used to support our capability assessment, but practitioners also need to be able to understand and utilize the organization's approach to compliance as a planning and communication aid. Many organizations have experienced a strong move away from single-focus compliance and enforcement over recent years and towards analytics, agility and flexibility. As highlighted in a 2015 paper by Deloitte, organizations have also reported an increased emphasis on 'integrity and ethics' rather than on following a 'letter-of-the-law' approach to compliance.[20]

This, together with the impact which emerging technologies are likely to have on the organization's approach to compliance, will be relevant to how any capability assessment is received and will need to be clearly attached to any improvement planning which takes place as a result. Related questions for the practitioner might include the following:

- Has compliance been viewed as a barrier to change or innovation, and if so, have new strategies been adopted in response to the rise of disruptive technologies?

- Are opportunities being missed due to 'gold-plating' of assets or arrangements and by generally doing more than is required? If so, has the organization's actual compliance position been obscured?
- Are staff able to innovate and take risks in the knowledge that corporate appetite relating to compliance is clearly defined and well understood? How is this being reflected across new technology applications?

Other resilience models and approaches can also help the practitioner assess and discuss resilience-related topics. The additional uncertainty associated with disruptive technologies can be viewed in terms of conflict or tension, for example between the known and the unknown aspects of a compliant position, and the management of tensions within a resilience context forms an integral part of the approach outlined by Cranfield/BSI – this being the potential conflict or schism between compliance (often viewed as consistency) and flexibility.

Both of the external sources for resilience frameworks referenced within this chapter are worthy of further examination and the reader is encouraged to engage with them and others they might find, if only for an alternative and informed perspective on change. Unlike many such sources, both recognize and embrace the strategic nature of resilience and the need for organizations to approach challenges in a holistic and inclusive manner.

Models of organizational resilience tend to focus on many things and seek to tie together strands of organizational activity considered to be most relevant in establishing and maintaining resilience capability. However, it is all too easy to get lost in this detail, to focus on the definitions and the mechanics and the process of assessment and to forget the success and growth aspects of resilience and the need for it to be grounded within the organization's reality.

The final chapter, Chapter 8, engages with the principles of performance improvement and aspects relevant to how an organization can best seek to close gaps in resilience capability.

Endnotes

1 Denyer, D and Pilbeam, P (2015) *Managing Change in Extreme Contexts (Routledge Studies in Organizational Change and Development)*, referenced in Denyer, D (2017) *Organizational Resilience: A Summary of academic evidence, business insights and new thinking*, BSI and Cranfield School of Management. Available from: www.cranfield.ac.uk/som/case-studies/organizational-resilience-a-summary-of-academic-evidence-business-insights-and-new-thinking (archived at https://perma.cc/H8KF-WZD6)

2 Organisation for Economic Co-operation and Development (2000) *Reducing the Risk of Policy Failure: Challenges For Regulatory Compliance*. Available from: www.oecd.org/regreform/regulatory-policy/1910833.pdf (archived at https://perma.cc/F8UD-3YLA)

3 Kinsella, B (2019) Why tech giants are so desperate to provide your voice assistant, *Harvard Business Review*, 7 May. Available from: hbr.org/2019/05/why-tech-giants-are-so-desperate-to-provide-your-voice-assistant (archived at https://perma.cc/Y6C8-HGS8)

4 Folke, C, Carpenter, S, Elmqvist, T, Gunderson, L, Holling, C and Walker, B (2002) Resilience and sustainable development: Building adaptive capacity in a world of transformations, *A Journal of the Human Environment*, **31** (5), pp 437–40. Available from: cepd.cap.utah.edu/wp-content/uploads/sites/10/2018/08/resilience_sustainable_dev_gunderson_holling_walker.pdf (archived at https://perma.cc/YLP9-5YAY)

5 World Economic Forum (WEF) (2018) *Insight Report, Our Shared Digital Future: Building an Inclusive, Trustworthy and Sustainable Digital Society*. Available from (as an abbreviated quote): www3.weforum.org/docs/WEF_Our_Shared_Digital_Future_Report_2018.pdf (archived at https://perma.cc/K3WU-HFAQ). Previously available from the WEF Mapping of Global Transformations reports. Available from: intelligence.weforum.org/ (archived at https://perma.cc/H58S-325E)

6 World Economic Forum (WEF) (2018) *Insight Report, Our Shared Digital Future: Building an inclusive, trustworthy and sustainable digital society*. Available from: www3.weforum.org/docs/WEF_Our_Shared_Digital_Future_Report_2018.pdf (archived at https://perma.cc/K3WU-HFAQ)

7 United Nations reports, such as Global Outlook Report (2019). Available from: www.un.org/en/climatechange/reports.shtml (archived at https://perma.cc/5VG7-TXRD)

8 Health and Safety Executive (2011) *High Reliability Organisations: A review of the literature*. Available from: www.hse.gov.uk/research/rrpdf/rr899.pdf (archived at https://perma.cc/7XMS-6QPL)

9 Weick, K and Sutcliffe, K (2007) *Managing the Unexpected Resilient Performance in an Age of Uncertainty*

10 D'Oliveira, T and Mário, C (2010) *Organizational safety: From safety culture to organizational resilience*. Available from: www.researchgate.net/publication/267926244_Organizational_safety_From_safety_culture_to_organizational_resilience (archived at https://perma.cc/QGG2-5DYC)

11 Centre for the Protection of National Infrastructure website (nd) *Reducing Insider Risk*. Available from: www.cpni.gov.uk/reducing-insider-risk (archived at https://perma.cc/VY5F-N4EA)

12 Kolodny, L (2108) Elon Musk emails employees about 'extensive and damaging sabotage' by employee, *CNBC*, 19 June. Available from: www.cnbc.com/2018/06/18/elon-musk-email-employee-conducted-extensive-and-damaging-sabotage.html (archived at https://perma.cc/CA4S-HWRE)

13 Ormsby, A (2008) Palm oil protests target Unilever sites, *Reuters*, 21 April. Available from: uk.reuters.com/article/uk-britain-unilever/palm-oil-protests-target-unilever-sites-idUKL2153984120080421 (archived at https://perma.cc/SE4V-LST4)

14 PWC (nd) *Supply Chain Resilience*. Available from: www.pwc.com/us/en/services/consulting/risk-regulatory/supply-chain-resilience.html (archived at https://perma.cc/75ZY-BH3N)

15 The Resilience Shift (2017) *Resilience Return on Investment (RROI): Agenda setting scoping studies summary report*. Available from: www.resilienceshift.org/wp-content/uploads/2017/10/046_Resilience-Return-on-Investment.pdf (archived at https://perma.cc/LJ8J-4DN5)

16 Rand Corporation (2014) *The Hurricane Sandy Rebuilding Task Force's Infrastructure Resilience Guidelines: An initial assessment of implementation by federal agencies*. Available from: www.rand.org/content/dam/rand/pubs/research_reports/RR800/RR841/RAND_RR841.pdf (archived at https://perma.cc/A3GP-9C8Q)

17 Resilient Organisations (2007) *Resilience Management: A Framework for Assessing and Improving the Resilience of Organisations*, research report 2007/01. Available from: ir.canterbury.ac.nz/bitstream/handle/10092/9488/12610600_resilience%20management%20research%20report%20resorgs%2007-01.pdf?sequence=1 (archived at https://perma.cc/YCV3-SAN8)

18 Resilient Organisations (nd) *Building Adaptive Resilience: High-performing today, agile tomorrow, thriving in the future*. Available from: ir.canterbury.ac.nz/bitstream/handle/10092/12208/Building_AdaptiveRes_PRINT2.pdf?sequence=1 (archived at https://perma.cc/G6TV-3RX2)

19 Denyer, D (2017) *Organizational Resilience: A summary of academic evidence, business insights and new thinking*, BSI and Cranfield School of Management. Available from: www.cranfield.ac.uk/som/case-studies/organizational-resilience-a-summary-of-academic-evidence-business-insights-and-new-thinking (archived at https://perma.cc/H8KF-WZD6)

20 Deloitte (2015) The changing role of compliance. Available from: www2.deloitte.com/content/dam/Deloitte/gr/Documents/financial-services/gr_fs_the_changing_role_of_compliance_en_noexp.pdf (archived at https://perma.cc/T8GE-JWSB)

8

Application and implementation

This final chapter addresses the need for managers and practitioners to consider the realities of working with a structured assessment/ maturity model, and also the initiatives or programmes required to drive resilience performance in their organizations. I touched briefly on programmes and a structured approach in considering the nature of transformation in Chapter 7, specifically with reference to external consultancy providers, and whilst this may be the reality for some organizations, others will be approaching the need to deliver change, having deliberately set out to assess and understand resilience capability themselves and without the need for third-party assistance. Either way, I am assuming at this point that the organization is in receipt of a report which highlights gaps, deficits or weaknesses in its resilience capability and for which there is some appetite for improvement.

The starting point for any meaningful improvement effort involves a degree of appreciation as to what needs to be done, and as such this requires us to revisit some of the assurance detail we first introduced in Chapter 6, but only in so far as it helps to emphasize the importance of ensuring that the correct resources and capabilities are present to deliver that assurance activity. If viewed as a simple technique, which is of course a monumental oversimplification, the reasonable expectation of managers and others within the organization likely to be exposed to resilience assessment would be that it was accompanied by some form of preparation and forewarning – plans, training, support and communications, for example. Similarly, the expectation of those likely to be in receipt of any findings is that the improvement exercise is completed at pace and with the minimum of disturbance and cost.

The other main consideration is that improvement resources are inevitably limited, and that any resilience-oriented activity is likely to be competing with other discrete activity and expenditure, much of which might already have been determined as critical in helping the organization achieve its strategic objectives. The organization's true capacity for 'additional' work or offline activity is always a difficult thing to measure but that does not mean that capacity constraints, real or imagined, will not be flagged on a regular basis as the organization seeks to challenge and prioritize any new undertaking. The notion of 'limited capacity', not to be confused with 'resilience capability', is fundamentally a comment about the organization's resources and the availability of specific skills, such as those which the organization relies upon to manage and deliver its projects.

This chapter considers the resources and capability available within the organization, for the purposes of delivering improved performance, and how this might be organized, what a delivery programme might look like and the associated requirements for performance data and other information. It is vital that the resource and planning requirements associated with delivering improved performance are not confused with those dedicated to response and recovery activities following an incident – this is about improving capability, not responding to or recovering from a crisis event. Obviously, the resources in question might in some degree be the same, but the requirement and their application is quite distinct.

The chapter begins with a recognition of the need to ensure that resilience is clearly and consistently hosted across the organization, emphasizing the need for a clear strategy which allows the Board to capture and articulate its priorities and plans. Just as it is essential to establish a strategy for assessment, as outlined in Chapter 6, so it is for implementing and bridging the capability gap of which management have now been appraised. Implementing strategy requires the setting of improvement objectives and it is these which will alert stakeholders inside and outside the organization as to the Board's immediate areas of concern and to the initiatives which will probably feature for inclusion in future agendas and business updates.

Improvement strategy

If we approach strategy as a process rather than as a singular document or statement, then we are more likely to be on the correct path. Strategy describes the manner through which understanding is gained and through which decisions are made – it speaks to the steps which allow the intentions of the Board to be distilled and articulated and it results in the organization's priorities being confirmed. Set against clearly defined objectives, it is strategy which allows individual initiatives to take shape and which enables the organization to develop meaningful improvement plans.

The challenges faced by the organization will only become apparent when capability has been properly assessed, and it is the need for assessment and reporting of resilience capability which should mark the beginning of this process. I touched upon the need for an assessment strategy already in Chapter 6 and will return to the subject again later in this chapter; it really does colour everything, going well beyond how the organization engages specifically with the assessment activity. How the organization chooses to go about the assessment will have an enormous impact on the quality and usability of the information which management and the Board get to consider. In turn, this will influence how the organization thinks about improvement objectives and what these look like in respect of the ORCM or other model of resilience capability and maturity.

As mentioned already, resilience is a holistic concept and one which seeks to describe the organization's capability in the context of the communities, markets and sectors within which it operates. The strategy for resilience should be similarly holistic in nature and recognize the needs, expectations and capabilities of those within its broader network. Importantly, therefore, strategy has to factor in the organization's ability to address the challenges it has identified, informed by its network, which in turn will determine what it believes are actionable objectives. It is at this point perhaps that one of the characteristics of the strategy process becomes more apparent – this is not a quick process, or at least not if it is to yield meaningful and lasting value.

It is likely that the Board will be involved in building resilience strategy over a series of meetings or events, and for most organizations this will inevitably take some time. The validation of assessment information and the creation and completion of a formalized report takes time enough, particularly when the inevitable review and rework of the report is taken into account. The subsequent consideration and discussion at Board level simply adds to the cycle. Practitioners need to ensure they do not remain idle during what can be a protracted process as the detail and findings from the assessment need to remain current and reflective of changes which may have taken place within the organization. Efforts should be made to ensure that any updates or amendments are available for consideration as the report is considered and that any significant alterations are highlighted.

Outside of significant structural change, it would perhaps be unrealistic to expect the assessment of behaviours and attitudes within the organization to change significantly over just a period of a few months – our relationship with the organization of which we are a part tends not to change that quickly. However, it is quite possible that the assessment and reporting (and consideration) of resilience capability takes place either side of financial or regulatory reporting deadlines. Similarly, it is quite possible that new products or services will have been released to market, that new assets will have become operational or that specific events will have taken place which reflect on the suitability of the organization's skills and competencies. Such changes need not be considered material, but it is not unreasonable for the report's audience to expect us to have considered their potential impact on the findings.

Just as the resilience of the organization only makes sense within the context of the environment which supports it, the Board's strategy for improving resilience capability should always be considered within the context of the organization's existing priorities and initiatives. I have already identified some of the key internal connections for resilience in Chapter 7; for example, safety and security and the significance of crisis management capabilities and contingency planning activities. What is particularly important is that the strategy is clear and coherent; it needs to make sense to those inside and outside of the organization and the way in which it seeks to draw together the threads of existing plans and initiatives should be obvious and well informed.

There is no predetermined model or approach to how the organization might seek to integrate existing activities into a broader improvement strategy to boost resilience capability, and nor should there be. Introducing a coherent strategy for resilience reveals nothing about what the Board might consider appropriate in respect of additional governance or programme-level structures, and there should certainly be no presumption that any activity loosely connected with resilience should now be consumed or delivered under a single 'banner'.

How the organization intends to position itself to deliver improved resilience capability will of course be translated into a series of aims and objectives. Regardless of the nature of these objectives, be they tangible or somewhat aspirational, they should be anchored not just in the reality of the organization but also in the model chosen to facilitate the most recent assessment. This not only allows for consistent use of language as strategic-level objectives are cascaded down through the organization, but also makes for consistent assessment comparators, ie comparing like with like in the future.

Resilience describes a successful organization. However, in defining an approach and committing the organization to a particular course of action, the Board also needs to agree how exactly success will be determined, at least in terms of known capability gaps. To some readers this will appear to be such an obvious point that it should barely warrant a mention, particularly given that we have already highlighted the need for improvement objectives to be established, but reality suggests this point is frequently neglected, sometimes entirely.

As already outlined, any gap in resilience capability will be a function of the organization's chosen assessment approach, and the way it is understood and described will be determined by the model or framework against which the assessment has been undertaken – what we find will be determined by the type of examination carried out and on the tools we have used. The same, of course, will be true when it comes to wishing to confirm the progress that has, or should have been made going forward.

With this mind, the strategy of the Board should therefore embrace the fullest meaning of what it means to 'implement' a plan or solution, and 'success' should ultimately be defined in relation to how improvements in resilience capability can be evidenced. Implementation cannot be considered or presented in isolation of an intended outcome and is only meaningful in the context of what has actually been achieved. For example, a plan may consist of a sequence or series of individual actions. To be considered as complete or executed, it would not be unreasonable for the customer to require some sort of confirmatory evidence. However, 'implementation' is not activity-based, but rather it is outcome-based. For something to have been implemented points to a successful outcome having been achieved and something which can therefore be validated. A new policy can be said to have been implemented only once the outcomes highlighted within it can be consistently demonstrated – simply having the policy defined, agreed and publicized is not enough, and therefore cannot qualify as success.

We have already said that assessment of resilience will likely change over time, for example as the assessment process itself matures, and so strategy and the objectives which it supports should not be viewed in static or fixed terms. As the Board's understanding of resilience assessment and organization capability changes, this is likely to be mirrored in some way by a maturing of performance measurement – that is, the emergence of new or enhanced performance information from across the organization. As new information becomes available to the Board, either through routine performance reporting or through ad hoc re-assessment, a review of the improvement strategy should follow.

It is therefore not unreasonable to expect resilience objectives to change in the near term, and for some of those changes to be potentially quite significant. This final point also draws attention not only to the maturing of performance measurement but also to the fact that a working appreciation of resilience – sufficient to allow for some strategically important decisions to be made – is likely to be a challenge for some Board members, and leads us rather nicely to a consideration of 'resources and capability'.

Resources and capabilities

The need to address questions of resource and capability provides a recurring theme for practitioners throughout the strategy process, beginning with the resilience assessment itself and the detail of how this is commissioned. The detail contained in Chapter 6 alerts the reader to some of the considerations when planning and delivering an assessment of resilience capability, and its relevance begins with the expectations (both implicit and explicit) and understanding of the Board. The resources and capabilities we are interested in here are those which can be brought into play in pursuit of the organization's strategic resilience objectives: the funding, the plant and equipment, the knowledge, in fact anything which is harnessed for the purposes of achieving a desired resilient state.

The decision to invest in an assessment of resilience capability will only have come about following some degree of analysis and discussion of the organization's position and consideration of the available options. Such a decision may have been informed by external consultants and Board members may have been largely reliant on those external experts to capture and explain the relevance of the assessment work and even the potential value which improved resilience capability could realize for the organization. It is therefore not unrealistic to expect the initial assessment activity to be the result of a 'pitch' by a consulting firm, keen to persuade and to demonstrate its expertise in what remains a developing field.

In deciding to undertake an assessment and the form which that assessment will take, which of course need involve no more commitment than to acknowledge the receipt of the assessment outputs, the Board will be working with existing information, good or bad, regarding the resources available to it. Funding limitations and the capabilities and working relationship with internal audit teams are likely to feature, together with the short-term timelines which are often influenced by specific events and new product releases or pending regulatory changes. But this is just the first and most obvious aspect of resource and capability consideration. The Board will have a raft of decisions to make as it organizes and configures its assets in pursuit of improved resilience capability and one of the key challenges will be to recognize what actually is available at the outset and what can realistically be achieved as a result.

If we assume that Board members are committed to an assessment taking place, based on at least some 'base' level of technical understanding about resilience, and unless wholly delegated, we must also believe that they feel sufficiently appraised of the technical skills of internal assurance teams to make a decision about who should be charged with undertaking the assessment. In doing so, the following considerations should also be apparent:

- Is the Board keen to maintain control over the assessment and subsequent reporting activity, something which is usually much easier when dealing with an internal function (however independent they may feel) than with an external consultant?
- How would any future (re-)assessment activity be delivered and would this entail some degree of knowledge transfer or technical upskilling? If so, when would this best be delivered?
- Is the Board persuaded of the need to compare resilience assessment directly against other (competitor) organizations, and if so, what implications might this have for how and by whom the assessment is to be carried out?
- How likely is it, based on the organization's APPROACH, RESULTS, etc that nothing at all will be done as a result of the assessment – is it genuinely nothing more at this stage than a one-off assessment exercise?

Before leaving the topic of assessment, it is worth reconsidering how assurance in a wider sense is undertaken and perceived, touching again on some of the points raised in Chapter 6. Firstly, and following on from the points immediately above, it is worth considering whether the Board has a genuine starting point or position from which it will receive the outputs of any assessment. Much, of course, will depend on the quality and depth of the existing assurance activity over which the Board presides, and in some cases this may have had a significant influence on how the assessment of resilience capability was framed and initiated.

Detail of the organization's current assurance planning processes can provide an important insight with regard to the potential value which the Board derives from the control and risk information which is reported to its members. The Board's understanding will likely be influenced by how assurance plans are established and whether activity is routinely mapped to the organization's strategic risks or business processes. With reference to the technical 'Three Lines of Defence' model for assurance, consideration should also be given to the way in which internal and external functions are afforded responsibility for delivery.[1]

The model provides an important reference point for considerations of resilience assessment as it helps to explain the allocation of existing assurance resource within the organization, and as such, how risk ownership and reporting is approached. The principles outlined within the model are universally applicable, and therefore represent a reality for every organization even if the model itself is not necessarily referred to by management or knowingly applied. Reference to how the model applies to an organization can help in understanding and explaining the following:

- assumptions around independence and the delivery of governance, and whether independence is valued more highly than the quality of the outputs;
- role and make-up of the organization's Audit Committee and how active it is in seeking assurance across specific areas of risk;
- type of reporting in place and the ability to separate conflicting opinions in the report without undermining its meaning or impact.

The second factor to consider in relation to the points introduced in Chapter 6 concerns the quality, depth and purpose of assurance within organizations, which can vary enormously. As the quote below highlights, although assurance activity often appears to be very structured and deliberate, it can be unclear how the process itself is organized or controlled:

> At the moment, there is a sense in which assurance simply happens. It is not a planned activity in the way in which parts of it are executed. For example, most internal audit departments normally prepare an annual plan which is presented to and discussed with the Audit Committee. However, there is rarely an overall, documented plan for the totality of assurance that is required at board level and which the board needs to provide to other stakeholders.[2]

Assuming there is some element of deliberateness and direction in the organization's planning and delivery of assurance, any commitment to undertake an assessment of resilience is likely to have an impact on existing arrangements. For example, the assessment may seek to include or make reference to other assurance work which forms part of the current plan, or some planned work may have to be adjusted or postponed. Given the inevitable impact which assurance activity has on the wider organization, as the associated workload can prove to be significant for those functions required to take part in testing or in making data available, the planning of any work should also take account of the overall capacity to absorb new or ad hoc requests.

Finally, considerations of resource and capability will be evident for as long as resilience is being studied within the organization and will extend from the first time resilience is discussed at Board level, right through to the routine validation and reporting of performance improvements. For most organizations this will include specific reference to the following:

- the availability of programme and project management skills and the capacity for managing and delivering offline initiatives or other work packages which sit separately from day-to-day activity;
- levels of employee and stakeholder engagement and how this influences the manner in which messages are communicated;

- existing capital plans and investments and what this means not only for the availability of funding but also the likely impact on future resilience performance;
- potential costs associated with implementing resilience-related actions, including those of training and the often significant costs, both direct and indirect, associated with any structural reorganization;
- restrictions associated with regulatory parameters or previous commitments and undertakings within which the organization operates.

Programme delivery

For those considering how best to close gaps in resilience capability, there is likely to be a lot to think about, not least the organization's recent history of managing change and performance improvement. There is also, of course, the structures and mechanisms likely to be needed to execute any new action plans sanctioned by the Board. Given the strategic nature of resilience it would be a mistake to think about such plans or remedies in a purely tactical way, and it would therefore be wise to engage with the Board on the 'how' of resilience improvement, and not just the 'what'. To avoid this particular pitfall, practitioners should begin by considering those delivery requirements (and existing project and programme management structures) appropriate for transformational change – ie that which either references a profound, complete or radical change, or which suggests a new direction or a different level of effectiveness.

Whilst the terms 'initiative', 'project' and 'programme' are frequently used interchangeably, it is worth us being as clear as possible with the labelling and terminology we use. For the purposes of delivering improvements in resilience capability, a programme should be considered in the following way:

- Programmes tend to be strategic in nature and linked to investment decisions. They are clearly and obviously aligned with the organization's business plan and may therefore also have a specific external focus.

- Programmes tend to involve a collection of projects and employ umbrella-style governance and aggregated reporting across a range of activities and disciplines.
- Programmes tend to focus on benefit delivery and not just outputs and may therefore reflect business opportunities as much as specific failure risks or emerging threats.

Given the nature of the changes we are likely to be considering, and the benefit or value associated with the actions we are proposing to take, it makes sense for us to approach our resilience gap actions as constituting a 'programme', rather than as merely discrete projects or initiatives. After all, these are actions of strategic importance and ones likely to involve significant investment. And herein lies the hidden benefit of a programme approach to improvement delivery. Not only does it make sense from an oversight, resource utilization and risk management perspective, but through sponsorship and some unique governance touches, it is also the most effective way of maintaining Board-level engagement and support.

In accepting the need to establish a programme of work, the organization will want to consider some of the more practical elements, such as reporting timescales and organizational structures. However, some of the earliest considerations should be focused on confirming sponsorship at Board level and installing a senior, independent chairperson who can assist in bringing different elements of the organization together and who carries the authority and oversight necessary to minimize the risks of programme objectives being missed. For smaller organizations or those with limited project experience/ resources, the additional challenge will be to adopt the principles of good programme management without viewing it in overly prescriptive or bureaucratic terms.

Reporting to the chairperson, the purpose of a programme board is certainly not a symbolic one and nor is it about creating unnecessary structures or additional, costly steps in the delivery process. Run correctly, the programme board provides information on progress to the organization's main Board via the programme sponsor, and in order to do this the chairperson should be able to rely upon some element of independent, ongoing assessment and support. Furthermore, the programme board provides the mechanism through which decisions are taken in respect of individual project elements, central resource allocation, sequencing of events, etc.

Through effective oversight and governance, the chairperson is able to offer independent advice both to the delivery teams and project manager(s), and also to the programme's sponsor. Working with the support of project managers and assessors, and through being able to interpret the needs of the programme sponsor, the chairperson should feel equipped to make recommendations and decisions about individual projects. Importantly, this independent oversight should extend through to the latter phases of the programme where it will be necessary to validate the achievement of improvement objectives.

As noted above, delivery structures and what passes for a 'programme' will inevitably appear different, one organization to another, dependent upon size, complexity, and of course the organization's maturity. Also, for some organizations the execution of resilience gap actions may look very similar to a product development programme, whilst in others it may display similarities with how major new contracts are delivered. Practitioners should therefore not be tempted to equate the need for a programme-oriented approach with a something which is in any way automatic or bureaucratic or which suggests a mandatory list of features.

Stage-gates or phase reviews are common to many projects and programmes and are important in support of our resilience efforts as they allow the programme board to reconnect with the Board's requirements and to review progress through the lens of the ORCM or other assessment model. It is likely that most improvement programmes will be structured quite generically and what unique references there are will only have meaning within the organizational context within which the programme is set, such as references to specific resources or locations or structures. Indeed, the assessment model may not be referenced at programme level.

The scheduled, periodic review of programme activity has both a governance and a resilience purpose. At the technical level, the review affords the chairperson the opportunity to make informed decisions and recommendations about progress, both in respect of objectives already achieved and also readiness to progress. Phases would normally seek to reflect the generic project or programme life cycle, from concept, feasibility and funding approval, through to trials and full implementation of the chosen solution. Often based on input from independent programme assessors, such reviews can be expected to have the following elements in common:

- risk analysis and material changes;
- test and validation activity;
- regulatory or statutory approvals;
- marketing and communications planning;
- systems requirements;
- operations planning.

From a resilience perspective, structured reviews allow the chairperson to consider the programme within the context of the resilience model used to engage with the organization and provide the assessment report and recommendations. This is particularly important where changes within the organization, or indeed externally, have a potential impact on the detail of the resilience assessment. For example, certain elements of the ORCM tend to be more sensitive to near-term and circumstantial changes, such as RESULTS and STRENGTH, and it is these which the review should likely focus on:

- RESULTS – crisis events or significant changes in published sales/profit figures can have a significant impact on investment plans, product releases, etc.
- SKILLS – redundancy programmes or M&A activity can have a negative impact of the availability of skilled and knowledgeable resources.

- STRENGTH – anything which calls into question the health or integrity of the organization's assets can result in major corrective programmes being initiated.

However unique each programme is in time and place, practitioners should still expect generic principles of good project management to be applied, including defined responsibilities and ownership, due dates and deliverables captured in the form of a plan, processes for monitoring and reporting on progress and a comprehensive risk management approach. Assuming such principles are in evidence, and similar to how resilience assessment is considered, one of the biggest challenges for the organization in respect of programme delivery is likely to be in how it seeks to assimilate existing initiatives and project work.

Widely acknowledged as a live issue for many programmes, the presence of existing projects can make for rather a complicated context within which to consider the needs for coordinating delivery efforts. As part of its overall improvement strategy the Board and the chairperson of the programme board may decide to cancel certain activities whilst seeing others consumed into the wider resilience portfolio. In such an environment, it is not unusual for existing projects to effectively 'start over', in that they may have to justify themselves again, going back to an earlier business case. This is not necessarily a bad thing, particularly if it reflects a new dimension in Board thinking, but of course it may simply be reflective of a new tightening in non-resilience funding.

In common with most work programmes of this type, resilience-related efforts will therefore need to balance the requirements to plan for delivery alongside whatever else is happening within the organization with the requirements to monitor and report on progress and the need to validate the effectiveness of implementation. The curiosity of project and programme activity is that the weakest element, from a resilience perspective, is so often associated with the way in which lessons are learned and improvement delivery actually confirmed. This is not a commentary so much on the success of previous improvement efforts, but rather on the way in which management's attention tails off so quickly following the release of a new product or the signing of a new contract, and it is something of which practitioners should be acutely aware.

The lack of focus around project and programme learning, and the back end of the plan in general, is probably not helped by the nature of previous improvement efforts. The reality for many organizations is that improvement efforts are operational or tactical in nature, or at least that is the only level at which demonstrable improvement can actually be confirmed. The fact that the back end of the plan has become an unfashionable place must reflect on the organization's overall resilience capability, given the significance of technical skills and a learning culture, but it is also important for the following reasons:

- The risk of incurring avoidable costs can actually be elevated towards the end of a project. Withdrawal and support costs can amount to a significant proportion of the overall budget and the potential for consequential loss or committed costs following handover or launch can even undermine the organization's viability.
- Value associated with customer experience and employee engagement, for the majority at least, is only apparent once a service or change is visible and has gone live.
- Regardless of what else may have changed in the meantime, the Board should still be seeking to confirm the detail and scale of the capability improvements which they originally sanctioned.

Stage-gates and phase reviews are vital to achieving both near-term and long-term success. Project and programme phases should not be allowed to reduce in value at some point convenient to one or more party involved and the independent chairperson should be the first to challenge any pressure to the contrary. The same discipline should be applied to reviews during the latter stage of programme engagements and those involved should be expected to value the learning potential which they offer.

Organizational design (and re-design)

In terms of an overall approach to closing resilience capability gap actions it is difficult to separate organizational design considerations from those relating to resources and capability and programme delivery. However, design (or more accurately 're-design') has a significance all of its own, not least because it is so often presented to the world as being essential in delivering competitiveness and growth potential for the organization – exactly those elements that we use to define resilience.

Transformational change is regularly presented as a structural design project or initiative, and vice versa. Furthermore, many people's experience of such initiatives, my own included, results in the adoption of a rather cynical perspective, preferring to believe that it is less transformational and more of a convenience – a process and mechanism through which management can exert cultural as well as cost control over the organization's activities rather than to seek change in any other sphere.

Organizational design creates the alignment of structures and reporting lines deemed most appropriate for delivery of the organization's strategic objectives, and it is routinely considered both in output terms, that is the resulting 'lines and boxes', and in change terms, that is the process and sequencing of events through which a new design is delivered and populated.

It is probably fair to say that the relationship between organizational design and organizational resilience is somewhat unclear. Whilst references to competitiveness and realizing growth potential through re-design are entirely consistent with our understanding of resilience, the act of re-designing can of course be a very complex, expensive and hugely impactful tool for management to consider. A Board determined to land a new structure as a means of hitting whatever targets they may have set may or may not be interested in evaluating the impact of such change across the broad spectrum of resilience characteristics or criteria.

For example, design initiatives can be used to attempt change at a decision-making or cultural level, and of course as a means of reducing costs, absorbing new product or service lines or as a way of better reflecting regulatory requirements. Whilst it doesn't always prevent such approaches being badged as such, it is generally less clear how and when they are used to progress learning capabilities, to improve safety performance, instil a compliant mindset or truly facilitate innovation and adaptation.

As we did in Chapters 3 and 5 for the notions of leadership and service quality, we can use a simple mapping to illustrate how the relevance of organizational design is reflected within the ORCM, albeit it does not have a specific category or entry of its own. The detail of internal structures and hierarchies may not immediately be evident from the labels used for the nine features and concepts within the ORCM, but there is an undoubted significance which is reflected within the following elements:

- The STRENGTH of the organization can be influenced by various aspects associated with organizational design, including size and scale and the ability of the design to release spare or otherwise redundant resources. The resilience of individuals within the organization is also a key characteristic and this itself can be greatly influenced not only by the structures and the allocation of specific resources (ie the 'lines and boxes' of the design) but also by how changes to the design are managed and delivered over time.

- As a simple extension of the above, the PERSONALITY of the organization will also be influenced by notions of staff loyalty, engagement and turnover, each of which links to design and the history of design within the organization.

- AWARENESS within the organization provides a useful example of a linkage which is both quite tactical on the one hand, and on the other one which speaks to strategic governance. Visibility, understanding and reporting all require resources, some of which might be quite specialized. Similarly, organizational designs must also provide for the adequacy and suitability of those formal channels through which information and decisions are transmitted.

The significance of design is also emphasized by reference to components of our resilience definition, namely those of re-shaping and growth. A new design and how it is delivered for the organization will obviously constitute some degree of re-shaping, but we should exercise extreme caution in reading too much into this. The truth of course is that many change activities, however disruptive they might be, offer little in the way of genuine re-shaping and may be so subtle that with the exception of some different contact names the nature of any change might be completely lost on the outside world.

As discussed in Chapter 7, the idea of transformational change certainly suggests an environment within which a new structural and hierarchical design might be appropriate. The compelling need for organizations to adopt a forward-leaning digital strategy in order to help engage and interact in new ways both internally and externally would appear to offer a meaningful example. After all, why would anyone expect an existing design to facilitate the sound execution of a strategic change such as this?

In returning to our definition of resilience, there is also a response and growth aspect to organizational design. A flatter, less complicated structure might make it easier for management to re-allocate resources or to hasten the decision-making or project delivery processes. Outsourcing of key activities may improve the ability to adapt to near-term fluctuations in demand through pushing the supply challenges on to (more capable) partner organizations. It may be somewhat more difficult for us to understand how design actually enhances the organization's ability to make and deliver other changes.

The answer might be suggested in how organizational design activity is conceived and how its success is confirmed. We would expect any change to be accompanied by some sort of justification – the 'real' justification, and not the one presented to staff who are simply being asked to re-apply, once again, for their jobs. We would also hope that the delivery and execution of that change would be monitored in such a way that achievements could ultimately be reported on. With resilience reflecting the full breadth of organizational activity, the list of considerations for design activities is not a short one, but one which should include the following:

- Does the design create the conditions in which the organization's resilience ambitions can be realized? Which aspects of the design will be used as indicators of resilience capability?
- Which roles within the organization have a particular relevance to resilience capability including the leadership cadre and those with specific responsibility for addressing resilience gap actions? How does the design equip and support them in these endeavours?
- How does the design deliver the flexibility and capacity necessary to execute ad hoc and committed programmes of work, and how does it support the maintenance of required skills across the organization?
- Which characteristics within the design promote speed of decision-making and innovation in solving problems? How does the design ensure that appropriate levels of risk are being considered?
- How does the design produce an environment necessary to build a learning organization and one which produces a proactive stance in respect of compliance?

These are not intended to be deliberately difficult or obscure questions, and at some point or other we will each have come across claims about organizational design which touch upon one or more of them. Furthermore, we will each likely have experience of such claims never actually being proven or validated.

Data and information management

A key consideration in seeking to close gaps in resilience capability is the data landscape within which the organization operates – that is, understanding the value and potential of the organization's information and the data it is drawn from. This is not so much about the perils of data and how the organization shares it or seeks to protect it, but rather it is about the significance of information in helping us to assess, monitor and report on resilience capability. The dangers here are not of data loss or of repeating data mistakes made by the organization in the past; they are of the accuracy, completeness and accessibility of data and how this might ultimately influence our understanding of the organization and how resilient it is. From the standpoint of this chapter, the biggest single danger for the organization is not having the data from which to make an assessment in the first instance; the second biggest danger is not having the data from which ultimately to evidence improvements in capability.

As outlined in Chapter 5, the organization's data assets provide us with an opportunity to examine the ORCM along its entire length – from data as a STRENGTH and something against which SKILLS can be assessed, through to the organization's APPROACH to data and to considerations of it as a RESOURCE. The organization's engagement with external stakeholders, for example through routine reporting, will provide insight into some of that data and into how the organization views it. Organizations will also probably have taken a public position on data and how they intend to use it, whilst others will have been established or re-invented themselves to take advantage of new data markets.

How the organization's information and data is managed has become increasingly important from a resilience perspective, so much so that embracing cyber-security and data-privacy requirements is broadly recognized as offering competitive advantage in sectors such as financial services and retail.

Picking up on previous comments regarding compliance, organizations can quickly find themselves defined by their approach to data within an environment frequently dominated by litigation and service outages. Part of the reason for this, of course, is the exponential growth in both volume and application of data and the failure of many organizations to appreciate data as an asset of value.

In common with any assessment endeavour, the initial assessment of resilience capability will be dependent for its relevance, completeness and accuracy on the available data, as will the organization's ability to monitor resilience conditions going forward. With the help of existing reports, one of the first challenges faced by practitioners will be to establish the detail of the wider data landscape from which resilience information will need to be drawn. Whilst there are likely to be certain standout sources, such as assurance reports and annual accounts, the very first pre-assessment data requirement might well involve establishing an inventory of quantitative sources against the elements contained within the ORCM or other assessment model – many of the qualitative sources being established specifically for the purposes of the assessment.

Some of the linkages to the resilience assessment model will be obvious, albeit interpreted within the unique context of the organization, and will suggest broad measurement categories associated with volume indicators, such as number of training days or number of qualified personnel. The model structure itself will likely influence how straightforward this identification actually is, it being based at least in part on the labels and references contained within it. Practitioners will also be hugely dependent on the process knowledge they are able to bring to bear during planning for the initial assessment – it is knowledge of local information flows which will define what might actually be possible within the time allowed.

Within any such quantitative inventory, the word which should perhaps be underlined first is 'potential' – that is, even when data sources have been confirmed, questions will usually remain about access and accuracy and of course there is rarely any guarantee that what is available today will necessarily be available going forward. The unfortunate reality for many practitioners is that they will be forced to compete with numerous other pressing demands being considered by SMEs and those responsible for data collection and reporting, and even the explanation associated with existing data sets can be a time-consuming exercise. Add to this the practitioner's request to consider how any new data can be released and the task can quickly become an uncomfortable one.

Once mapped to the organization's chosen assessment model, the practitioner is likely to be aware of immediate gaps, or areas within which data appears to be problematic for some reason or another. Such gaps can usually be filled, to some degree of satisfaction, by the use of proxies – that is, organizational characteristics, activities or other information which offers to substitute for direct measurement or records. Proxies can allow the practitioner to reconstruct their chosen assessment model, at least in part, using alternate references. Some proxies will offer relatively close associations, whilst others may require a significant degree of creativity, and therefore interpretation.

In itself, the use of proxies can prove to be a challenge, particularly for the recipients of the assessment outcomes. Whilst we owe it to ourselves to be transparent in how we have used data to inform our assessment of resilience capability, full disclosure of proxy data or information may prove to be a significant distraction in some circumstances. We should therefore seek only to fill gaps where it makes sense to do so, and to test the proxies we intend to use as thoroughly as possible. One example of a 'borderline' proxy – ie one which may just be too creative – is the use of training data.

It is probably fair to assume that all resilience assessment models include reference to 'leadership', whether directly or as an influencer across a range of characteristics (as is the case for the ORCM). Whilst it is quite possible to generate leadership-related data through qualitative sources, this should probably be supplemented with quantitative sources if possible – the challenge being the ability to identify them. At first sight, the thought of using 'training delivery versus plan' might seem rather too tenuous, or just plainly inappropriate. However, with a little imagination it is quite possible to consider 'delivery to plan' as a reasonable proxy for 'management commitment' – ie management's ability and willingness to see through commitments to competency and development of staff. When combined with other similar measures, this may then provide a reasonable basis for building a commentary around the organization's PERSONALITY and APPROACH, and therefore leadership style.

Beyond the requirement to directly assess resilience capability, data now demands a recognition that elevates it beyond simply a consideration as part of the organization's ICT or digital strategy. Data for today's organization is much more than that and it has a growing influence over our baseline capability, our vulnerability to specific threats and our ability to recognize and seize upon market opportunities. For example, Big Data is dramatically changing the way in which data is collected and processed, and the ways in which resilience capability is considered can itself by changed by the introduction of data when considered and analysed in massive amounts. One memorable quote from 2013 stated that over 90 per cent of the data in the world had by that point been created in the previous two years, and a report in *Forbes* in 2018 suggested there are in the region of 450,000 tweets sent on Twitter and over half a million images shared on Snapchat every minute.[3,4]

A fascinating example of volume data is provided in a 2016 article which seeks to examine the use of data within a disaster-type scenario, in this case the 2015 Nepal earthquake.[5] Here, Big Data analysis was used to investigate the detail of over 36,000 tweets and other social media entries and responses from 205 managers involved in disaster relief activities. The earthquake is reported to have killed nearly 9,000 people.[6]

The almost universal adoption of social media platforms to help manage our communications not only releases huge quantities of information into areas where there was previously very little, it also forces us to reconsider the transactions and relationships upon which the resilience of organizations is built. Whilst the article cited above references supply chain relationships within the context of a disaster response effort, it is not only the speed with which such information is available but also the new insights and perspectives which it can provide.

Retail provides another example of where significant new volumes of data are now available, much of which has presented itself in parallel with the enormous changes being experienced in the sector with the expansion of e-commerce. Analysts are seeking to find more and more effective ways of anticipating behaviours and trends, and as consumers we are gradually being conditioned to accept a retail experience which is more unique, at least in part, to us. And all of this should provide an important focus for practitioners in the pursuit of resilience gap actions, as many of the organization's data volume opportunities have an external and/or transactional element to them.

Many organizations invest heavily in Twitter, Facebook and other social media channels as a way of engaging with customers, and to a lesser extent organizations increasingly employ internal platforms as a means of encouraging communication amongst staff. Each exchange obviously has the potential to generate data which can then be mapped to our chosen resilience model as part of assessment and gap-closure activities, and something which has a particular application when it comes to confirming the results of improvement action.

Conclusion

It was never going to be possible to capture every perspective or improvement angle within this final chapter, as, whilst the definitions and modelling of resilience lend themselves to a degree of prescription, the detail of their application will for ever be part of the unique circumstances of each organization. However, the chapter has been able to present some common pointers for consideration and also highlighted some of the challenges associated with thinking through the outcome of a resilience assessment and of seeking to implement change.

The improvement strategy devised by the Board will really dominate everything about the closure of gaps in the organization's resilience capability and will be largely dependent upon not just the assessment, of course, but also by the quality of the Board's understanding – that is, their understanding of what is achievable from a resource and data perspective and whether they have an existing structure capable of delivering on their resilience ambition. This is largely about Board-level awareness and competence – leaving all of this detail to be unpicked at a programme level or delegated to functional managers is simply not appropriate and will almost certainly result in delays and missed opportunities.

Having mentioned 'ambition', it is also probably worth stating that resilience goals should be evident as part of the organization's improvement strategy, and it surely makes sense for this strategy to be clearly detailed as well. Ambition in a resilience sense works very much as it does for other risk-related considerations, and therefore no prior expectation or judgement is necessary with regard to how the Board intends to apply it. Assuming the Board has confidence in the assessment it has been presented with, it will be free to decide on those objectives which help to define the organization's direction of travel and therefore where the true resilience gaps exist.

Regardless of whether an organization's resilience ambitions remain muted or not – after all, each organization is in a unique place and has to account for its own decisions – we should absolutely expect the organization's approach to be defined by some largely generic improvement-related considerations. These will include the following:

- Strategy needs to make sense in respect of the day-to-day realities of organizational life and it should be considered in terms of how it can promote a resilient mindset and provide staff and other stakeholders with something to coalesce around.
- Whilst remaining flexible and open to adjustment, strategy should take the organization beyond an initial set of goals and objectives and should look beyond the next assessment.
- Having already committed resources to delivering an assessment exercise, the opportunity costs associated with any new improvement programme should itself be assessed in some detail and with the highest level of honesty and transparency.
- In examining the organization's structure and the resources it has at its disposal, consideration should also be given to the requirements for managing and coordinating a new programme of improvement activity, and what sort of internal changes (enduring or otherwise) are required to enable it.
- In seeking to make available the data necessary to support a meaningful assessment, it should be clear whether this is existing data, extracted from regulatory reports for example, or if it is newly established.
- Similarly, it is important to determine if data perspectives can be repeated, how the accuracy and completeness of data can be validated and what the data permits in terms of external benchmarking. Consideration should also be given to whether traditional methods of data coding and analysis might no longer be appropriate.

Given the strategic nature of resilience capability and the interconnected nature of the characteristics and behaviours associated with resilience, as identified in Chapter 5 in relation to the ORCM, it would usually be inappropriate to consider individual actions in isolation, or as forming discrete and independent initiatives. Similarly, it would be naïve not to consider how organizational design works to permit and encourage the required change and how it might also act as a barrier.

Two final points for consideration. Firstly, if organizational resilience is fundamentally a question of how successfully we are able to manage strategic risks, then our efforts in seeking to achieve new levels of resilience capability must be consistent with our overall approach to managing risk across the organization. That is not to suggest that risk appetite should in any way be uniform, but rather that the positions adopted for safety and compliance, for example, are consistent with what we are endeavouring to achieve for resilience – something which will only become truly apparent following an assessment. An obvious point perhaps, but many organizations continue to struggle with risk delivery and the introduction of new and broader ways of thinking about risk do not necessarily make that any easier.

From a safety or compliance perspective, Board members may be entirely comfortable with assuming accountability for the risks taken on their behalf, confident that the organization's appetite for exposure in these areas has been defined and well communicated. However, this is not always the case and even when it is, the execution at local level can look different from that which was intended. The way in which resilience throws a wrapper around a number of other risk categories, and the range of influences and behaviours which go to define it, tends to amplify any disconnect which exists across the organization's wider approach to risk.

Secondly, in seeking to make sense of an assessment outcome and chart a future course for the organization, the Board is likely to be addressing subjects which may be difficult or uncomfortable, not least the detail of failed attempts at change which precede it. There is also the continuing rush to upgrade technologies and the nature of change as it is experienced within the organization, often appearing both chaotic and relentless.

One of the most popular strategies in seeking to introduce structural change into an organization is to (wherever possible) avoid dwelling on the past, and whilst this may have a convenience to it which can be attractive to management, it usually only serves to suppress and to hide. Resilience capability and the ambition to deliver improvement provides a unique opportunity to revisit why so many initiatives or change methodologies have failed to achieve much more than modest gains in process efficiency. An approach which is genuinely holistic, commercially-centred and which seeks to address strategic-level risks can easily be contrasted with past experiments which have been fragmented or divorced from the external context within which the organization operates.

Similarly, a focus on organizational resilience can also help to make sense of the change-burden under which so many organizations work. The explosion of data and the bewildering pace of technological change can act to blind the Board and management to many of the organization's needs. A good assessment model allows the practitioner to present the current contribution and/or maturity of each resilience element within the context of an overall 'score', and to examine the interplay of individual aspects of organizational activity and performance. The model should also drive the action-planning process for organizations by highlighting the known improvement and development capacity of each defining feature and the contribution of each behavioural element.

In drawing to a final conclusion, and of course for the benefit of the reader, it is probably worth revisiting the entirety of the book at this point, at least in brief summary. Fundamentally, these chapters seek to provide a reasonable level of subject detail, without ever becoming overly forensic, and to introduce the various elements of a unique and highly adaptable assessment model, sufficient for it to be of practical use to both practitioners and Board members alike.

This latter point, for me at least, is hugely significant. The primary objective has always been to facilitate a self-assessment of resilience capability regardless of the organizational context within which it is being considered. The ORCM is comprehensive and flexible enough to allow this, and hopefully I have provided the pointers and ideas necessary for it to be understood and applied. Perhaps the single biggest challenge for practitioners in seeking to deliver meaningful and consistent assessments, and that which the book therefore aims to address, is not expertise or mastery of the subject but rather access to and intimate knowledge of an appropriate assessment framework or model.

If, having digested the entire book, readers feel better able to address the fundamental questions outlined at the very beginning, then it will have served its purpose. As practitioners seeking to lead a discussion with the Board, our ambition should be to answer the following: What is resilience, from an organizational perspective? What does it look like and how resilient is the organization with which I work – that is, how can it be measured and how can resilience capability be improved?

Endnotes

1 Chartered Institute of Internal Auditors (2019) Governance of risk: Three lines of defence. Available from: www.iia.org.uk/resources/audit-committees/governance-of-risk-three-lines-of-defence/ (archived at https://perma.cc/HY4K-5RTE)

2 Alexander, D (2018) Assurance Mapping (referencing material from a post financial crisis report by the OECD), presented at a Chartered Institute of Internal Auditors event, 2 February. Available from: www.iia.org.uk/media/1689589/assurance-mapping-david-alexander.pdf (archived at https://perma.cc/7WCT-YP8B)

3 SINTEF (2013) Big Data, for better or worse: 90% of world's data generated over last two years, *Science Daily*, 22 May. Available from: www.sciencedaily.com/releases/2013/05/130522085217.htm (archived at https://perma.cc/6QAX-FABK)

4 Marr, B (2018) How much data do we create every day? The mind-blowing stats everyone should read, *Forbes*, 21 May. Available from: www.forbes.com/sites/bernardmarr/2018/05/21/how-much-data-do-we-create-every-day-the-mind-blowing-stats-everyone-should-read/#279bf35160ba (archived at https://perma.cc/2GSR-STVG)

5 Papadopoulos, T, Gunasekaran, A, Dubey, R, Altay, N, Childe, S and Fosso-Wamba, S (2016) The role of Big Data in explaining disaster resilience in supply chains for sustainability. Available from: kar.kent.ac.uk/57191/1/JCP%20resilience.pdf (archived at https://perma.cc/UFJ8-TB3S) (doi.org/10.1016/j.jclepro.2016.03.059 (archived at https://perma.cc/9KSZ-KXNC))

6 ActionAid (nd) Earthquakes in Nepal 2015. Available from: www.actionaid.org.uk/about-us/what-we-do/emergencies-disasters-humanitarian-response/earthquakes-in-nepal-2015 (archived at https://perma.cc/8M7M-RDG8)

INDEX

4Sight model 161, 241

accountability, trust and 93
adaptation, approach to resilience 41, 42–43
Adaptive BC 22
Affinity Health at Work (AHAW) 55, 57–59, 60
Alibaba, re-invention of retail (case study) 114–18
Allison, James 67
Amazon 64, 115–16, 117
ambition, why it pays for organizations 69–71
analogies for resilience
  driving analogy 141–41
  false analogies 47–51
animal welfare protests 231
Apple 168
Apple stores 108
application and implementation 247–75
  Board improvement strategy 271–75
  Board priorities and plans 249–53
  data and information management 266–71
  improvement strategy 249–53
  organizational design (and re-design) 263–66
  programme delivery 257–62
  resilience goals 271–73
  resources and capabilities 253–57
  risk management approach 273–74
approach
  concept within the ORCM 143, 162–65
  questions for assessment data-gathering 193
artificial intelligence (AI) 166–67
  growth and impact of 156
  machine learning 226
  safety implications of 224–26
assessment of resilience 175–97
  applying capacity measures to the ORCM features 196–97
  benchmarking performance 205–08
  BP example 120–22
  data gathering and analysis 187–91
  defining an appropriate assessment strategy 208–10
  defining the assessment process 183–87
  early planning of reporting objectives 186–87
  external assessment 175
  indicators of potential resilience capability 196–97
  ORCM as a self-assessment tool 175–77
  organizational health approach 180
  planning for 183–87
  practices relevant to the ORCM concepts 191–96
  provision of assurance 177–79
  qualitative data-gathering 191–96
  qualitative input 186, 188–90
  quantitative data-gathering 196–97
  quantitative input 186, 188, 190–91
  reducing subjectivity 196–97
  reporting phase 197–202
  role of subject matter experts (SMEs) 185, 186, 189
  selecting the correct assessment strategy 179–83
  strategy for assessment 175–76
  tenure of the organization 91
  use of focus groups 188–90, 191–96
  who should carry out the assessment 179
  see also Organizational Resilience Capability Model® (ORCM)
assurance
  arrangements within organizations 255–56
  assessment and 177–79
attention deficit, feature of the ORCM 143, 155–56
auditors 179
augmented reality 115
Australian Government Organizational Resilience (AGOR) website 55–57
  definition of organizational resilience 41–43

awareness
    concept within the ORCM 143, 160–62
    of the business environment 117–18
    questions for assessment data-gathering
        193

benchmarking performance 205–08
    elements of resilience 207–08
    industry peers 208
    use of case studies 207
    use of models and indices 207
Besos, Jeff 64
BIE website 221–22
Big Data analysis 269–70
Blackberry 118
Bloomberg New Energy Finance (BNEF) 28
Board
    bridging concept in the ORCM 159–60
    decision to invest in resilience capability
        assessment 253–55
    improvement strategy 271–75
    priorities and plans 249–53
Boeing
    cyber-attack 125
    problems with the 737 MAX aircraft
        122
Boohoo 107
'bouncing back' notion of resilience 48, 51,
    52, 54, 65, 69, 95, 104
BP 53
    Gulf of Mexico disaster 2010 74–75
    recovery from the 2010 Gulf of Mexico
        disaster (case study) 103–04,
        118–22
    Texas City disaster (2005) 119, 120
brand loyalty 94
Breach Level Index website 23
British Standards Institution (BSI) 59, 76
    *Standards Outlook 2017 – Governance
        and Resilience* 93
    resilience model 213–14
    organizational resilience report (with
        Cranfield) 239–41
BS 67000 (guide to city resilience) 61, 62,
    164
business-as-usual objective 40
business continuity 20–22, 44
    focus on the status quo 69–70
Business Continuity Institute (BCI) 26
    definition of organizational resilience 45
Business Continuity Maturity Model
    (BCMM) 21
business failure and survival rates 29

capabilities for strategic resilience 253–57
capability gaps 257
    performance improvement 247–75
car manufacturing 108
case studies
    Alibaba 114–18
    BP Gulf of Mexico 2010 disaster
        recovery 103–04, 118–22
    House of Fraser collapse in 2018
        105–09
    impact of the WannaCry virus in 2017
        123–26
    insights about organizational resilience
        102–05
    London transport network resilience
        126–31
    Mercedes Formula One (F1) team
        109–14
    selection of case study material 131–34
    sources of 105
    use in benchmarking performance 207
CEO attitudes survey, views on
        organizational resilience 59–60
change
    capability to deliver transformational
        change 218–23
    demographic change 27
    gradual versus transformational 49
    importance of enthusiasm for 77–80
    nature of change for organizations
        49–50
    readiness for 77
    resistance to 78
    technological change 28
    transformational change 40, 49,
        218–23, 263–66
change champions 79–80
change fatigue 78, 80
change management
    nature of the change 41–43
    role in organizational resilience 38–40
chatbots 115
Christchurch, New Zealand, earthquakes
    (2010–11) 161, 237–39
civil society organizations (CSOs) 27–28
cloud computing 218
collaboration
    mutual aid agreements (MAAs)
        167–68
    resilience and 163–64, 165–66
collectivism 91
Collins, Jim 18
Comet 108

communications, influence on learning outcomes 166
community, engagement through social media 168–69
community resilience 91
compliance
    as a strategic issue 72–74
    bridging concept in the ORCM 158
    in a period of technological revolution 214–18
    positive and negative views of 72–74
    understanding what it looks like 214–18
compliance mindset, indicator of resilience capability 86
consultancies, services related to resilience 24–26
context of organizational resilience 15–30
    consultancy services 24–26
    data vulnerability 22–24
    material science 16–18
    resilience can be built and it can be destroyed 18–19
    societal influences 26–28
    standards compliance 20–22
continuous learning 83–86
Cranfield School of Management
    organizational resilience report (with BSI) 239–41
    resilience model 213–14
crisis management approach 41–42, 44
crisis prevention 74, 75, 76
crisis response, influence on short-term and long-term success 74–76
critical infrastructure, London transport network resilience (case study) 126–31
cryptic definitions of organizational resilience 44–47, 54
culture of organizations 85–86, 164–65
    role in building or destroying resilience capability 18–19
    trust in organizations 91–93
cyber-attacks 22–24
    impact of the WannaCry virus in 2017 123–26

Daimler 110–11
Danske Bank 20
Darwin, Charles, misinterpretation of his ideas 47–50
Darwinian evolutionary theory 39
data assurance 191

data collection and analysis 113–14
data gaps and problems
    dealing with 268–69
    use of proxies 268–69
data issues, lack of understanding and transparency 23–24
data management 266–71
    Big Data analysis 269–70
data security 94–95
data vulnerability 22–24
    scale of 29–30
definitions of organizational resilience 34–62
    ability to thrive and prosper 44
    adaptation 41, 42–43
    AGOR definition 41–43
    Author's definition 51–54
    breadth of approaches 35–37
    business-as-usual objective 40
    concepts of risk 43
    crisis events viewed as shocks 41–42, 44
    crisis management approach 41–42, 44
    cryptic references 44–47, 54
    endurance 45
    event-focused definitions 38–40
    event life cycle approach 38, 39
    event-plus approaches 41–44
    evolution 41, 42–43
    false analogies 47–51
    learning aspect 45, 47
    misinterpretation of Darwin's ideas 47–50
    nature of change 49–50
    persistence 45–47
    role of personal resilience 50–51
    role of the organization 43
    soundbite references 44–47, 54
    timescale 43
    use in discussions within organizations 35
    Wikipedia definition 38–40
definitions of resilience
    material science perspective 16–18
    mechanical approach 16–18
    something which can be built and destroyed 18–19
    system perspective 218–19
demographic change 27
Denyer, David 161, 239–41
digital economy 219
digital technologies
    disruptive technologies 215, 219–21
    innovations 118, 169
    transformative effects 219–21

digital trust 94–95
direction
    concept within the ORCM 143, 158–60
    questions for assessment data-gathering 192
Disaster Recovery Journal (DRJ) 26
disaster response, use of Big Data analysis of social media 270
disruptive technologies 215, 219–21
driverless vehicles 219, 225
Dudley, Bob 119–20

eBay 22
e-commerce 108
    Alibaba (case study) 114–18
Economist Intelligence Unit (EIU) 59
    definition of organizational resilience 45
employees
    mental health and wellbeing 88–89
    resilience of 151–52
endurance, view of organizational resilience 45
environmental concerns 27, 104
Equifax 22, 23
ethical behaviour, trust 92–93
European Union (EU), Economic and Social Committee 27
event-focused definitions of organizational resilience 38–40
event life cycle 38, 39
event-plus definitions of organizational resilience 41–44
events, response to 17–18
evolution
    approach to resilience 41, 42–43
    inappropriate application to organizations 47–50
    misinterpretation of Darwin's ideas 47–50
    theory 39
Extinction Rebellion movement 232

Facebook 116, 117, 270
    data breach in 2018 23
fake news 162
financial crisis of 2008 92, 168
financial services, importance of trust in 94–95
financing, access for businesses 168
focus groups 188–90
    group size and make-up 195
    number of questions 195
    qualitative data-gathering 191–96
    reinforcing the objectives 195

scheduling of sessions 196
understanding the questions 195–96
foresight, 4Sight model 161
four Rs of resilience 17

globalization 93
Google 24, 116
governance, role in resilience 72–74
Greenpeace 231

Hayward, Tony 75
high reliability organizations (HROs) 223–26
hindsight, 4Sight model 161
Hong Kong, anti-government demonstrations 232
horizon scanning 68–69, 76
House of Fraser, collapse in 2018 (case study) 105–09
Huntington Life Sciences 231
Hurricane Katrina 17

implementation *see* application and implementation
information management 166, 266–71
information resources, approaches to 37
information sources 55–60
infrastructure planning 27
initiatives 257, 258, 261, 263
innovation, digital innovation 118, 169
insiders acts, security issues 299–31
insight, 4Sight model 161
interviews
    qualitative data-gathering 191–96
    use in assessment 188–89, 191–96
investment in resilience 233–36
ISO 22301(Security and resilience – Business continuity management systems) 20, 21, 22
ISO 31000 (Risk Management Guidelines) 163

knowledge management 47, 83–86
knowledge transfer
    during project delivery 84–85
    when staff leave the organization 83–84
Kodak (Eastman Kodak Company) 105

leadership
    influence on organizational resilience 80–83
    influence on team performance 111–13
    retention of talent and 82–83

significance in the ORCM 156–57, 159–60
learning
  aspect of resilience 45, 47
  concept within the ORCM 143, 165–67
  continuous learning and resilience 83–86
  lessons from disaster events 85–86
  machine learning and AI 166–67, 226
  questions for assessment data-gathering 194
  triggers for action and change 85–86
Lehman Brothers bank collapse in 2008 92
lessons from disaster events 85–86
Liebreich, Michael 28
London transport network resilience (case study) 126–31

machine learning 166–67, 226
Marks and Spencer (M&S) 109
material science, perspective on resilience 16–18
maturity, re-invention capability and 71
Mercedes Formula One (F1) team 67–68
  case study 109–14
Ming Zeng 117
models and frameworks 34
  comparing alternative models 213–14, 236–41
  see also Organizational Resilience Capability Model® (ORCM)
Mulberry 108
municipalism 91
Musk, Elon 230
mutual aid agreements (MAAs) 167–68

narcissism 81
National Health Service (NHS) UK, impact of the WannaCry virus 123–26
natural disasters 17
natural selection, inappropriate application to organizations 49
Nepal earthquake (2015) 270
networks 151
New Retail, Alibaba case study 114–18
Nike 117, 168
Nokia 105, 118

Olympus 20
operational resilience 70–71
organizational behaviour, misinterpretation of Darwin's ideas 47–50
organizational culture 85–86, 164–65
  role in building or destroying resilience capability 18–19
  trust in organizations 91–93
organizational design (and re-design) 263–66
organizational resilience
  ambition and 69–71
  approach to 30
  approach to risk 65–69
  attitude towards change 77–80
  barriers to success 97
  benefits of 96
  compliance as a strategic issue 72–74
  continuous learning and 83–86
  elements to take account of 96–98
  key considerations 64–98
  leadership influence on 80–83
  organization size and 89–91
  personal resilience and 86–89
  short- and long-term implications of crisis response 74–76
  trust and 91–95
Organizational Resilience Capability Model® (ORCM) 65, 140–72
  application in organizations 170–72
  applying capacity measures to ORCM features 196–97
  approach to reporting 199
  assessment practices relevant to concepts 191–96
  Board as a bridging concept 159–60
  bridging concepts 157–58, 159–60
  compliance as a bridging concept 158
  concepts contained within 143, 156–69
    approach 143, 162–65
    awareness 143, 160–62
    direction 143, 158–60
    learning 143, 165–67
    resources 143, 167–69
  data and information management 267–69
  definition of organizational resilience 51–54
  driving analogy 141–41
  features contained within 143, 148–56
    attention deficit 143, 155–56
    personality 143, 151–52
    results 143, 153–54
    skills 143, 152–53
    strength 143, 150–51
  introduction 140–42
  leadership 156–57, 159–60
  overview 143

quality of the organization's product or service 169–70
resilience maturity scale 46–47, 142–48
  Step 1: Immediate Fail 145
  Step 2: Early Casualty 145–46
  Step 3: Limited Progress 146
  Step 4: Still Stopping Short 146–47
  Step 5: Gets Further Than Most 147
  Step 6: Just Keeps Going 147–48
self-assessment approach 140–42
self-assessment tool 175–77
significance for organizational design 264–65
organizations
  more than the sum of the parts 86–89
  proactive versus passive role 43
oversight, 4Sight model 161
Oxfam 105

palm oil trade protests 231
performance improvement 247–75
  Board improvement strategy 271–75
  Board priorities and plans 249–53
  data and information management 266–71
  improvement strategy 249–53
  organizational design (and re-design) 263–66
  programme delivery 257–62
  resilience goals 271–73
  resources and capabilities 253–57
  risk management approach 273–74
performance information, access to 23–24
persistence
  distinction from resilience 46–47
  view of organizational resilience 45–47
personal development 54
personal resilience 45–47, 54
  connection with organizational resilience 50–51, 79–80, 86–89
  personality and 151–52
personality, feature of the ORCM 143, 151–52
Peters, Tom 133
Piper Alpha disaster (1988) 120
political movements 27
populism 27
product quality 233
  inclusion in the ORCM 169–70
Professional Evaluation and Certification Board (PECB) 88
programme, definition 257–28

programme delivery 257–62
project management 261
  knowledge transfer 84–85
projects 257–63
PwC 222, 232

qualitative data-gathering 191–96
qualitative input 186, 188–90
quality of products or services 233
  inclusion in the ORCM 169–70
quantitative data-gathering 196–97
quantitative input 186, 188, 190–91

regulation, disruption of new technologies 214–18
re-invention, capability in organizations 70, 71
reporting
  approach to 197–98
  assessment process 199
  benchmarking performance 205–08
  caveats 200
  data balance 201
  early planning of reporting objectives 186–87
  external context 198
  format and style 200
  graphic presentation of data 202–05
  objectives and scope 199
  opinion-based or information-only 199–200
  ORCM approach 199
  Q&A 201
  role of sponsor 198
  solutions and recommendations 201
  wider reporting 201–02
reputational damage, related to data issues 22–24
resilience
  as a relative concept 29
  definitions of 16–19, 218–19
  material science perspective 16–18
  mechanical approach 16–18
  something which can be built and destroyed 18–19
  systems perspective 218–19
  see also organizational resilience
resilience capability, variation in different parts of an organization 29
resilience capability gaps 257
  performance improvement 247–75
Resilience Expert Advisory Group (REAG) 55, 56

resilience goals 271–73
resilience maturity scale 20, 142–48
  Step 1: Immediate Fail 145
  Step 2: Early Casualty 145–46
  Step 3: Limited Progress 146
  Step 4: Still Stopping Short 146–47
  Step 5: Gets Further Than Most 147
  Step 6: Just Keeps Going 147–48
Resilient Organisations (RO), New Zealand 55, 160–61
  resilience models 213–14, 237–39
resources for strategic resilience 253–57
  concept within the ORCM 143, 167–69
  questions for assessment data-gathering 194
results, feature of the ORCM 143, 153–54
retail sector
  re-invention by Alibaba (case study) 114–18
  use of social media 270–71
risk
  significance of our approach to 65–69
  strategic risk 54
risk management 30
  appetite for risk 162–65, 177–78
  approach to 273–74
  provision of assurance 177–79
  strategic risk management 65–69
  threat management 97
  WannaCry cyber-attack in 2017 123–26
  wider concept of risks 43
risk-taking behaviours, organizational safety and 226–28

safety, relationship with resilience 223–28
safety-mindedness of organizations 164–65
Sandberg, Sheryl 23
security
  insider acts 229–31
  role in organizational resilience 228–33
  supply chain security 231–33
self-assessment *see* assessment of resilience; Organizational Resilience Capability Model® (ORCM)
self-awareness 162
service quality 233
  inclusion in the ORCM 169–70
shocks, crisis events viewed as 41–42, 44
Siemens 20
situational awareness 160–62
size of organizations, influence on resilience 89–91
skills, feature of the ORCM 143, 152–53

SMEs (small and medium-sized enterprises)
  access to funding for growth 168
  failure rates for small businesses 29
  influences on resilience 89–91
Snapchat 270
social change 28
social media
  Big Data analysis 270–71
  community engagement 168–69
  use in crisis prevention 76
social movements, influence of 26–27
society, influences on organizational resilience 26–28
soundbite definitions of organizational resilience 44–47, 54
stability concept 71
Standard Chartered 73
standards compliance
  alternatives to 22
  significance for resilience capability 20–22
strategic risk 54
strategic risk management 65–69
strength, feature of the ORCM 143, 150–51
stress and change 78
subject matter experts (SMEs) 185, 186, 189
success, component of resilience 144
super storm Sandy (2012) 17, 163, 236
supply chain resilience, role of trust 93–94
supply chain security 231–33
supporting resilience 212–43
  capability to deliver transformational change 218–23
  comparing alternative models 236–41
  compliance in a period of technological revolution 214–18
  grounding within the organization's reality 241–43
  importance of security 228–33
  investment in resilience 233–36
  relationship between resilience and safety 223–28
Svanberg, Carl-Henric 119
systems perspective on resilience 218–19

technology
  compliance in a period of technological revolution 214–18
  data security 94–95
  digital trust 94–95
  impact of voice technology 216–18

safety implications of new technologies 224–26
technological change 28
vulnerability associated with 29–30
terrorism 127, 129–31
Tesla 230
threat fatigue 97
threat landscape for organizations 66–69
threat management 97
Three Lines of Defence assurance model 178–79, 255
timescale, long-term thinking about resilience 43
transformational change 40, 49
    capability to deliver 218–23
    organizational design (and re-design) 263–66
Transport for London (TfL) 128–31
Tripwire website 30
trust
    accountability and 93
    role in organizational resilience 91–95
Twitter 270

Unilever 231
urban resilience, London transport network (case study) 126–31

value of becoming resilient 96
values of organizations 164–65
voice technology 216–18
Volkswagen (VW) emissions scandal 20, 85–86
vulnerability management 30

WannaCry virus impact (2017) (case study) 123–26
Welch, Jack 81
Wikipedia, definition of organizational resilience 38–40
Wolff, Toto 110–13
World Economic Forum (WEF) 219, 220
World Health Organization (WHO), European Small Countries Initiative 91

Zuckerberg, Mark 23

Lightning Source UK Ltd.
Milton Keynes UK
UKHW050038100123
415066UK00003B/10

9 781789 661842